MULTINATIONAL MANAGERS
AND
POVERTY IN THE THIRD WORLD

Multinational Managers
and
Poverty in the Third World

LEE A. TAVIS, EDITOR

UNIVERSITY OF NOTRE DAME PRESS
NOTRE DAME   LONDON

Library of Congress Cataloging in Publication Data

Main entry under title:

Multinational managers and poverty in The
Third World.

    1. Underdeveloped areas — International
business enterprises — Social aspects —
Congresses.   2. Underdeveloped areas —
Poor — Congresses. I. Tavis, Lee A.
HD2755.5.M8345   658.4'08'091724   82–50288
ISBN 0–268–01353–5   AACR2

Manufactured in the United States of America

To Sparky

Contents

Foreword

THIS BOOK REPORTS ON the activities of a mixed group of managers, missionaries, academicians, and policy advisers who have taken on a most important task: to work toward a better vision of the potential role for multinational corporations in global development. They work toward a vision of a world where a billion people do not have to be illiterate, because we have the means to eliminate that condition; where a billion people do not have to be hungry, because we have the technology to grow food, especially if we grow it in places where the people are hungry. We cannot approve of a world where fifteen million people will die needlessly this year, most of them children, most of them in poorer countries, most of them under the age of five.

I have followed with interest the activities of this seminar since its inception. That a group from such varied backgrounds and global views has held together is a real tribute to the participants. Without this kind of communication there is a tendency for emotional challenges and defenses of multinational activities in the Third World that contribute nothing to achieve our vision.

Although I cannot accept the extreme view so often espoused by many of my religious colleagues that multinationals are monsters, debilitating and ruining the poorer countries, I do empathize with their attempts to bring justice in a world which is not going to be at peace without justice. Any world in which 20 percent of the population controls 80 percent of the total life resources of a small planet cannot say that the arrangement is a formula for peace.

Somehow, these concerns for justice must be implemented by those in the trenches—the multinational managers—many of whom are dedicated to a concept of world justice and fully understand that international involvement means international responsibility. These managers are working in an economic structure that they neither invented nor, if it were up to them, that they would necessarily wish to maintain. The people I have known personally who are directing multinational corporations have been responsible people. They must operate under unusually difficult circumstances: in political, economic, and social systems with rules and values very different from our own. Yet many of them try to do business in a moral way. If we are to upgrade the poorest among us at a time when our resources are becoming ever more scarce, the potential contribution of the multinational corporation must be used to its fullest.

In my comments at the first seminar workshop, I spoke of the difficulties of mediating the conflicts surrounding the multinationals' presence in poor countries and the appropriateness of Notre Dame as the site for this work. Universities are, by nature, mediators. Just as a priest mediates between the two great extremes, finite and infinite, in universities truth emerges through the nurturing of ideas, the interpretations of opinions, and the interplay of opinions and thoughts that may go in quite opposite directions. The beautiful thing about a university is that one can disagree without being disagreeable.

I applaud the insight and understanding generated by this seminar as indicated in the materials reported here, and I hope that the participants' deliberations will both enhance their own creativity and help to clarify the issues as debated in the broader moral sphere.

Rev. Theodore M. Hesburgh, C.S.C.
The University of Notre Dame

Acknowledgments

THE MOVING FORCE BEHIND the initiation of this seminar was C. R. Smith, past president of American Airlines. His example, as a pioneer in both military and commercial air transport, and through a long association with the University of Notre Dame, reminds academicians, particularly faculty in the professional schools, that we must not only work with concepts and analyses, but must move toward the implementation of our ideas. It is not enough to outline an ideal world, we are called to change the world through interaction with the profession which we serve relative to the issues of our concern.

Two of us from the University of Notre Dame initiated the seminar from which the materials reported in this volume are drawn: Father Don McNeill, the Director of the Center for Experiential Learning, and myself. Early in our acquaintance in 1976, we found that although we shared a common concern for the persistent poverty in the Third World, our views of potential solutions, particularly the role of multinational corporations, varied substantially. Now, thanks to the other seminar participants, we both feel that we have a much surer grasp of the problem and hope that we are moving toward agreement on some solutions. Father Don's comprehension of the process of learning through experience pervades the seminar activities.

Content credit goes to the participants as well as to the designated authors. In this seminar, no idea has gone unchallenged. The materials presented in this volume do, indeed, reflect a full range of world views brought to bear on the issues, thanks to the unusual intensity of the participant debate. These interchanges have been captured in the discussion summaries, all of which have been prepared by Therese Tavis.

We are grateful to all the participants in the seminar, and

wish to commend them for their contributions of time and spirit and talent. The seminar participants are listed in the Appendix. We owe a special debt of thanks to the management of the multinational firms which offered the support of their names, their funds, and, most importantly, an extensive commitment of their executives' time, to a project with high risk and no possibility of direct return. All are to be commended.

American Cyanamid
Caron International
Castle & Cooke, Inc.
Caterpillar Tractor
Chase Manhattan Bank
Continental Bank
W. R. Grace & Co.
Johnson & Johnson
Ralston Purina

These firms, of course, cannot be held responsible for statements in this volume. The materials reflect a full range of views on the role of multinationals in the Third World.

Lee A. Tavis
University of Notre Dame

Introduction

IN OCTOBER 1978, a diverse group of multinational corporate managers, academicians from a wide variety of disciplines, missionaries, and others directly involved in Third World development, convened at the University of Notre Dame to initiate a dialogue directed toward identifying ways in which socially conscious multinational managers (executives of firms whose products or services are both produced and sold in underdeveloped as well as developed countries) might respond to poverty in Third World countries where their firms have investments. Many managers are vitally concerned with the desperate living conditions of the poor in these countries and believe that the presence of their firms may provide opportunities to exercise some ameliorating influence. A major challenge facing these executives is to respond to the living conditions of people attempting to survive at the boundaries of physical existence, while continuing to ensure the profitability of their firms' operations.

Since the initial meeting, the group has continued as a seminar, and it has undertaken a variety of activities. Organized under the Notre Dame Center for the Study of Man in Contemporary Society, it is now in its fifth year of discussion and research. We believe that our deliberations have progressed to the point where we should share our concerns and analyses with others.

BACKGROUND OF THE SEMINAR

The seminar has been structured to develop a dialogue that would continue with a high degree of intensity over a long period of time to deal effectively with the complexity of the poverty issue and its problematic links to the private sector. It intends to focus the attention of participants with fundamentally different world views on alternative actions that could be initiated by multinational firms. The participants recognize that each human holds the right to some minimal survival standard of living and that those of us who are not trapped in absolute poverty must attempt to aid the desperately poor. This moral congruence is what has held the group together.

Given the large presence of multinational firms in all corners of the world, the issue of their relationship to national economies has become of primary significance. When one begins to discuss the issue within any gathering, the need for dialogue becomes obvious. Beyond the general affirmation that multinational firms contribute to economic growth, there is not much consensus among multinational managers, economists, social theorists, church groups, labor or Third World leaders as to what influence multinationals do or should exert on national economics, or on particular groups within the host countries, such as the poor. Each observer assigns a role to the multinational which supports that individual's normative view of how the world should be structured. And most observers would impose their own rules on the firm without considering the managerial response and responsibility, or what actions could be initiated within the firms themselves.

Currently there is little communication between managers—who, often through direct experience, are keenly aware of and concerned with the crushing poverty of the Third World—and organizations such as the United Nations or missionary groups, which are conducting effective analyses of these problems. Positions have become entrenched. Most attempts at dialogue turn into confrontations with little communication taking place, even when the participants share a genuine concern for the poor. It seemed that a university could provide a proper forum to bring these groups together, and that the University of Notre Dame, with its commitment to global justice and peace, was particularly suited to this purpose. And thus the seminar was launched.

The most important element undergirding the commitment of the seminar to the world's poor is the quality of the participants. The group membership is well balanced in terms of executives, academicians, and others involved with Third World development. Ten firms have representatives among the executive participants. These managers have extensive operating experience in Third World countries. The Notre Dame faculty members involved represent a broad spectrum of the University's disciplines: They are drawn from the Departments of Accountancy, Economics, Finance, Government, Marketing, and Theology. In addition, participants with experience in Third World development come from the United Nations, the Center of Concern, the Council of the Americas, the U.S. Department of State, the International Finance Corporation, the University of Texas, and the Maryknoll and Millhouse Fathers. A list of participants is in the Appendix.

The process of structured interaction among a group with such disparate world views evolved serendipitously as a result of our activities. A number of participants consider the process to be as important as the content. The seminar is indeed unique in terms of the diversity of its participants, the level of trust that has developed among people with vastly different interpretations of world events, and the organization of research teams made up of practitioners as well as theoreticians.

The seminar has now moved through seven phases: four workshops built around three research periods. The first workshop, held 2–4 October 1978, was designed to outline the problems and clarify the relevant issues. Its purpose was to set a conceptual structure for the potential role of multinational involvement with Third World poverty. This first workshop was followed by a year-long research phase during which seminar participants undertook studies of the multinational presence in the less-developed countries as a transition from the conceptual discussion of the first workshop to specific courses of action available to the multinationals. The research was planned by task forces, each one with membership balanced between executive and nonexecutive participants. The goal of the research task forces was to establish as objective a data base as possible, the reliability of which could be broadly agreed upon by all seminar participants. The alternative interpretations of these data took place in the follow-up workshop, as each participant was challenged to apply his or her own interpretation of the data to the issue at hand and to suggest strategies and implementation procedures for the multinational response to Third World poverty.

The second workshop, on Multinational Action Alternatives, was held in October 1979. We then extended the research phase for two more periods, and met at workshops in 1980 and 1981.

This volume contains papers presented at the first three meetings and the reports of research undertaken.[1] Presentations are followed by a summary of the subsequent workshop discussions.

THE MANAGERIAL PROBLEM

In developing the seminar, it was realized that multinational managers are in a unique and tension-creating situation. Their firms, as the key economic integrators in a politically fragmented and increasingly nationalistic world, are an inextricable constituent of both the progress and the problems of the international economic order.

Multinationals have contributed in a major way to economic growth in both developed and less-developed countries since World War II. Technological capabilities and the ability to convert technology to productivity through the organization of complex productive systems and to marshal financial and other resources on a worldwide scale to support that production have been a cornerstone of worldwide economic growth. In the coming decades, the multinational contribution to worldwide productivity will be even more important as greater demands are made on natural resources.

The same global contribution and integration, however, make the multinationals a component of the persistent maldistribution of resources. The dramatic worldwide economic growth of the past quarter century has not touched the lives of millions of people in both urban and rural areas who live at the boundaries of physical existence. For them, economic development has not paralleled economic growth. The widely held trickle-down theory of economic development does not seem to be working, at least in a time frame considered acceptable in light of the deplorable conditions in which so many people now exist.

The extent of poverty in the Third World is stunning. This kind of poverty cannot be allowed to continue. The most fundamental human right is to survive, and, no matter where the minimum standard for basic human needs is set, millions and millions of people fall far short of that threshold.

Multinationals are tied to the poor through the patterns of development in the Third World countries. As an economic bridge between the developed and less-developed countries, they provide the means by which international resource balances are operationalized. As a major factor within many less-developed countries, multinationals are closely tied to local development issues.

For individual firms, the linkage to the poor depends upon the company and the particular country's development pattern. A firm producing medical supplies or pharmaceuticals in a less-developed African country, for example, would have close linkages. Its products are a necessary consumption item for the poor and they must be usable under the most squalid, unsanitary conditions. The local production of these goods would create additional direct ties to the poor in the areas of employment, training, finances, etc., and indirect ties through the country's development process. A multinational agribusiness would introduce modern production technology into the technically primitive cultures and economies of remote rural areas. A bank lending to agricultural cooperatives is closely linked to rural living standards. Other kinds of multinationals, such as firms extracting minerals for export, would be a major factor in a country's balance of payments, though it might have fewer direct ties to the internal sector.

Thus, multinational enterprises with investments in the Third World have direct and indirect linkages with the people, and they may be in a position to help. Managers who accept the poverty challenge will need to balance their continuing fundamental responsibility to enhance worldwide productivity against their search for positive responses to the issues arising from the conditions of the poor in the Third World. The actions undertaken by managers will be the results of their own intentions constrained by the realities of the multinational environment and their own ability to initiate action within the corporate structure.

Content of the Volume

The paper and discussion summaries presented here follow the issues as they unfolded in the seminar. Part I addresses the poverty issue and how it relates to the environment of the multinational corporation. It poses the problem, outlines the very real pressures for change in the international environment that are altering the opportunity and the constraints facing the multinational firm, and analyzes the belief systems of groups involved in this change.

Part II enters into a discussion of how multinationals can and should respond to poverty within the confines of the national and international environments. A number of participants share their views as to the potential for multinational response. The responsibility of corporations to respond, and the degree of freedom available to managers to direct their response, are debated, as are the managerial techniques required for incorporating their concern into the decision process.

Part III is a case history, describing and analyzing the Castle & Cooke Dolefil pineapple-raising operation in the southern Philippines. The major research activity of the seminar, this project was undertaken as an attempt to look beyond the multinational economic impact to its social effects, as well as to provide a concrete example on which to focus the conceptual discussion. The data are presented as objectively as possible, and are then interpreted from different perspectives by three seminar participants.

Part IV briefly outlines the nature of the debate concerning the presence of multinational corporations in Third World countries. It considers the various levels at which analysis can take place, and it addresses the question of why the debate is so contentious that it seems to hinder rather than enhance the conditions of the truly needy.

Lee A Tavis

Note

1. Papers from Workshop IV, held in October 1981, and Workshop V, scheduled for 1982, will appear in a second volume of this series.

PART I:

The Multinational Environment

IN PART I THE critical elements of the multinational environment are reviewed. The first papers set the nature of the problem: the characteristics of persistent, severe poverty in the Third World. In his paper Father McCormack statistically documents the magnitude of poverty and examines its ties to a major causal factor, population growth. Jameson then concentrates on the way economic and social systems create poverty, and urges that, if this historical pattern is to be broken, we must learn more about the social and economic structures of countries of the Third World.

From these discussions of poverty, we turn in Father Henriot's paper to a consideration of how the global economic system is changing and the challenge of restructuring the world's economic order.

Next, we have two discussions on the vast topic of the transfer of technology from developed to less-developed countries. This is an issue that touches on every aspect of the multinational firm's presence in national economies and relates directly to employment and the pattern of development in the host country as well as to the success of the corporation. Hayden raises the issue of conflicting objectives between supplier governments in the developed countries and user governments in the Third World. The discussion paper on the United Nations Conference for Science Technology and Development draws on the rich experience of members of the seminar group with that Conference.

In the final paper of Part I, Francis and Manrique present a consideration critical to a full understanding of the multinational corporation in its environment: the belief systems of those who will share in molding the future role for multinationals. This project arose from a concern with the rancor of the argument. The seminar group observed that much of the "debate" was not really a debate at all, because the discussion regarding the impact of multinational corporations on less-developed countries consisted in some groups making comments that were not even heard by others. Thus this paper attempts to identify the topics or issues that have been sufficiently defined and agreed upon to support meaningful debate, and to anticipate areas of agreement that are masked by the emotionalism of the argument.

1. Poverty and Population

REV. ARTHUR McCORMACK, M.H.M.

MOST PEOPLE ARE AWARE that many countries in the world are poor. When famine or disaster strikes, generosity on a personal and national basis is prompt to alleviate it. Even in normal times the plight of hundreds of millions is serious, and for that reason the United States contributes well over $2 billion per year to the developing countries and, since World War II, has given nearly $30 billion in food aid alone. Still, it may be useful to give a more detailed picture of world poverty and relate it to population increases so that the true extent and urgency of the problem may be realized and the case for the multinational contribution fully defined.

DEVELOPING COUNTRIES AND THE THIRD WORLD

Until recently the poorer countries of the world were more often described under the overall title of the Third World. But this is actually an inaccurate description. The Third World is actually composed of three worlds. It is valuable to explain the distinction.

One world consists of countries which are not all poor; indeed, they are very rich. There are some developing countries within the Organization of Petroleum Exporting Countries which at present have huge incomes because of their oil

This paper is an updated version of chapter 2 of Father McCormack's book *Multinational Investment: Boon or Burden for the Developing Countries?* (New York and London, 1980; copyright Arthur McCormack).

revenues and cannot be regarded as "poor," yet technically they have been classed with the Third World. Kuwait and Abu Dhabi exemplify this sector of the Third World. These states are not really the Third World in the true sense.

The majority of developing countries—over 100 of them —do not produce oil and many are poor, some extremely so. The really poor people are concentrated in the Third and Fourth Worlds[1]—the worlds of non-oil-producing developing countries. The Third and Fourth Worlds, along with the oil-exporting states, comprise three worlds, or sectors of the Third World as it is generally referred to.

The Third World, in this more specific examination, includes states with a dualistic society, such as the Philippines or Brazil, where a group within the population has a high degree of the developed world's affluence but many millions of the population—by far the majority—have yet to experience any of this affluence to any great extent. The Philippines would perhaps resent the title "developing country," though in official bodies it is listed with that bloc. If one sees the prosperity and the luxury high-rise buildings in Manila, one would think one was in a rich country. Even poor people seem to "get by" and those with some education seem to have a quite tolerable life. But if one visits the slums of Manila or the rural areas throughout the country, one sees that there is desperate poverty and that, for nearly half the population of 45 million, life is often a precarious battle for survival.

The Fourth World is that in which even the dualistic façade is missing; nothing in this group of states masks the absolute destitution of the people in these states. In countries such as Bangladesh and Kampuchea, thousands of people die every day because the barest of human needs cannot be met.

It is important to recall that the Third World is not merely one set of states existing on equal economic and social levels. Perhaps it can be said that those states in the specific Third World (as outlined here) are the developing world, while those in the Fourth World are not really "developing," and are known as the poorest countries.[2]

THE STATISTICS OF POVERTY

Gross national product (GNP) per head is a poor guide in these cases. It is not income per capita but food per stomach or money per pocket that is the real indicator. It is with this reservation in mind that one should study the World Bank table below which, using the rough guide of GNP per head per year, highlights the realities of poverty in much of the world. This table shows that only 54 countries (out of 178) with a total population of 1,088 million are prosperous, with per capita incomes of $3,000 or more. At the other end of the scale, 74 countries with a total population of nearly 2.5 billion have per capita incomes of less than $700 a year (one tenth of the lowest figure for rich countries).

Table I

Per Capita Income of Rich and Poor Countries

Income group	Number of countries	Population mid-1978 (millions)	GNP 1978 (U.S. $000 millions)	Average GNP per capita 1978 (U.S. $)
Less than $300	36	2,008	415	210
$300 to $699	38	493	232	470
$700 to $2,999	50	571	841	1,470
$3,000 to $6,999	29	536	2,222	4,150
$7,000 and over	25	552	5,083	9,220

Source: World Bank Atlas, 1979.

Note: Due to rounding, the amounts in this table may not equal the amounts or aggregates of the figures appearing in the regional tables. For geographical location of the countries listed, see regional maps.

Among the countries in the lowest class are the "least developed countries" and some which come under the U.N. designation of countries "most seriously affected" by the rise in oil prices (1973) and by general inflation.[3] The total population of the "poorest" countries is 609 million. Their average GNP per head is less than $100 per year.

Putting the above figures into more human terms, they mean that more than one-fourth of the people of the world have an annual income less than that which many Americans get per week. One in seven lives in a country where the average per capita income per year is less than that of a "poor" worker in the United States per week.

The GNP per capita is an imperfect measuring instrument, as I have already pointed out, because it is an average. Some people may be very much richer than, for example, $200 per year; many may be very much poorer. In making comparisons, one has to allow for a different cost of living in developing countries as compared to developed countries; on the other hand, even the poor in developed countries share in the general amenities found in more affluent nations.

Having made all these allowances, it nevertheless remains clear that perhaps at least two billion people do not have the financial or other resources for a life which will enable them to fulfill their possibilities as human beings. They are dogged by preventable ill-health, inadequate or unsuitable food, and little leeway to allow for natural disasters.

These are the facts—the world as a whole still lives in a state of underdevelopment. Estimates may certainly vary and different yardsticks may be used to measure them; but statistics on poverty and hunger never convey sufficiently the despair on which they are based. Such statistics are not mere figures to be juggled.

THE HUMAN SITUATION

I have had the melancholy privilege of visiting and walking around the slums of the developing world on three continents and have actually lived and worked in one of them in West Africa. Though by no means a picture of unrelieved gloom—for human nature does triumph over the most materially deprived conditions and the ingenuity of the inhabitants can make their environment less unbearable—this is a situation that cannot be tolerated.

We must look beyond the statistics to the human dilemma represented by them. Many of the peoples in these countries are poor, hungry, subject to disease, living in conditions unworthy of human beings, illiterate and underemployed. In presenting our statistics, it must never be forgotten that this is a problem concerning people who live in a million villages and in urban slums where conditions are well below the level of what most of us in the West would regard as the extreme limit of poverty.

Within the circle of underdevelopment, there are the

absolutely poor. Their self-perpetuating plight simply cuts them off from whatever economic progress there may be in their own society. They remain largely outside the whole development effort, neither able to contribute to it nor benefit from it. Malnutrition saps their energy, stunts their bodies, and shortens their lives. Simple preventable diseases maim and kill their children. Squalor and ugliness pollute and poison their surroundings.[4]

Surely, then, one of the immediate priorities for the human race must be to work for the alleviation of the plight of the underprivileged. The goal must be not only to give immediate help but also to enable them to secure for themselves the essentials of existence.

It is difficult to visualize such poverty or its relation to ourselves. These places are far away and do not seem to impinge on our lives. Moral concern, Christian concern, indeed simple human concern should make us want to eliminate such poverty. But human nature being what it is, moral concern too often tends to be turned aside by self-interest. For example, if you cut your finger while reading about a terrible earthquake, the pain of the smaller incident will wipe out the impression of the larger.

But self-interest is also involved. The developing countries are showing signs of passing from "deference to defiance"; and if hundreds of millions decide not to accept the division of the world into the "haves" and "have nots," decreasing world stability would affect us all. I am not thinking so much of Robert Heilbroner's suggestion of nuclear blackmail (though one could not rule that out),[5] but of confrontation and conflict between developed and developing countries, which the former might win—and in doing so might suffer so much that it would be a Pyrrhic victory.

The above facts show that economic and social growth in the developing countries are needed and should be among mankind's top priorities. Not that economic growth and development are ends in themselves, but for many they are preconditions of a decent living with the possibility of enjoying the most basic human rights.

The present state of affairs need not continue. The means are there to remedy the harshest realities of this tragic human situation if rich and poor countries cooperate. Man's ingenuity and efforts can vastly improve the situation if all who are in a position to do so help according to their own potential. Multinationals—those powerhouses of efficiency, skill, and inventiveness—have a part to play.

THE POPULATION FACTOR

The population factor, which is crucial to any consideration of the world situation, has tended to be ignored or played down in relation to multinational corporations. (For example, the word "population" does not appear in the index of the monumental work on multinationals, *Global Reach.*)[6] But the immense poverty I have described above is compounded by the vast numbers which exist in the world today—over 4 billion people, up from 1.6 billion in the year 1900, of whom nearly 80 percent live in the less-developed countries. What is more, this population expansion is still going on.

Population has exercised a powerful influence throughout history, and population pressures have been one of the major causes of mass migrations and of wars. As long as absolute numbers of migrants were not large, there was always somewhere to go. Now, although the land resources of the earth are by no means exhausted, there are no longer many places suitable for migration. Utilizing still empty spaces such as the Sahara Desert or the huge valley of the Amazon River would involve arduous and expensive operations and would have unforeseen effects on the earth's ecosystem.

The huge population increase of the past 150 years has put us in an unprecedented situation, and many new problems have arisen as a result.

The Growth of World Population

Population increase during the early part of the Christian era was sluggish. The Christian writer Tertullian warned of the dangers of overpopulation in the year 209 A.D., when the estimated population of the world was 200 million! Now the population is 20 times that number. It is not only the huge increase but the speed of the increase, especially in this century, which makes it extremely difficult even for underpopulated countries, like some African nations, to absorb rapidly increasing numbers.

It took well over one thousand years after Tertullian's time for the world population to rise from 200 to 500 million. But from the mid-seventeenth century onwards, mainly due to the medical and hygienic measures, a swift acceleration took place. The next increase of half a billion took less than 200 years (i.e., to 1830). Since then 3 billion more have been added. It now takes only one decade to add nearly a billion people. The third column of table 2 shows the reality of the population explosion.

Table 2

Population Increase A.D. 200 to 2000

Year	Population (millions)	Years to Add One Billion Persons
200	200	
1650	500	
1830	1000	
1850[1]	1200	1,650
1900	1600	
1920[1]	2000	90
1950	2500	
1961	3000 (or 3 billion)	41
1976	4 billion	15
1988	5 billion[2]	12
2000	6 billion[2]	12

Source: The author; compiled from a number of United Nations sources.
1. Approximation.
2. Projection.

The best projections for the year 2000 are roughly 5.8 billion to 6.25 billion, i.e., an increase of about 2 billion. It could be higher if measures to control population are not successful.

Rates of growth have gone down somewhat in the past 10 years, but world population, at its present rate of growth of 1.7 percent, is scheduled to double in 41 years' time from its present level (table 3).

Population Growth in the Developing World

In a finite world of limited resources and space, such a rapid multiplying of the numbers of people cannot go on indefinitely. At the moment, however, I wish to consider two main facts that are of immediate consequence. One is that the world will have about 2 billion more people in the year 2000 than it has now. No matter what measures are taken, these people will need to be provided for. Even if the increase could be reduced to 1.5 billion, my point remains valid.

The second fact is that this unprecedented growth has been and is taking place mainly in the developing world. Of these 2 billion, about 1.6 billion will be in Africa, Asia, and Latin America. There are more people now in the developing countries than there were in the entire world less than 15 years ago. (The 3 billion mark in world population was passed in March 1961.) And the increase continues at a staggering rate.

Table 3

World Population Situation, Mid–1979

	Estimated Population (millions)	*Rate of Natural Increase (percent)*	*Years to Double Population*	*Projections to Year 2000 (millions)*
World	4321	1.7	41	6168
Africa	457	2.9	24	831
Asia	2498	1.8[1]	38	3588
Latin America	352	2.7	26	597
Europe	483	0.4	173	521
North America	244	0.7	99	289
United States	220.7	0.6	116	260.4
Russia	264	0.8	87	311
Oceania	23	1.3	53	30

Source: Population Reference Bureau, Inc., *1979 World Population Data Sheet,* Washington, D.C.

1. Includes Japan, Singapore, and Hong Kong, whose low rates of increase lower the average.

The present population and rates of growth for selected developed and developing countries are shown in table 4. While none of the developed countries has a rate of population growth higher than 0.9 percent, all of the developing countries shown have a rate of 1.1 percent or more. Most have 2.5 percent and some have 3 percent and more.

Incidentally, one must also note that rates of increase become even more significant when related to absolute numbers. For example, India, with a growth rate of 1.9 percent and 660.9 million inhabitants, has a much greater problem of assimilation than Kuwait, with its 1.1 million inhabitants increasing at nearly twice that rate. At its present rate, India will have just over 1 billion people by the year 2000.

To put this into perspective, it may be useful to note that rates of population increase follow a compound interest pattern. For example, at a rate of increase of 0.1 percent it would take 690 years for population to double; with a rate of increase of 1 percent, it takes only 70 years for the population to double. When the rate of increase is 4 percent, it takes a mere 17 years for population to double. The pattern and its impact can be illustrated by the contrast between Germany and Mexico. With a rate of increase of 0.2 percent in 1979, the Federal Republic of Germany would double its population in 350 years (2329). Mexico, with a rate of 3.4 percent, would double its population in just over 20 years. The United States would double its population at present rates in 116 years.

CONSEQUENCES OF THE POPULATION EXPLOSION

The population explosion is a great complication — indeed, one of the main causes of world poverty. Mrs. Indira Ghandi once said that because of the rapid increase in population, "We have to run to stay in the same place." The Prime Minister of India was using, consciously or not, the words of Alice in *Through the Looking Glass.* When the fantasy world of Alice in Wonderland has caught up with real life, we can appreciate the seriousness of the situation. At present rates of growth, India must provide 10,000 extra school places, 1,000 new housing units, 1,000 more hospital beds per day for the next 20 years merely to accommodate the population increase of nearly 13 million per year — to say nothing of trying to im-

Table 4

Rates of Population Increase
in Selected Developed and Developing Countries

Country	Natural Rate of Increase[1] (percent)	Population Mid-1979 (millions)	Projection for Year 2000 (millions)
DEVELOPED COUNTRIES			
Japan	0.9	115.9	128.9
Canada	0.8	23.7	29.0
United States	0.6	220.7	260.4
Italy	0.4	56.9	61.2
France	0.4	53.4	57.2
United Kingdom	0.0	55.8	56.6
Federal Republic of Germany	0.2	61.2	63.4
DEVELOPING COUNTRIES			
Kuwait	3.7	1.3	3.1
Mexico	3.4	67.7	132.3
Brazil	2.8	118.7	205.2
Bangladesh	2.9	87.1	155.1
Nigeria	3.2	74.6	148.8
Bolivia	2.8	5.2	8.9
Tanzania	3.0	17.0	33.1
Indonesia	2.0	140.9	210.5
Egypt	2.6	40.6	63.5
India	1.9	660.9	1,010.5
China	1.2	950.0	1,193.0
Chile	1.6	11.0	15.1
Argentina	1.3	26.7	32.9
Uruguay	1.1	2.9	3.5

Source: *1979 World Population Data Sheet,* Population Reference Bureau, Inc., Washington, D.C.

1. The rate of natural increase will differ little except in special cases (such as Vietnam) from the rate of population growth (which includes migration).

prove the lot of the millions already living in poverty. The facts are there even when one cannot condone the methods Mrs. Ghandi took in 1975 and 1976.

The consequences for the developing world can be seen in every aspect of life. The 1976 United Nations Vancouver Conference on Human Settlements did not give much attention to population (like several other U.N. conferences which wanted to avoid controversy), but it is in the cities that one can see most vividly the consequences to the developing countries of rapid population increase. The population of Mexico City in 1950 was 2.9 million. It was 10.9 million in 1975. According to reasonable projections, it will be 31.5 million by the year 2000 at present rates of growth. Other cities in developing countries have similar population pictures, of which table 5 offers a small sample of the most populous. At the beginning of the twentieth century the world was a rural civilization; by the end of the century it will be an urban civilization. It is projected that by the start of the new millennium, over half of the population of the world will be in towns and cities of 100,000; that 60 cities will have populations of over 5 million people. Of the top 30 cities of the world, those in the developing countries will vastly increase in population while those in the developed countries will remain fairly constant or even decline somewhat.[7]

Table 5

Population Growth in Selected Large Cities of Developing Countries

| City | Population (millions) | | |
	1950	1975	2000
Mexico City	2.9	10.9	31.5
Sao Paulo	2.5	9.9	26.0
Lagos	0.3	2.4	9.4
Manila	1.5	4.4	12.8
Djakarta	1.6	5.6	17.8
Shanghai	5.8	11.5	22.1

Source: United Nations Fund for Population Activities, *Population and the Urban Future* (New York: United Nations Fund for Population Activities, 1980).

The Special Case of Food

There is not the space here to fully document the effect of population increases in the areas of food, employment, education, health services, the environment, and the growth of slums in the cities of the developing world. Some time ago I wrote a book on these subjects in which I devoted a chapter to each one.[8] But a few impressions may help to visualize what common sense tells us. We have seen how poor these countries are, and we know some of them actually experience hunger and starvation in bad years. If there is barely enough food for guests who are invited to a party, the solution is surely not to double the guest list.

Because of population dynamics, many more people—indeed, half the number who are on earth—are going to come to life's banquet whether we like it or not, short of absolute catastrophe and despite population control programs. However, we do have a choice at least regarding some of the increase.

It is clear that it does make a difference whether the number of additional people by the year 2000 is 1.8 billion, 2.25 billion, 2.4 billion, or even more. These figures can be affected by family planning programs in keeping with religious beliefs and cultural values—and these programs are essential.

At the same time, people who now exist must be given enough to eat and other basic necessities for a decent human life. The additional 2 billion people due to arrive by the end of the century, and who will come no matter what measures of birth regulation are used, must also be cared for. Sometimes preoccupation with the ways of reducing the rate of natural increase obscures this second immense task, a task in which multinationals, if they were given the chance, could assist considerably.

Obviously, the primary need is for more food. Thanks to technology, which has vastly increased food productivity, severe famines such as those that struck India in 1952 and China in 1962 are largely a thing of the past. Enough food can now be produced and made available to alleviate the worst famines. But the famines of 1972 and 1974 showed that grain stocks can become so low, transportation so difficult, and the ability of poorer countries to acquire supplies of food so restricted by their poverty that crisis situations can still arise. The famines of 1972 and 1974 which hit the African countries of the Sahel (Senegal, Mauritania, Mali, Upper Volta, Chad, and Gambia), and India and Bangladesh were not so terrible as those in the past, but they were bad enough. And worse still, the reserves of grain in the United States were at one time down to a 27-day supply.

Each year world population increases alone call for over 30 million more tons of grain, and this figure will rise as greater numbers each year compound the total increase. It is within the realm of possibility to feed this burgeoning population, but it will require immense efforts and worldwide cooperation.

The situation of plenty due to the bountiful harvests of 1976 and 1977, which led President Carter and Secretary of Agriculture Bergland to withdraw land from cultivation in order to avoid a glut and the accompanying depressed grain prices, did not occur in 1980 when the harvests were adversely affected by severe drought conditions. The 1981 food crop from California was hurt by the appearance of the Mediterranean fruit fly. These cases demonstrate how previously bountiful harvests can be hurt by the environment.

Acute fears of famine were lessened by the abundant harvests of the late 1970s but this did not mean that famines similar to 1972 and 1974 could not happen again. Critical shortages of food occur in many parts of Africa today—South Africa, Uganda, Nigeria, Tanzania, and Somalia—as well as in the southeastern Asian states of Indonesia and the Philippines. The world's attention became focused in 1980 on the plight of the 765,000 people living in Somalia who were unable to find enough food for subsistence due to overcrowding after war with Ethiopia and the onset of a severe drought.

A Washington-based agricultural consultant, E. A. Jaenke, warns that the world's next food shortage could be in the making right now and will occur within the next two or three years if there are bad harvests in one or more major grain-producing lands. The report of a three-week meeting of the Food and Agricultural Organization in Rome in December 1977 gave a similar warning. While confidence was expressed that the Organization was doing everything possible, the report stated that "the world food situation remains fragile and there are no grounds for complacency."

A report to the United Nations in November 1980 warned the developed states to begin creating world grain reserves because the world production is falling behind consumption at the rate of 2 percent in 1979 and a projected 3 percent in 1981. With this drop in production, world grain supplies will soon be at the 1972–74 levels when the world suffered from shortages. The result will be higher food costs for all, but they will especially hit those countries that cannot afford to pay any more.

Table 6 shows the statistical reasons for concern. It gives the amount of food, measured in tons of grain, that will be needed to feed the anticipated population increase in the years up to the end of the century, taking the United Nations median population projection.

Table 6

World Population and Food Needs, 1975 to 2000

	Developed	Developing	Communist	Total
POPULATION (MILLIONS)				
1975	765	2002	1200	3967
2000	926	3674	1632	6232
Total Increase	161	1672	432	2265
Total Increase (percent)	21.0	83.5	36.0	57.1
Average Annual Increase (percent)	0.8	2.5	1.2	1.8
TOTAL GRAIN CONSUMPTION (MILLION METRIC TONS)				
1975	399.3	367.9	448.5	1215.7
2000	492.9	765.5	619.0	1877.4
Total Increase	93.6	397.6[1]	170.5	661.7
Total Increase (percent)	23.4	108.1[1]	38.0	54.4
Average Annual Increase (percent)	0.8	3.0[1]	1.3	1.8

Source: U.S. State Department, *Foreign Agricultural Circular on Grains*, Washington, D.C., September, 1977.

1. Includes increase of 85.0 million metric tons required to raise the population of developing countries to minimum nutritional standards.

The fact that in 1975 the developing countries produced only 347.3 million metric tons of grain while their consumption was 367.9 million tons shows the great difficulties the developing countries will have to feed their people. A somewhat lower shortfall was experienced in these countries from 1976 to 1977—377.2 million tons consumed against production of 360.8 million. The position for 1977–78 was, however, worse still: production was estimated at 350.3 million tons against consumption of 386.0 million.[9]

Nevertheless, from the point of view of food production alone, it would be possible to feed the extra people who will populate the developing countries over the next 20 years. The problems will arise in the ability to pay and in transportation and distribution difficulties. But food aid and supplies from developed countries cannot be a permanent solution, although they will be needed for a long time to come.

The true solution is to increase the productivity of the farmers of the developing countries most in need. In this way food will be available on the spot. It will become an asset to these countries so that they do not need food imports for which they must use precious foreign exchange. That this can be done is shown by the concrete example of the Philippines and India: Improved strains of rice and wheat plus fertilizer and water can lead to much greater crop increases than comparable inputs in the developed countries. But "modernizing" the 700 to 800 million farmers in the developing world cannot be done overnight, nor can it be done without great economic and social changes. Moreover it cannot be done without political stability: One of the reasons that the ideological, brutal "cultural" revolution of 1966–1969 in China was called off was its disruptive effect on agriculture.

There are countries at present receiving food aid because political and military priorities are preferred to feeding their own people. To say the world cannot feed its peoples to the end of the century is unduly pessimistic. But for it to do so will require a far greater commitment on the part of all countries and a reordering of priorities.

Employment

Food is not the only basic need affected by rapid population increase. Perhaps the most intractable problem of this decade is unemployment, and it is directly affected by population increase. High population growth rates in the past are now throwing large numbers of young people into a job market which is beyond developing countries' powers of absorption. This situation will continue for the rest of the century. Some estimates suggest that at least 20 percent of the world's work force is out of a job. Not only is this a tragic waste of resources, it also poses some severe social problems.

Between 1967 and 1970 unemployment in Latin America soared, from 2.9 to 8.8 million, partly because of the population explosion. During the 1970s, 165 million Indian youths entered the job market, compared with 117 million in the 1960s. This is in addition to the fact that unemployment in India had risen from 11.4 percent in 1961 to 15.5 percent in 1969 (and this calculation is probably a conservative one). Incidentally, this should indicate that development projects should be labor-intensive, not capital intensive as in the West.

Unemployment in Mexico is typical of what is happening in many developing countries. More than a third of Mexico's work force of 16 million (the population of Mexico is 62 million, with an annual growth rate of 3.4 percent) is either unemployed or underemployed. Each year some 800,000 youths pour into the labor market, which can absorb only a fraction of them. Perhaps as many enter the United States illegally and are subject to fear and blackmail. On the other hand, some people in the United States wonder if their country should be used as a safety valve for problems caused by over-reproduction.[10]

Added to this unemployment picture is a very high rate of population increase in Mexico. By the year 2000 Mexico's population will double and the population of Mexico City will triple. The combination of rapid population increase and widespread poverty is a potent cause of great social unrest and probable political upheaval. To have a seething population on its doorstep would be a very undesirable situation for the United States as well.

It could possibly be through increasing the productivity of farmers in developing states that both the food and unemployment situations could be best improved since raising productivity could be accomplished through labor-intensive tasks. Not only would this put more people to work and increase the badly needed output of food in the developing countries, but this labor-intensive solution would preclude the importation of capital-intensive solutions that almost invariably mean machinery and/or technology which the developing countries cannot afford. If they did not import such items (expensive and sophisticated machinery as well as highly specialized technology) from the developed states, the developing countries could lower their external debt and could concentrate on funding domestic projects rather than paying off their creditors abroad.

To do this, however, the developing states must have aid in searching for new strains of crops, developing irrigation systems, and finding alternative energy sources, since they simply cannot afford to pay for existing ones at current world prices. When a new strain of rice is developed, the other prerequisites for growing it must be found since the rice cannot be grown without fertilizer and irrigation. With the increasing cost of energy vital to improving yield in states with a growing number of people, provisions should be made to meet energy needs in order to increase both employment and food production levels. If these things are not done, both social unrest and large-scale famines may soon result.[11]

Multinationals—One Way Out of the Poverty Trap?

The vast problems that face the world for the rest of the century will take all the resources of human ingenuity and a wise choice of priorities to resolve them. Dynamic leadership will be needed. It is these considerations which lead me to suggest that an institution which has shown outstanding capabilities in the past should—indeed, must—play the part.

Giovanni Agnelli, the president of Fiat in Italy, has put this succinctly:

> We live in a world of mass poverty, rapidly rising population, growing resource scarcity and accelerating inflation. Global planning to assure the most efficient possible use of resources is desperately needed to cope with these problems. It would be wrong to assert that multinational companies can solve these huge problems by themselves, but it is hard to see how these problems can be so solved without the management skill, the technical know-how, the financial resources and

the worldwide cooperation networks that the multinationals possess.[12]

For multinational corporations to solve these problems will require an appreciation of the fact that overall population increase among the poor is not the advantage for business that population increase in itself might seem to be. The extent and rapidity of the increase in the less-developed world might well be a recipe for disaster. It need not be. Self-interest and moral concern should make multinationals use their power to help ensure that it is not. Ultimately, they have no more important goals than this. A novel idea, perhaps? Yes, but since when have multinationals been allergic to novel ideas?

NOTES

1. The Third World and Fourth World: Originally the term Third World was used (first by George Baladier in 1956) to describe the countries which did not belong to the First World, the industrialized countries, or the Second World, the Communist bloc countries. In the course of time, the term Third World became synonymous with the poor developing countries. However, since 1973, when some of these countries became poorer on account of the quintupling of oil prices (and oil-producing countries became very much richer), the use of the term Third World has become misleading as it could include countries such as Tanzania with an annual income per capita of $130 and Kuwait with an annual income per capita of $12,000. Since 1973 it has been more accurate to regard the Third World as those countries which are not among the poorest countries (and yet, at the same time, are not oil-producing countries), and the poorest countries themselves as the Fourth World. If we wish to retain the division of blocs of nations into "worlds," the oil-producing countries would then be regarded as the Fifth World. To use the ambiguous term Third World now can cause confusion.

2. *1980 World Bank Atlas,* p. 4.

3. Jyoti Shankar Singh, *A New International Economic Order: Toward a Fair Redistribution of the World's Resources* (New York: Praeger, 1977), p. 93.

4. Robert McNamara, Speech, Board of Governors of the World Bank, Washington, D.C., 1975.

5. Heilbroner says that there "seems little doubt" that underde-

veloped nations will have a nuclear capability "within the next few decades and perhaps much sooner." The question will then arise as to how that capability might be used, and, he says, "I will suggest that it may be used as an instrument of blackmail to force the developed world to undertake a massive transfer of wealth to the poverty-stricken world." Robert L. Heilbroner, *An Inquiry into the Human Prospect* (New York: W. W. Norton & Company, 1974), pp. 40–44.

6. Richard L. Barnet and Ronald E. Muller, *Global Reach: The Power of the Multinational Corporations* (New York: Simon & Schuster, 1974).

7. United Nations Fund for Population Activities, *Population and the Urban Future* (New York, 1980). The book is the result of a conference held in Rome, 1–4 September 1980. It was attended by the mayors of 47 of the 60 cities that are projected to have over 5 million people by the year 2000. The information is derived from a chart in the book which shows the top 30 cities and their growth from 1950 to 2000.

8. *The Population Explosion: A Christian Concern* (New York: Harper & Row, 1973).

9. U.S. Department of Agriculture, "World Agricultural Situation," October 1977. Due to the "Green Revolution" the Philippines exported rice in 1977, and India was self-sufficient in grain in 1970. For a discussion of food needs and population growth, especially with regard to developing countries, see Keith Abercrombie and Arthur McCormack, "Population Growth and Food Supplies in Different Time Perspectives," *Population and Development Review*, September-December 1976.

10. Louis Turner, *Multinational Companies and the Third World* (New York: Hill & Wang, 1973), pp. 160–163.

11. *New York Times*, February 23, 1981, p. 19.

12. John Humble, *The Responsible Multinational Enterprise* (London: Foundation for Business Responsibilities, 1975), p. 73.

2. Poverty: The Result of Economic and Social Structures

KENNETH P. JAMESON

IN 1850 THOMAS CARLYLE denominated economics as "the dismal science." Let me make three points to provide some context on how very dismal the economics of poverty can be: we know very little about poverty and those afflicted by it; the poor have always been with us and our economic systems have created them; and, in examining poverty we must also examine the issue of social structures.

Father Arthur McCormack has said that indeed if we are talking of poverty, we have to talk about it in terms of how it affects people, how it affects the individuals involved, rather than simply looking at large-scale aggregate statistics. To try to do that, I give you one example of what poverty means. The example is taken from northeastern Brazil in an area that in the early '50s and again in the '60s became a sisal boom area. Large portions of the land were planted in sisal. The overall impact of this boom was an increase in the concentration of land with many people losing their land and going into wage labor. One such wage laborer is Miguel Costa; he works in sisal. He and his wife and four children live together. If one estimates what their caloric requirements are for growth and maintenance, they need about 12,592 calories per day to live normally. But, with his income the most they can purchase is 9,393 calories, which is about 75 percent of their total needs. Miguel's needs are met, because if they were not met, he would gradually become weaker and become unable to work. His wife's are also met. What happens in such a poverty situation is that the caloric deficit results in a reduction of the calories the children can take in. Its impact, the real implication of such poverty, is that the parents are starving their children. They are starving them not because they want to do it, but because that is the only response they can have in the situation that they are in. The impact on the children can be seen in terms of their growth. For example, their three year old son is about 85 percent of the average size of children of that age; their six year old, 70 percent; their eight year old is 62 percent. In other words, the growth of the children, or the retardation in their growth, gets progressively worse as they grow older. They will eventually end up with problems in terms of energy, intelligence, and so forth. What I have described is the human dimension of poverty and we must keep it as our context in considering poverty.

With this "dismalism"—the reality of poverty—in mind, I want to make three points individually. The first is that we know very little about poverty and impoverished people, but we do know that our social processes are creating poverty all the time. It is even difficult to count the poor. We are becoming adept since the 1950s at compiling aggregate statistics: gross national product, savings rates, etc. We do not, however, know very much about poor people. A few anthropologists have studied poor people in their situations and gradually are unmasking more information. The point that I would like to make is based upon the evidence that we do have, based upon the experience we do have. We can make a case that there has always been poverty; obviously, certain areas of the world have always been poor. They will probably continue to be poor, unless something remarkable happens. There are people who have always been poor; the Tasaday in the Philippines have always been poor. There is a substratum of poverty that has always been with us.

One of the things that we are coming to understand, however, is that poverty is not simply a static situation of continuance of poverty. We are actually creating poverty in the present era: in a very real way, if we can talk in global terms, our economic systems and the way they function are actually creating poverty.

The evidence, again, has to be impressionistic, but some obvious examples exist. One example is that some of the Indian tribes in Brazil, having been "discovered," have had their lands taken away. And in some cases there have been actual

attempts to wipe out the tribes. We would say that the degree
of their poverty has indeed increased as a result of this economic development into the Amazon region of Brazil. Miguel
Costa is another example. He had been a small farmer, existing at a subsistence level, but able to protect himself in terms
of security by allocating his resources in different fashions
during drought, etc. Then he had some margin; now, as a
wage laborer, he has no margin. If he cannot go to work some
days, he does not earn anything and his family situation becomes much worse. He is an example of an increase in poverty.

One of the best studies on this was done by the British
economist-anthropologist, Margaret Haswell, on the Gambia.
She did her initial work back in the 1940s on nutrition and
agriculture in Gambia, and returned in the 1960s and 1970s to
see what was happening in one particular Gambian village.
Her basic conclusion is that in the Gambian village there is a
new form of poverty, what she calls institutionalized poverty,
meaning, in her terms, that, while the people who live in the
village now have higher aspirations, on the other hand they
have experienced no change in their ability to satisfy those
aspirations. Their objective conditions are virtually the same,
but because of those higher aspirations many of the support
structures that could cushion them in a drought or in some
sort of a disaster have been taken away. The communal support system is now gone. It has been destroyed by the structural changes to the economy which in turn have seriously al-
tered the social system on which the communal support system
rested. The introduction of Western-type business enterprises,
particularly the multinationals, depended on the free market
economy, which could not coexist with the previous communal
society. Instead, the traditional society in the Third World
areas has been permanently put in a secondary place because
people are forced to choose between the system they know
best and the one that is being imposed on them by the developing industries. Eventually, the traditional society is not
merely institutionalized into a secondary position, but eventually it disappears, and the poverty which has accompanied the
secondary position (poverty induced by introducing the new
technologically advanced life style and a new consumer-
oriented ideology which cannot be part of the communal society) becomes the normal condition. So the situation in the

Third World, in this case of the Gambian village, has become much more precarious in this twenty-year period.

My first point, then, is simply that we must realize that we are creating poverty and that this is a challenge which we will have to deal with.

The second point I would like to make is that this is nothing new. The poor have always been with us and we have always been creating poor people through our economic systems. Indeed, if we go back to 1850, back to the time of Thomas Carlyle, and try to understand the determinants of poverty and what was going on with poverty at that time, we find many analogies to what is occurring today. One study of historical evidence attempted to learn as much as possible about poor people in 24 countries in the 1850s. It concluded that in periods of economic transformation and economic change, the poor lose. In the 1850s, the poor lost.

Another lesson from that study is that the poor are highly affected by the availability of land. Where there existed access to the major resource at that time, land (which is still the major resource in many of the Third World countries today), the loss to the poor was less than in situations where there was no access to the asset of land.

In addition, the study found that the history of these 24 countries presented no automatic mechanism which incorporates the poor into the overall growth and development of the country. In other words, the poor can be marginalized very easily and there is no tendency to bring them into the general development that is going on.

In addition, it was in the period of most rapid growth that the poor were hurt most, around the period of the 1850s. It was in the countries which were growing most rapidly that the poor were suffering the greatest losses. But the basic social, political, and economic structures of the situation could mediate and have an import on the final experience of poor people.

In some sense I suppose, we can take solace in the fact that the poor have always been with us and these processes have always been going on. So we say, "What's new? What was happening in the 1850s is happening in 1981 as well." In some sense the challenge to us is not to say, "Well, that's life. That's nature. That's the way the economy and political structure works." Rather, it is a challenge to say, "Well, it may have worked that way before but the difference in 1981 is that we now have the ability to begin to ameliorate these tendencies which operate to the detriment of the poor. We can break out of this historical pattern." In a very real sense, I think that is what we are examining in this book.

My third point picks up on the whole question of social structures. The topic of the volume is multinational managers and how they can relate to poverty. I would like to point out that throughout these essays one should keep in mind that what a multinational manager might do will be highly conditioned by the given social and political-economic structures of a country. What that suggests is that if we are going to think about poverty and deal with it, we have to look at countries that have been successful and try to ask ourselves why they have been successful. Luckily, at this point we have enough information, enough background, so that we can begin to ask those questions. We do find a number of countries in which the dismalisms are much less and in which the situation of poverty has been dealt with much more successfully than it has in the aggregate statistics that are mentioned. Examples are Taiwan, Korea, and perhaps Sri Lanka and Costa Rica. These are success stories where there has been growth accompanied by an amelioration of or a decline in the amount of poverty. We have to understand why it happens in some countries and not in other countries, for that will affect the impact of the multinational manager.

I would also suggest that you owe it to yourselves, we owe it to ourselves, to realize that many of the countries in which there has been a decline in poverty have a very different social structure from that which we are accustomed to. They are the socialist countries. Many of them have been relatively successful in lessening poverty when compared with many of the non-socialist Third World countries. To be sure, the record is mixed on the socialist as well as on the non-socialist sides, but some of what has been learned in China and Cuba in terms of delivering basic health services, basic nutrition, and in agricultural production must be studied and be taken seriously. I'm not sure if we can draw any recipes for the multinational managers from those experiences. Perhaps it is better not to do so, but at the least we must realize that whatever multinational managers can do will certainly be mediated by the given social and economic structures of the countries they are dealing with.

I would like to end by expressing the hope that this type of a context will be helpful. It is, again, a type of aggregate context. But we have to realize what poverty is. We have to realize how it stands within the historical context. We have to realize that there are political and economic structures that are going to affect what anybody can do in terms of dealing with poverty.

3. Restructuring the International Economic Order

REV. PETER J. HENRIOT, S.J.

IN HIS FOREWORD TO the *World Development Report 1978,* former World Bank President Robert McNamara described the development challenges in the following words:

> The past quarter century has been a period of unprecedented change and progress in the developing world. And yet, despite this impressive record, some 800 million individuals continue to be trapped in what I have termed absolute poverty: a condition of life so characterized by malnutrition, illiteracy, disease, squalid surroundings, high infant mortality, and low life expectancy as to be beneath any reasonable definition of human decency.
>
> Absolute poverty on so massive a scale is already a cruel anachronism. But unless economic growth in the developing countries can be substantially accelerated, the now inevitable increases in population will mean that the numbers of the absolute poor will remain unacceptably high even at the end of the century.
>
> The twin objectives of development, then, are to accelerate economic growth and to reduce poverty.

The purpose of this paper is to explore the second objective of development—to reduce poverty—as it relates to alternative world models, particularly the one expressed in a

---

A summary of the general discussion after the presentation of Father Henriot's paper is contained in the Addendum to this chapter.

New International Economic Order (NIEO), and to probe what might be some of the policy implications for multinational corporations that take seriously the challenge of global poverty.

I should at the outset disclose how I approach the topic. I am by training a political scientist; but I will be using some economics, from the point of view of political economy. I am by additional training a priest—and I will be considering some ethical issues, from the point of view of social justice. I am also by temperament an activist; hence, I will be advocating social change, from the point of view aroused by strong feelings about present injustices. Thus, I have my biases.

The basic question being asked in discussions of world development is one which I consider to be the major ethical issue confronting the people of the United States in the remainder of the twentieth century. That question is: What stance will we take in the restructuring of the world's economic order so as to effect a more equitable distribution of resources to meet basic human needs? I believe that this question of the global restructuring of the economic order impinges deeply upon the domestic scene in this country and will increasingly enter our politics in the years immediately ahead; it will be with us all of our lives.

It is crucial that an examination of the role of multinational corporations in meeting world poverty takes place within a global context of the call for a restructuring of the world's economic order. The focus in development debates is increasingly turned to the international structures of trade, aid, money, investment, and decision-making: these structures comprise the international economic order. The restructuring is being called for by many of the developing countries in the South, a call which is being rebuffed by many in the North. No North-South dialogue or decision is possible today without taking into account, whether positively or negatively, this call for structural change.

This paper examines three elements of the topic: First, How does the question of restructuring arise? Second, What are the dimensions of the debate around this question? And, third, What are some possible implications for the choices and activities of multinational corporations?

RESTRUCTURING

The first point is: How does this challenge of restructuring the global economic order come to us today? I believe that
in the United States, whether we belong to a policy community, a business community, an academic community, an ethical
values community, or simply an ordinary citizen community,
we all find ourselves continually more enmeshed in a world
struggle for which we lack a comprehensive picture, adequate
tools of analysis, a sufficient array of policy responses, and
convincing guiding principles. Without this comprehensive
global picture, we tend toward piecemeal, immediate, prag-
matic solutions. Lacking tools of analysis, we tend to see the
problem simply as a malfunction within the system, one that
we can adjust and modify to gain satisfactory results. Lacking
an array of policy responses, we tend to find ourselves locked
into certain positions without questioning them (e.g., the operation of a free market economy). Lacking guiding principles, we tend to be frightened by some of the implications of
calls for fair and equitable distribution of resources and the
provision of basic human needs for everyone.

Consequently, people in the United States seem to be increasingly in confrontation with a large portion of the world.
The axis of this confrontation has shifted in recent years from
an East-West arena to a North-South one. This means a
movement away from a previously dominant world view which
could be described as "pentagonal", not only in the sense that
it is the Pentagon's world view of the centrality of military-
strategic issues, but also pentagonal in that it concentrates on
the five major powers: the United States, the European Community, the Soviet Union, the People's Republic of China, and
Japan. The world today faces the realities of a confrontation
between the industrialized rich world, which includes the
Soviet Union and the Eastern European states, and the poor
nations—the developing countries, Latin America, Asia, and
Africa: the so-called Third World.

The United States is trying to come to grips with the policy implications of a globe on which the key confrontation is
not simply East versus West, but is increasingly North versus
South. Our foreign policy has not yet adequately adjusted to
this new situation. The United States still tends to see events in

Africa, Asia, and Latin America within an East-West context even when North-South language is used. For example, the situation in Angola a few years ago was viewed by the administration and in many foreign policy circles not primarily as a North-South problem of decolonization and development, but primarily as an East-West issue of military strategic significance. Political turns in Latin America are frequently weighed in terms of possible Marxist (Soviet and/or Cuban) influence, rather than in terms of social development and self-reliance.

Often the business community in the United States appears to be more perceptive than the government. The multinationals recognize that the North-South conflict is the central arena of the emerging world economy in terms of resources and markets. They have struggled to understand and to adapt to the changes in North-South relations. Some have fought these changes drastically (e.g., the sordid case of ITT in Chile); but others have adjusted fairly well, at least in short-term arrangements (e.g., majority control of investments by host countries). But all these corporations must respond to a "new assertiveness" that is being exercised by the developing nations. It will be helpful to study the background for this new assertiveness, which is based upon (1) a complaint they have, (2) an analysis they offer, and (3) a clout they exercise.

The Complaint

The complaint developing countries have is that the global economic order simply is not working to their advantage. It is important to note the reasons given for this complaint, whether or not we agree with them. Third World leaders point primarily to the widening and increasingly dangerous gap between rich nations and poor ones. Today, some 25 percent of the world's population controls 80 percent of the world's wealth and trade, 90 percent of its industry and services, and almost 100 percent of its institutions of research. The World Bank reports that some 800 million people are trapped in "absolute poverty." In many parts of the Third World, the situation continues to deteriorate.

During the 1960s the gross output of the world increased nearly $1 trillion. Eighty percent of that increase went to nations with a gross national product per capita of over $1,000, the rich nations. Less than 6 percent of that increase went to the poorest nations of the world with GNP per capita of under $200 per year. Nearly two-thirds of the people of the world live in nations where, in the last two decades, the annual increase in GNP per capita has been less than one dollar a year. The poor nations are remaining poor.

In looking at the present international economic order, the South points to a variety of grounds for its complaint that this order does not operate to its advantage. In trade patterns, as an example, some 80 percent of the foreign exchange earnings of the developing countries comes from the sale of their raw materials. Yet, in the last decades while the non-oil-producing countries of the South increased the volume of their exports by more than 30 percent, their earnings for those exports increased by only 4 percent. Because of the fluctuating prices of basic commodities, they were selling more and making less profit; simultaneously, they were finding their own purchasing power undercut by inflation in the rich nations. For example, in 1960 Indonesia could sell 25 tons of rubber and earn enough to purchase six tractors from Europe or the United States. Today, the earnings would purchase only two tractors. Guatemala could in 1960 purchase one tractor with the earnings from three tons of bananas; today, nine tons of bananas would have to be sold to bring the equivalent earnings.

Other trade that developing countries engage in, such as manufactured goods, faces many obstacles in the industrialized world. Discouraging tariff and non-tariff barriers are effective obstacles. For instance, unprocessed cocoa from Ghana can enter West German markets with an import duty of 4 percent, but cocoa manufactured into chocolate bars faces an import duty of 12 percent. The developing countries lose an estimated $20 to $30 billion a year in export earnings because of such barriers. An economist at the World Bank has said that the structure of international prices shows that the developing countries receive back about $30 billion a year for the export of their 12 principal commodities (tea, coffee, cocoa, etc.). Consumers in the developed countries pay for these same commodities (in a slightly more processed, packaged, and advertised form) close to $200 billion, with the estimated $170 billion difference going to the international middleman—the service sector, multinational, etc. Former

World Bank President McNamara has sharply criticized the excessive and increasing protectionism in the developed nations. New quotas have been imposed in recent years by many European nations and by Canada and the United States against imports such as clothes, textiles, footwear, and other manufactured items from developing states.

Most people know that foreign aid has been declining, though many may not realize just how much, and with what effect. In 1960 the total flow of Official Development Assistance (ODA) from North and South was 0.52 percent of the gross national product of northern countries; in 1977 this percent had fallen to 0.31. The United States is today among the lowest of the low in ODA flows, with only 0.22 percent of its GNP going to help the poor nations. The greatest part of aid is in the form of loans, not of outright gifts, increasing the serious problem of the South's indebtedness. The outstanding debt of the poor nations by the end of 1978 was approximately $250 billion, and it is expected to increase by two-thirds by the end of 1985. Debt service is costing the non-oil-producing developing countries $37.1 billion a year, and it is consuming a large percentage of their foreign exchange earnings from exports. The South is actually returning considerably more to the North in interest and principal payments on previous loans and in purchases of goods than it is receiving in foreign aid, which raises the question of who is aiding whom.

Another part of the complaint is the issue of monetary relationships. The South complains that their currencies have not been protected from the consequences of the wild fluctuations of the dollar and the pound sterling on the international market. In 1971, $150 million of international reserves held by the poor nations were wiped out by President Nixon's unilateral action devaluing the dollar. Moreover, the creation of new international monetary reserves—the Special Drawing Rights (SDRs), the "paper money" of the International Monetary Fund used to facilitate trade—has primarily benefited the rich nations. Of the $102 billion of reserves created from 1970 to 1974, only $3.7 billions, or less than 4 percent, went to developing nations.

Finally, the developing countries complain that the structures of investment have not benefited them. A common litany of accusations made against the multinational corporations by

some Third World leaders argues that foreign investors do
three things to the local economy. First, they thrive on local
savings instead of bringing capital into the country (less than
$1 in $4 of MNC investment came from the parent company
in the 1960s). Second, they make the developing countries still
more dependent on the industrialized world for finance and
technology. Third, they import a consumer ideology to the
masses which is destined to create explosive frustration because of the very luxury—and elite-oriented economic structures they are helping to put into place.

The Analysis

Given this many-faceted complaint of the poor nations of
the world, what is their analysis of the situation? Their basic
conclusion is that the rules of the game are stacked against
them. Trade patterns, commodity price agreements, aid
agreements, investment patterns, monetary relationships,
decision-making arrangements—all are the structures of the
international economic order, the rules of the game. The
developing countries want a new set of rules which can be
achieved only by restructuring the international economic order. Backing up their conclusion are two sorts of analyses, one
moderate and the other more radical.

The moderate analysis notes that the poor countries did
not participate in making the international economic order,
and that it was not primarily designed to meet their interests.
The international monetary system, for example, was established by the rich nations at Bretton Woods in 1944. At that
time, most of the developing world, including huge countries
in Africa, on the Indian subcontinent, and in Indonesia were
colonies of the rich nations, and their economic futures were
evaluated primarily in terms of their colonial relationship. The
nations of the South argue that the old order largely maintains
and that the present international economic order cannot be
expected—even with the best of good will—to operate in
their favor. It cannot simply be modified or adjusted; it must
be significantly changed.

The radical analysis goes one step further. According to
this view, "development" and "underdevelopment" are flip
sides of the same coin. The present structures of the international economic order are not simply accidents of history; they

are the necessary consequences of the economic designs of the developed world. The rich get rich *because* the poor stay poor. The lines of dependency of the South upon the North cannot be expected to change with simply minor adjustments in the system. Radical analysts see underdevelopment as an intentional condition imposed by the rich.

Whether a moderate or a radical position is taken, the analysis basically comes forward with the same message: The present international economic order is not capable of providing the environment within which the poor nations can raise themselves up to a better standard of living for all their people; hence, it must be changed.

Clout

As loudly as one may complain, and as cogent as one's analysis may be, no effective change will occur unless strong pressures can be exerted. This requires "clout," real political power. The new assertiveness of the developing nations is being noticed precisely because of its new clout. For several years, especially since the 1972 meeting of the United Nations Conference on Trade and Development (UNCTAD III) in Santiago, the developing nations have been arguing about the bargaining for some more significant changes in the international economic order. But it was only in the fall of 1973, with the actions taken by the OPEC (Organization of Petroleum Exporting Countries) nations on the price of oil, that the demands of the South began to be heard. The Third World nations were moving dramatically toward a trade union model of negotiating, and they were finding strength in solidarity. Their clout came from acting together, even though in many instances their immediate, short-term interests may have conflicted (as has been the case with rises in petroleum prices).

The Group of 77, the South's negotiating bloc within the United Nations (which now actually consists of more than 110 nations), has demonstrated a surprising sense of solidarity. They have shown it in pressing their demands and in backing them up with both well-developed reasoning and pointed threats of boycotts, embargoes, etc., which would affect the North's economic prosperity. An important demonstration of solidarity occurred in April 1975, when the oil-consuming nations of the North invited the oil-producers of the South to an

energy conference in Paris. The United States and other industrialized nations had hoped to confine the agenda solely to
the issue of the rising price of oil. The OPEC states, however,
wanted to talk not only about the oil in their own interests, but
also about additional commodities in the interest of other
Third World states. The conference collapsed in the face of
this solidarity, paving the way for two significant events in the
immediate future: one was the conciliatory speech of U.S. Secretary of State Henry Kissinger to the UN Seventh Special
Session in September 1975. The second was the convening of
the Conference on International Economic Cooperation
(CIEC) the following December in Paris to discuss a wide
range of North-South issues. The solidarity thus displayed by
poor nations has forced the rich states to take seriously the
evolving debate over the international economic order.
Though the CIEC dialogue floundered for two and a half
years, the talks resumed in Mexico in October 1981. Despite
predictions of splits within the Group of 77, the developing
nations seem to be holding together as firmly as ever.

An Answer: A New International Economic Order

With the new assertiveness of the South, growing out of a
complaint, based upon an analysis, and backed up with some
clout, what are the dimensions of the debate regarding a restructuring of the global economic order? The major dimensions of the debate appear after thoroughly examining the
elements of the call for a new international economic order.
The call originated from the Sixth Special Session of the
United Nations General Assembly that met in April 1974. This
Special Session met to address the increasing distress of the
developing countries, as prices of oil had skyrocketed directly
before the Special Session, as have grain prices more recently.
The poor countries were faced with the fact of their increasing
impoverishment and with the need for new solidarity among
themselves in dealing with the rich nations. With the united
efforts of the Third World nations, and with reservations from
the industrialized nations which included the United States,
the Special Session passed a program calling for the establishment of a "New International Economic Order" (NIEO) which
involved the restructuring of trade patterns, commodity price

agreements, aid arrangements, investment patterns, monetary relationships, and decision-making methods. The program calls for a new set of rules of the game, not just for more fairness according to the old rules. Central to this thrust was the demand for an "equality of opportunity" in the development struggle through a restructuring of the present order.

A look at some of the key elements of the new set of rules as contained in the NIEO helps to clarify the debate. First and foremost, NIEO calls for the respect of the full sovereign equality of each nation in participation in all decision-making that affects its future. In addition, the developing states demand: full sovereignty over their own natural resources, along with the right to expropriate foreign investments if that sovereignty is damaged; free choice of the economic and social system deemed appropriate by each nation, not determined by outside influences or by internal subversion aided by outside influences;[1] the right to claim compensation for previous colonial domination on the part of the North; the control over the investment activities of multinational corporations (raising questions relating to the exhaustion of resources or the impact on employment); the guarantee of stable and remunerative prices received for raw materials; linkages of the prices paid for basic commodities (e.g., rubber, bananas, cocoa, coffee, etc.) with the prices paid for essential imports from the North (e.g., tractors, machine tools, etc.) in order to combat the effect of inflation in the industrialized nations;[2] the renegotiation of, or a moratorium on, debt service, or outright forgiveness of debt (such as offered to U.S. farmers during the Great Depression); better access to markets of the North through preferential tariffs; reform of the international monetary system; and support for producer associations such as OPEC, or a copper or bauxite producers' cartel.

These elements of the New International Economic Order had been repeatedly urged before; now they were offered in one package. A new phrase, New International Economic Order, entered into the discussions at international meetings. My colleagues and I at the Center of Concern, who have been involved in the series of major UN conferences on these issues over the past few years, have often heard the particular topics put into the context of the New International Economic Order. It is useful to mention these meetings and to explain their relationship to the NIEO debate in order to

make more concrete the persuasiveness of this call for a restructuring of the international order.

The World Population Conference held at Bucharest in
August 1974 took up the critical question of the world's population, now doubling every 35 years, and declared that population must be stabilized. The World Food Conference at
Rome, also held in 1974, acknowledged that poor states need
to produce more food for themselves while also buying from
the rich nations. At the 1975 International Women's Conference in Mexico City, women from the rich states spoke of improving the woman's position in what they perceive to be
given minimal levels of living standards. Simultaneously,
women from developing states insisted on merely establishing
the rights of education for all (particularly in areas where illit-
eracy is between 50 and 70 percent), of jobs for all (where
unemployment is between 25 and 35 percent of the population), and of medical aid for all (where basic health services
are woefully inadequate). The Conference on Human Settlements, meeting at Vancouver in 1976, discussed the quality of
life around the world, rural as well as urban, but focused on
urban areas where the population doubles every 16 years. The
1979 UN Conference on Science and Technology in Vienna
struggled to promote international cooperation in applying
science and technology while working for international development.

Each of these recent conferences, along with similar meetings on employment, deserts, water, and health, has based its
particular interests on an over-all pattern of socio-economic
change in the Third World. That change can only occur within
a context of restructuring of relationships between rich and
poor states—a new international economic order. Each conference showed increasing awareness that a piecemeal approach to a new international economic order, tinkering with
one specific issue here or there, does not meet the needs of a
global order today. A piecemeal approach offers no guarantee
that all the pieces will add up to a whole structure. A more
systematic approach is necessary.

The effort toward a new ordering of the international
economic structure is not the total solution, nor is it a perfect
program. I am very much aware of serious shortcomings in
the proposals individually and in the package as a whole. It
has an excessively nationalistic tone, with individual sover-

eignty emphasized by the poor nations in ways which may be counterproductive to true global cooperation. No assurance is given that increased benefits for the nations of the South will not go only to national elites, but will also go to the majority poor. Serious questions about the prudence, as well as the justice, of expropriation actions can be raised. The search for commodity price stabilization on the part of the developing nations may not address the more difficult issues of international division of labor, self-reliant development programs, and long-term international economic planning. Finally, the impact that implementing an NIEO would have on the citizens in the industrialized world (e.g., workers in the United States) remains unclear, along with the question of who will bear the burden of the impact.

These reservations and questions aside, the fact remains that the call for a new international economic order remains the principal focus for the North-South dialogue on the restructuring of the global economic order. Yet, the United States has been very reluctant to engage in serious NIEO negotiations. The official positon has frequently reflected the characterization of the Third World's struggle which it was given by Daniel Patrick Moynihan prior to his appointment as United States Ambassador to the United Nations, when he referred to the struggle as being based on "the politics of resentment and the economics of envy."

At the time that the UN Sixth Special Session approved the NIEO call in April 1974, the United States entered several very strong objections. The United States delegation argued that no overhaul of the system was necessary, that it had basically worked well enough, and that only minor adjustments might be called for. Vigorous objection was made to several points, in particular to the endorsement of expropriation of foreign investments. In December 1974 the UN General Assembly, approved the Charter of Economic Rights and Duties of States (CERDS), a restatement of the NIEO. The United States government voted against the Charter. Mentions of the NIEO in UN conferences at Bucharest, Rome, Mexico City, etc., were repeatedly objected to by this country.

With the collapse of the original Paris talks in April 1975, and with the recognition of its growing isolation from its North Atlantic allies, the United States went to the UN Seventh Special Session in September 1975 with an expressed desire to engage constructively in the dialogue and debate. This constructive spirit continued into December, with the convened Paris talks, and with the Conference on International Economic Cooperation, and its on-going commissions to probe the practical issues of North-South dialogue. Then, in May 1976 the United States faced a major bargaining session on the NIEO at the meeting of UNCTAD IV in Nairobi, Kenya. There the Group of 77 pushed strongly for a comprehensive approach to the question of stabilizing prices for their basic commodities by urging the establishment of a common fund to support this stabilization. The United States government fought against such a common fund and proposed instead a series of negotiations on a commodity-by-commodity basis. The process continues today and was reviewed at the UNCTAD V meeting in Manila during May 1979, where again the call from the meeting was for a set of global responses to economic plight through a new international economic order.

The Eleventh Special Session of the UN General Assembly in August and September 1980 again advocated an NIEO by trying to develop an International Development Strategy for the 1980s, with participation by all nations, and to achieve agreement on a framework for global negotiations that would provide a centralized decision-making apparatus under UN auspices to consider items of global management. These items were to be raw materials, energy, trade, development, and money and financing. The Conference was unable to agree on procedural rules in the global negotiations because of resistance from the United States, West Germany, and Great Britain. In retaliation, the Group of 77 refused to approve the International Development Strategy in order to prevent the United States from claiming that the session had been a successful one. Had the measures been approved, the international system would have been moving toward the proposed new international economic order.

During 1980, major reports from independent commissions and multilateral institutions were issued supporting the call for major structural alterations in the international economic order. These reports included the President's Commission on World Hunger, the *Global 2000 Report* to the President, the International Monetary Fund's *World Economic Outlook for 1980*, the *World Development Report 1980* from the World Bank, and the *Brandt Commission Report*. Each gives evidence for developing states' claims that the world economy is adversely affecting them at an increasing rate, and that major changes to the international economic system are essential to improving the lot of the developing states.

The *Brandt Commission Report* is an example. This independent commission of international figures, headed by former Chancellor of West Germany Willy Brandt, worked for two years to evaluate the current social and economic conditions as well as the immediate needs of the entire world as it entered the 1980s. The report, issued in February 1980, particularly addressed the needs of the poorest nations as well as those of the middle income states. The findings indicated that the developing world suffers from shortages of food, from the lack of the basics for sanitation, from extreme fluctuations in both commodity prices and exchange rates, from the North's imposition of protectionist tariffs on manufactured products from the South, and from difficulties derived from balance-of-payments deficits. A major theme running through the report is the need for the South to secure proportionate privilege and responsibility in managing the international economic system; this power-sharing should be in management within a multilateral situation such as the World Bank. The report stressed that the solutions to these severe problems merit global solutions made under both political and moral considerations.

The *Brandt Commission Report* outlined an emergency plan for the years 1980 to 1985 intended to avert a catastrophe for the 800 million poor people in the world today. The four major aspects of the emergency plan include an immediate, large-scale transfer of resources (financial and natural) from the North to the South to aid the poor and to help amortize foreign debts of the middle income states; an international energy strategy including significant investments in the South to promote research and development of energy resources there; a global food program to provide at least a bare minimum for existence; and major reforms in the international economic system. The report warns of serious repercussions if the current conditions are not acknowledged and dealt with promptly. This report goes beyond previous international study groups by stressing that the implications of not heeding the calls for reform are dangerous for the North as well as for the

South. In short, the *Brandt Commission Report* of 1980 firmly advocates a new international economic order.

Is the NIEO still alive as an issue today? Some would argue that the impetus from the Group of 77 has been lost and would point to the stalled North-South dialogue as evidence of this. The renewal of the talks scheduled at Cancun, Mexico, in October 1981 may ease these concerns, however. Others would say that the widespread interest in a basic human needs strategy for development, focusing on internal measures to benefit the poorest in the developing countries, has distracted from the international structural reform movement symbolized by the NIEO struggle.

I believe we are seeing a new phase in the NIEO struggle, a phase which makes the structural reforms into means, not ends, in the overall development effort. World Bank economist Mahbub al Haq has referred to this new phase as a time when "reasoned analysis replaces initial heated arguments," and has called for a movement from discussion forums to decision-making forums. There is a surprising amount of consensus emerging on the minimal steps necessary to restructure the global economic order in such a fashion as to benefit both developed and developing countries. An economist at the Center of Concern, Phil Land, has outlined what he refers to as a "convergence" of values as expressed by such diverse groups as the Club of Rome, the Aspen Institute, the Dag Hammarskjöld Foundation, the Overseas Development Council, and the Third World Forum. This convergence points to bargaining positions which are possible on issues of trade, debt, monetary arrangements, and codes of conduct for investors.

Beyond the convergence proposals (many of them short-term), several long-term proposals are offered by leaders in both the industrialized world and in the Third World, such as those in the *Brandt Commission Report*. The latter proposals go directly to the heart of what is necessary to keep a global community functioning in a world where allocation of scarce resources and the distribution of the benefits of growth will continue to be central issues. They have relevance to the operation of multinational corporations. Among the long-term proposals frequently put forward are: a system of international taxation designed for some form of automatic transfer of resources, e.g., relating to benefits coming from the exploitation of the sea beds; an international central bank, that is, some sort of international monetary authority to deal more effectively and equitably with exchange, debt, reserves, etc.; and a global planning system to coordinate development strategies beneficial to all people and regions.

What are the implications of this movement toward a new international economic order for the operations of multinational corporations? The operations of MNCs have been and will continue to be affected by the aforementioned new assertiveness. Both directly and indirectly the NIEO touches on the environment within which MNCs function. Not all MNC managers in the industrialized world have understood the far-reaching consequences of this new situation. Many have actively opposed its direction. But any discussion of the role of multinationals in a development which comes to grips with Third World poverty must be placed within the NIEO context or risk irrelevance.

I personally am not yet convinced that the multinationals as now constituted and operating can in fact be a major force in meeting the challenge of Third World poverty. But, if I were at least to assume here for the sake of argument that they could play a constructive role vis-à-vis global poverty, then, in light of the NIEO world view here outlined, I would see several policy implications that need to be addressed.

In order to raise these policy implications, this paper can conclude with a few questions which point to some long-term issues to be faced as the NIEO debate moves into further hard bargaining stages. .I pose these questions to MNC managers.

1. The first and simplest question is whether or not the MNC manager is willing to acknowledge the fairness of at least some of the claims of the Third World for a restructuring of the economic order. By no means does this mean complete acceptance of the NIEO. But if little or no acknowledgement is made of the correctness of the complaint or the legitimacy of the direction for change, then the MNC manager will look outside NIEO considerations when deciding corporate policies. Such a stance cannot but bring increased frustration and eventual failure to any multinational efforts aimed at social goals. If, on the other hand, a more open stance toward the NIEO—critical, perhaps, but open—is taken, then at least some movement might be possible.

2. What is the perception of the MNC manager toward

the need for a "stable" environment for investment? Stability has been long sought after by corporations interested in operations in Third World countries, and understandably so. But in a time of rapid social change, stable conditions are not always the standard situations. The call for a new international economic order is not necessarily accompanied by the call for a new national ecomomic order. But this may very well be the case in many instances, with attendant "instability" in many of the established institutions of power. Multinationals cannot—should not—expect to dictate the terms of stability.

3. What is the reaction of the MNC manager to the question of multinational control over multinational corporations? This is a key NIEO issue. It must be admitted that today there is a common perception that a form of *laissez faire* capitalism prevails on the international scene, since the increasingly powerful multinational corporation is outside effective national and/or international control. Because of this perception, calls are continually made for "codes of conduct" for these corporations. Two of the most important proposed codes are those of a special UN Commission on Transnationals and of the Organization for Economic Cooperation and Development (OECD). The UN draft proposal reflects more the concerns of the Third World and concentrates on the requirements for a more self-determined, self-reliant development.

Addendum

DURING THE WORKSHOP Father Henriot expanded on his paper to present and criticize four models of development. The seminar participants discussed these models in small working groups, and reported their conclusions in plenary session. The presentation and small group observations are summarized below.

WORLD SITUATION

Attention to the gradual changes taking place in the economic and political structure of the world is of fundamental importance to multinational managers, for, not only will global restructuring impinge on profit opportunities but, of equal importance to the manager, the multinational is an instigator of the changes.

The global challenge is to have growth with equity. The trickle-down theory has been widely reputed to have failed. At issue is whether the process does not take place at all, or whether it takes place but too slowly. The lag in analysis may be explained in part by the nature of the theory in that it takes a while for the trickle-down to be observed.

Alternatively, participants pointed out examples where development has progressed more slowly but with more built-in distributional factors not operating on the trickle-down theory but on the gross national product per capita idea being more spread out (e.g., in Taiwan, Singapore, South Korea, Sri Lanka).

Multinational corporations alone cannot solve the poverty problem. It is up to them, in cooperation with the local governments, to carry on the crusade. If the topics of growth (increase in per capita GNP) and development (sharing of growth and distribution of social benefits among members of the nation) are considered as two separate goals, then they are not without their disadvantages. Questions arise, such as, Should and is it right for governments to restrict consumer choices? What do governments of developing nations want in terms of foreign investment?

Participants at the seminar agreed that MNCs do have positive contributions to make to development, yet they sensed that multinationals are becoming more and more hesitant to invest in the Third World, a reluctance caused largely by the animosity between firms and host countries that has grown over the years, aggravated by the related institutional response of the United Nations and the Group of 77. The majority of the present sovereign nations in the Third World were nonexistent twenty years ago. Today, we see corporations from former colonial powers creating foreign investment in countries that were once only export absorbers. Antagonisms appear on both sides.

A characteristic of foreign investment is the risk involved. Once welcoming sovereign nations change internally; then so do the rules governing foreign capital. Government and political realities prevent well-intentioned overtures toward private sectors. One finds that individual firms are backed by a much broader infrastructure and that relationships are not always bilateral. Developing nations, particularly smaller ones, can play the MNCs off against one another, using competition as the jousting instrument. Negotiating advantage does not always lie on the side of the MNC, especially when host countries act in consort.

Another reason for the MNC's hesitancy to initiate capital investment as well as to expand and continue in an established area, can be explained economically: capital is becoming more expensive, at least for United States companies. Moreover, the U.S. government has discouraged investment by new tax laws, additional red tape barriers, etc. Today new investment is a greater risk at higher cost.

DEVELOPMENT MODELS

What does development mean in light of the New International Economic Order? Several models have been explored.

First is the Economic Model, which puts the question of

why these countries are poor in terms of capital, and looks for answers in foreign aid. This is the model that guided take-offs for some countries. Its focus, however, was limited to numerical improvement, only one facet of development. To increase the GNP per capita does not necessarily mean all people's lives will be better.

The Social Model, which was popular in the 1970s, addresses the problem of marginality. The problem is internal to the developing nation: attending to rural development, income distribution, employment, agricultural needs; concentrating on national items. But the Social Model can sidestep or avoid the international structure.

Third, the Political Model addresses the issue of the NIEO. The problem is not internal, but is in the North-South relationship. The Political Model has given rise to the new assertiveness; but in calling for the NIEO, the call for the national order is frequently waylaid.

Finally, the Ethical Model advocates a more just, participatory, and sustainable society. The increasing scarcity of resources, the nuclear progress, and world political disorder, combine to make the problem global. The solution, then, is to shift away from energy intensive approaches, or from creating false wants, and to move toward the better use of human resources and respect for the environment. Moreover, internal reform is called for in order to distribute fairly the benefits of development. Granted, to move toward this last model may seem utopian, or require a change in human nature; but at least we can perceive the legitimacy in this effort to explore new paths.

In all the models described, one aim is eminent: the lessening of poverty. There is encouraging evidence that the trend may be in the right direction—that the number of poor people may actually decrease from a present level of about 760 million to an anticipated 600 million by the end of the century. These conjectures are based on assumptions such as the expansion of international trade, flow of credit, volume of concessional aid, international political disorders, and other structural pushes which reverberate in developing countries. Even if the numbers do diminish, they are still massive— hardly acceptable for a truly humane society. There are no excuses for shunning the gnawing reality of poverty.

NOTES

1. April 1974, the date of the UN Special Session, was only a few months after the events in Chile in September 1973.

2. This is the controversial issue of "indexation," a technical device familiar to citizens in the United States through the common practice of "cost of living index" for wages.

4. Technology Transfer: An Issue in Development

SAMUEL L. HAYDEN

SPEAKING FROM HIS EXPERIENCE as a participant in the study on technology transfer undertaken by the Fund for Multinational Management Education (FMME), Hayden stressed that the system of transferring technology is working and that a major restructuring is not needed.[1] Rather, Hayden suggested, the existing system should be made to work more efficiently.

His comments focused on the conflicts of objectives between Third World host countries and multinationals in regard to the transfer of technologies. Noting that the system needs to function in spite of these conflicts, he outlined the issues as seen from the host country's point of view and the response of the multinational.

COST OF TECHNOLOGY

Host Country: Include only the incremental costs of transfer in cost of technology.

Response: Technology is developed over long periods (15 to 20 years is not unusual) and should be priced according to its value and impact.

This is a summary report of Mr. Hayden's presentation and of the seminar discussion.

Control over Technology, Suppliers, and Technology Imports

Host Country: Reduce contract limitations on use of technology.

Response: There are global market liabilities to consider; the MNCs are responsive to, and responsible for, the product they produce and therefore want control over use and the resultant quality of product and service.

Host Country: Unbundle technology to obtain greater flexibility over imports.

Response: Companies sell products, not technology. Disembodied technology will cost more in the long run.

Host Country: Limit proprietary rights at the technology's source.

Response: The area of patent rights, property rights, etc. is essential to MNCs. Furthermore, removal of these restrictive clauses, en masse, will probably create a distrust between partners.

Host Country: Allow intervention of host country in technology transfer agreements; allow it to screen technology agreements and relationships in light of national development.

Response: Intervention complicates the industrial relationship between the user and the supplier; it adds a political dimension which makes it very difficult for communication between firms. As risk increases for the mutinational corporation, costs charged should also increase.

Host Country: Allow the host country the right to reject contractual obligations.

Response: It has been found that this results in a destruction of supplier confidence and a withholding of new technology.

Research and Development Facilities

Host Country: Relocate facilities to host countries.

Response: All right. We will relocate, providing there is a big enough market, and a strong infrastructure. There can be significant economies of scale in the development of technology.

APPROPRIATE TECHNOLOGY

Host Country: Provide us with labor-intensive, light-capital technology appropriate to our economy.

Response: Yet, what is appropriate to the cost structures or for the fundamental needs of the economy? And, who determines what is appropriate?

For a system that can accommodate these differences and still transfer technology efficiently, we must recognize that technology transfer is a person-to-person activity, and that it is based on contact and motivation of both suppliers and receivers. Transfer must be stimulated at the local level with an emphasis on the ability of the receiver to adopt and exploit this technology in conjunction with the multinational at the firm's level. This means that the focus of change should not be on the supplier side, but on the stimulation of demand at the local market level. Until this occurs, the conflict between the two stubborn and unwavering sides will continue to be unresolved.

The seminar discussion on technology transfer concentrated on the contribution of technology to the development process—the appropriateness issue. As one participant stated, "Multinational companies are the greatest transferrers of technology. They have information and processing systems that study local systems, then adapt to them." To tailor the technology to fit the environment where it will be utilized not only aids the local area, but the multinational corporation as well, as it furthers the efficiency of its production. Thus the bottom line from the point of view of the multinational should be appropriateness of the technology.

Still, "appropriate" technology cannot be described precisely. There will be some instances where the appropriate technology necessary for a certain product will be highly sophisticated, and both capital and energy intensive; a computer, for example. The feasibility of producing that product locally has to be determined before its appropriateness can be evaluated. Furthermore, the economic viability of appropriate technology is a major concern, as is the question of whether or not the appropriate technology is, in the long run, cost effective. Is "hand me down" technology for example, the most appropriate, or is it an insult to the Third World?

There are some sketchy answers to the question of developing technology in one milieu and then transferring it to another. Adapting technology to the environment as described above is one response, but it is not without complications. A different approach would be the installation of research and development centers in regions where the multinationals operate. In either case we are straining to see where a technology that is labeled appropriate after research or adaptation to a specified situation can be effective.

The question remains: "Appropriate to what?" Does it give jobs with dignity? Does it take account of the area's ecological problems? Does it remain cognizant of resource scarcity? These and other questions need to be fed into the meaning of appropriateness which itself is a factor in the meaning of development.

Ideally, the focus should be on the economic development of the Third World and not solely on the transfer of technology. It is only one element in economic development. One participant in the seminar stated that he thought "the question of transfer of technology is peripheral to the question of development and if the other conditions of development are present, the countries will obtain technology." From the MNC point of view, if technology is defined as the sharing of information about how to perform operations, then, with direct investment, the transfer of know-how comes naturally because it is necessary for efficient functioning of an enterprise.

NOTE

1. These observations are drawn from the research gathered through a Ford Foundation Project that focused on the international executive core. The research concentrated on how managerial skills are transferred from one organization to another in developing countries. The project included five countries: Brazil, Peru, Korea, Kenya, and Tanzania.

5. The United Nations Conference on Science and Technology for Development

SIMON BOURGIN, FRANK GRIMSLEY, REV. PETER J. HENRIOT, S.J.

IN AUGUST 1979 A MAJOR event in the relations between developing and industrialized nations took place in Vienna: the United Nations Conference on Science and Technology for Development (UNCSTD). Under the aegis of the Economic and Social Committee of the United Nations, the focus of the conference discussions was the ubiquitous topic of science and technology for development.

The United States delegation was based in the State Department. The members had undertaken a good deal of preparatory work for the conference so that they were in a position to speak in the name of the U.S. government as well as for the scientific and business community. Among the conference delegations, the presence of corporation executives in the U.S. delegation was unique: The U.S. managers did not find the foreign executives with whom they would ordinarily deal in matters of technology transfer present in the delegations of the other countries.

Attendance included nongovernmental organizations such as the Center of Concern, which serves in a nongovernmental consultative status with the Economic and Social Committee of the United Nations. Father Theodore Hesburgh, C.S.C., President of the University of Notre Dame, was

---

This paper summarizes the presentations by the panel members and the ensuing discussion.

the U.S. Ambassador and Chairman of the U.S. delegation. Jean Wilkowski was an ambassador to the conference and coordinator of U.S. preparation. Frank Grimsley, Vice President of Caterpillar Tractor, and Simon Bourgin of the State Department were members of the delegation. Rev. Peter Henriot, S.J., Director of the Center of Concern, monitored preconference activities and attended as an official observer.

At the seminar, Father Henriot, along with Frank Grimsley and Simon Bourgin, composed a panel to elaborate the purpose of UNCSTD, review its dynamics, and estimate its success. The following summarizes the comments of the panelists and the discussion among the seminar group. The views reflected in this summary do not, of course, necessarily represent a consensus of the seminar.

CONFERENCE PURPOSE

The United Nations may currently be perceived as a forum in which the developing countries work together toward a common goal: the restructuring of the international economic system so as to make it more equitable to the needs of all. In 1979 the Sixth Special Session of the General Assembly of the United Nations, meeting in New York, originated the call for the New International Economic Order, a major move toward that goal. The UNCSTD conference in Vienna was one more major event in shaping that restructuring. The meeting's purpose was to advance negotiations between developed and developing countries on the proposal of a new economic order by focusing particular attention on the important issue of science and technology for development.

So far as the world press is concerned, UNCSTD was very nearly a non-event. Only a smattering of the media attended, and, except for the science magazines, the proceedings went virtually unrecorded. This neglect may reflect some popular disenchantment with the United Nations as it is perceived today. The organization was created as a unifying body, a microcosm of national representatives discussing world issues, and in this fundamental purpose it has not changed. What has changed is its makeup: As decolonization proceeded, more than 100 developing nations were added to the 51 most developed nations which had signed the United Nations Charter in

1945. By the time of the UNCSTD meetings these newer members constituted an absolute majority at the UN and, operating as the "Group of 77" (actually, over 120 countries), they have sought wide changes in the global order, particularly in the economic and social sectors.

PREPARATIONS AND CONFERENCE: THE DYNAMICS

Diplomatic protocol dictates that fair and reciprocal ground rules be promulgated before any negotiations that are expected to succeed be approached. Thus, for UNCSTD a series of preparatory meetings were held over a three-year period wherein guidelines for the procedures and content of the conference were decided. Each participating nation produced a national paper in which it assessed its experience, needs, potential, and preliminary recommendations. From these papers was produced the draft Program of Action, several versions of which, heavily slanted toward Group 77 objectives, were considered in five UN Preparatory Committee meetings in Geneva and New York.

Two major strains of emphasis were evident during these meetings. The Americans were strongly in favor of strengthening the ability of the developing nations to absorb technology; it was hoped that infrastructure, on which capacity would be built, could be developed through a variety of channels. The Group of 77, on the other hand, emphasized access to technology. Primarily, this encompassed the terms under which multinationals should or could be permitted to operate in the host country. The list of demands presented at various times by the Group of 77 included free access to proprietary technology and nonconfidentiality of origin, in addition to permission to screen transfers in advance and to unbundle technology transfers whenever they thought necessary.

Echoing the call for free access is the Group of 77's belief that science and technology is the common patrimony of all peoples. (For most of the plenary sessions in Vienna, the heads of Third World delegations stressed the virtues of their systems and what is wrong with the multinationals.) They further believe that technology should be delivered to them either free or on preferred terms, since they emerged from their development mostly without a technical patrimony. The Group of 77 argued that technology had been paid for through its use in the developed countries and that its application in the Third World was an incremental extension of these resources.

If there is to be a cost associated with technology, a major issue is the nature of that cost. Third World countries want to know the cost estimated by the transferer to assess the reasonableness of the charge as it relates to the cost of developing that technology. A counterargument is based on market valuation. Here the value of technology is based upon demand— what the developing nations are willing to pay for it. Alternatively, how can a value be quantitatively determined for 75 years of development?

On the eve of the conference, after protracted and painful negotiations, the issues had narrowed. The views of the "77" and the industrialized countries showed a convergence in four areas: (1) the need to strengthen indigenous science and technology; (2) the need for industrialized countries to target more research and development to specific developing country problems; (3) the need to strengthen information systems in relation to developing countries; and (4) the need for higher priorities for science-and-technology-for-development programs in regional and international organizations.

On three other, far more important issues, there was a deadlock. The United States adamantly opposed sections of the draft Program of Action which called for regulation of multinational corporations and technology transfer on Group of 77 terms. The second issue concerned reform of the UN science and technology system, with the "77" claiming they were inadequately represented on the 50-member Science and Technology Committee. They asked that the committee be replaced by an intergovernmental committee of the whole, representing all UN countries.

Finally, to provide restitution for their late arrival on the industrial scene, and to help permit them to achieve equity, the "77" asked for a $2-to-$4 billion Science and Technology Fund, to be financed by automatic levies on the trade of industrialized countries. Just before the delegates met, a counterproposal to this demand surfaced: An interim fund of $250 million for a trial period of two years, to be raised voluntarily and administered by the UN development program; at the end of the period a committee of experts would appraise the real needs of the developing countries on a priority basis.

The UNCSTD conference, a mammoth affair involving several thousand delegates as well as several thousand nongovernmental representatives, made no progress on these issues in its first week. The "77" were threatening to go home by the middle of the second week, when the action began.

The U.S. delegation, working in the middle for a compromise, played a critical role. The Nordic countries, then the United States and Japan, came out for the interim $250 million fund, and finally the European-9 and the Russians and East Europeans as well. The "77" agreed on the last day of the conference. The seemingly intractable issue of the control of the multinationals and the transfer of technology were passed on unresolved to the General Assembly, which was to meet that autumn in New York.

SUCCESS

The UNCSTD conference in Vienna was a major event in the continuing North-South dialogues. It has worldwide significance in that the conference's topic has pertinent implications for all nations, developed and developing. Whether or not the conference can be judged successful depends upon the criteria of judgment. In no way did it advance the causes of strictly one side over another. In this respect it was a success.

Father Henriot evaluated the conference by delineating eight reasons for calling it a success and eight reasons for qualifying his enthusiasm.

The *first* reason for calling the conference a success is that conceptually, it elevated the role of science and technology for development. In the three-year process of extensive discussion, scientists and technologists faced the fact that a good deal of science and technology hasn't been for development in terms of meeting the basic human needs of people. Ninety-five percent of the research and development undertaken in the world today is done in the industrialized countries. Of this not much applies immediately to the basic needs of developing countries, or indeed to the really critical questions that we face in the industralized countries. The process of those three years of preparation turned the scientific and technological community to the recognition that science and technology has to be targeted to development for all of us. Conceptually that was an advance.

Second, some of this new understanding heightened the organizational role of science and technology for development. There had been an Office of Science and Technology in the United Nations. Now, as a result of the Vienna conference, its status within the UN has been raised to greater prominence and authority.

Third, the new committee includes all member countries of the United Nations. One of the emphases of the New International Economic Order is: "in the decisions that affect us [the Third World countries], we should have a say in making them." This means that if a committee is formed that is going to make decisions affecting the developing nations, representatives of these nations should be on that committee. Therefore, a UNCSTD success: a committee which is going to influence the developing countries in science and technology will include all the countries of the United Nations.

Fourth, new funds have been designated for science and technology. Although only $250 million, it is a significant start.

Fifth, in the discussion of science and technology for development, the role of women was highlighted. It was the only separate resolution passed by the conference. The recognition has been growing in recent years that any meaningful discussion of development as conceptually thought of and as organizationally put into effect must consider the female majority of the people on the face of the globe. You cannot transfer technology, you cannot have new technological advances in agriculture, for example, and ignore the fact that the people involved in 60 to 70 percent of agricultural production are women. This issue was debated in earnest by the U.S. delegation.

Sixth, a critical issue that was successfully aired was the massive commitment of the riches of human intellect, riches of natural resources, riches of time and organization, riches of science and technology that have been consumed by instruments of destruction. The whole issue of disarmament is central to development; there will not be any kind of development in human terms unless some of those riches and resources of mind, money and personnel, of time and organization, are diverted from instruments of destruction to meeting of basic needs.

Seventh, each round of the North-South negotiations brings clarity amidst the rhetoric of its confrontation. This conference followed suit by clarifying the questions surrounding the basic NIEO issues regarding the use of power, money, and resources. The Group of 77's demands were recorded so as to aid the negotiations, which, in turn, concisely presented the ingredients of a reform for the international economic system.

Eighth, a final reason for calling the conference a success is that the United States played a very positive role: in willingness to negotiate hard, in preparing very well, and in having a delegation that performed very well—participating whenever possible and exemplifying an unprecedented degree of openness. The very high quality of the United States delegation made it a leader in the discussions.

The eight reasons for calling UNCSTD a *qualified* success are:

First, there was an absence of communication between scientists and politicians; a distance existed between it being a science and technology conference and it being a political conference. Science and technology was not, in fact, the subject. It was more a conference on development and how different people understand development than a conference explicitly on science and technology. Some of the key breakthroughs were not dealt with in terms of how science and technology might be applied in specific situations.

Second, some of the issues related to the United Nations Conference on Trade and Development (UNCTAD) were not issues advanced in Vienna. After the May UNCTAD conference had ended in Manila with confrontation over many key issues, one might surmise that they would be raised in August on the agenda in Vienna. For example, of major earlier concern had been the code of conduct for multinational corporations—a continuing dispute. Yet this and other issues were not broached in Vienna.

Third, the role of the private sector, the multinational corporations, was not sufficiently treated. The topic surfaced in the committees, but discussion was limited—largely because the United States does not have much to say about control of corporations operating internationally. It does address controls on internal operations, such as antitrust laws or security and exchange commission regulations; but it is silent regarding controls on external operations and discourages others from discussing them.

Fourth, the issue of unemployment was never touched, even though a conference on science and technology for development should certainly have looked at this. The whole question of the impact of science and technology on employment was neglected.

Fifth, the financial arrangement—$250 million—was minimal. It was far less than the $4 billion the developing countries would have asked for. The $4 billion figure was the result of an extensive investigation and analysis such as a formula tied to the differences in balance of trade for manufactured goods. At the conference, where the developing countries were pressed very hard by the U.S. delegation and by others, this analysis held up reasonably well. Moreover, the conference did not deal with the developing countries' request for "automatic" financing based on something like an international tax system.

Sixth, the U.S. delegation was of a high caliber, yet not totally representative. There was a member of the AFL-CIO International from Geneva, but no other substantial labor participation. It is very difficult to talk about science and technology for development and hope to depict the U.S. point of view without a more active U.S. labor deputation. Other unions besides AFL-CIO have had a considerable amount of interest in international trade and questions of the transfer of technology. Moreover, although there was good scientific representation, there was little discussion of the appropriate technologies, little representation of alternative technology points of view.

Seventh, in reflection, the delegations from the developed world did not seem to recognize that we have also to learn in this whole discussion. There was something of a stance of "We made it, and we have to show you" (sometimes unfortunately reinforced by developing countries who would say, "You made it, please show it to us"). It must be a mutual learning process. We in the developed world need to learn from the Third World.

Eighth, finally, the conference stumbled into the hidden agenda of UN politics—personality politics. The secretary-general of the conference was not talking to the head of the key UN office dealing with science and technology. These conflicts simply hinder conference accomplishments.

Rapidly listed, these eight positive signs and eight questions for qualification point to the basic question that is being brought out in the United Nations in so many different ways—"How do we live as *one* people on the globe?" The United States has drawn on centuries of scientific patrimony beginning with the Greeks. How do other nations, all making up one world, draw upon this common patrimony? That question will haunt many more UN conferences.

6. Clarifying the Debate

MICHAEL J. FRANCIS AND
CECILIA G. MANRIQUE

ATTITUDES ABOUT THE IMPACT of multinational corporations
on poverty and development in the Third World have generated serious disagreement and controversy in international
forums, Third World countries, and in the developed world.
Raymond Vernon notes that "indeed, it is a little frightening to
observe the mounting flood of words on these subjects coming
from the typewriters of scholars, journalists, government
officials, and novelists."[1] But debate over these polarities car-
ries great importance because opinions influence public policy.
In the Third World, for example, the range of regulations for
outside investment varies with each country's political and
economic beliefs about transnational impact. Similarly, in
Western countries, tax policies, currency exchange restrictions, and other government measures are parts of the debate
itself.

Are multinational corporations instruments of economic
development or of economic domain in the relationship between the Western industrialized countries and Third World
nations? This chapter aims to clarify the steadily increasing
lines of argument in the debate. It does not determine which
point of view is valid or invalid, but only attempts to clarify
three areas:

(1) The main points of actual disagreement between
    those who support and those who criticize transna-
    tional corporations,
(2) the areas of agreement between these groups, and
(3) the issues that have not really been debated because

one side has simply not been responding to the other side's contentions.

Additionally, this study proposes a research agenda for the future by isolating actual disagreements from issues that one side or the other believes to be irrelevant. The subject areas considered in this paper include employment, diffusion of skills, levels of technology, demand manipulation, social class, codes of conduct, various effects on local government, capital, and the balance of payments. The sources of opinion are derived from the viewpoints of multinational executives, economists, journalists, and scholars.

METHODOLOGY

In order to understand the complex causal beliefs and assertions that have generated the attitudes of criticism or defense that characterize this debate, this paper uses a technique known as cognitive mapping. Stated quite simply, a cognitive map shows a line of reasoning. It charts a particular string of logical beliefs expressed by an individual (or group) on a single topic.[2]

Understanding the essential causal relationships that constitute a belief system is an important step toward the communication that can provide possible solutions for disagreement. But unfortunately, people do not normally speak in simple causal language. This study uses coding rules to reformulate normal language into causal assertions. As described by Margaret Wrightson, these rules are quite widely recognized by scholars.[3] They have been employed at the Institute of International Studies at the University of California at Berkeley and are being used in numerous research projects elsewhere.

Cognitive maps made according to such rules provide the quality of replicability which is a necessary component of the scientific method. This gives the methodology the characteristic of being "value free" in the sense that the opinions of those doing the research do not influence the findings. Thus, in the present context, a cognitive map of a businessman's analysis of foreign investment supposedly would be the same whether it was done by a transnational corporation admirer or critic.

Before describing the specific materials mapped, or even the selection of those materials, it would be especially useful to summarize the results of the research and to consider what the findings generally suggest and what they imply for future research into clarification of the debate.

There are few areas of agreement across the spectrum of views studied. But one important consensus rests on the question of whether MNCs (multinational corporations) diffuse skills in Third World countries. Except for one source among our selections, critics and defenders alike believed that MNCs did spread skills in host countries (although there were differences of opinion as to the importance of the skills and how widely they were spread).

Employment, technology, the influence of MNCs on local governments, and demand manipulation stood out as the areas of most direct disagreement. Certainly the technology question is currently (and quite appropriately) the subject of extensive debate and research in both the developed and less-developed world, as are the questions of employment generation by outside capital and the impact of MNCs on local producers and suppliers. Nevertheless, while these areas of disagreement are quite a vital part of the current debate, they do not suggest a need for a new research agenda.

On the other hand, two issues which were discussed extensively by one side and ignored by the other do suggest potentially fruitful areas for future research. The first concerns multinationals' self-imposed codes of conduct. While the sampling of sources for this essay may be skewed by the fact that each of the pro-MNC speakers happens to be favorably disposed toward codes of conduct, the fact that this matter is often completely ignored by critics suggests a need for further inquiry. Presumably, the basic question would be whether or not the existence of such codes actually alters the behavior of a corporation and, if so, in what manner? Obviously this is an extremely difficult area to investigate but that problem should not automatically place the topic out of bounds.

The other "partisan" issue in this study concerns the MNCs' impact on social class. MNC critics consistently claim that demand can be manipulated by the multinational corporations in a manner that is detrimental to Third World progress. On the other side, we find the belief in an enlightened, self-interested consumer who is better off protecting himself rather than being protected by any governmental agency. To research this controversy would be complicated because one presumably would have to determine (1) whether there is such a thing as "improper consumption" and (2) whether the MNCs' advertising abilities had demonstrable effects on consumption patterns. To sum up, can multinationals sell refrigerators to Eskimos? And, if so, do the Eskimos know something we don't know?

Critics see that impact as detrimental. Pro-MNC elements believe in the trickle-down theory and ignore the critics' claim that multinationals are perpetuating the existence of a class structure in less-developed countries which keeps the lower classes impoverished. To constructively examine this disagreement, comparative studies of lower classes from different countries would be very effective. Countries that have adopted a strategy of welcoming foreign investment might be compared with countries that have severely restricted or barred MNC operations.

A final comment needs to be made. The charts make it clear that there are great differences of opinion between three groups; (1) those who want significant government intervention in the economy with little dependence on outside private investment, (2) those who see MNCs as useful organizations which must nevertheless be carefully controlled by the host government, and (3) those who see MNCs as most beneficial when limited the least. The fact that these fundamental differences in perceptions make it impossible for one side to "convince" the other should not deter any interested party from participating in the debate. It is not the convinced whose minds will be influenced. In fact, in both the Third World and the developed countries there are many who are agnostics on this question. Well-conducted research will strengthen or weaken various parts of the case on either side. But in this process, the debate itself is elevated—a situation in itself of great benefit to the agnostic observers of the controversy. In particular, research which leads the two sides into discussing the same points of contention should be encouraged.

SELECTION OF MATERIALS

Materials were selected from scholars and businessmen who presented a number of differing points of view on the subject. The cognitive mapping technique provides a common ground for the understanding of these differences. To represent a favorable stance on multinational corporations and their operations in less-developed countries, published speeches of multinational executives were used.

Because so much diversity made the representation of a single consensus impossible, three sources were selected. This group includes one set of three public speeches by J. Irwin Miller, Chairman of the Board of Cummins Engine Company.[4] A person with a reputation for an interest in corporate responsibility, Mr. Miller is also respected as an advocate of internal codes of conduct for multinational corporations. The second set presents speeches by Lee L. Morgan, Chairman of the Board of Caterpillar Tractor Co.[5] He has also been publicly concerned about multinational corporation conduct and its role in Third World progress. The third selection is a 32-page pamphlet, *Beyond the New Mythology: The Multinational Corporation in the Mid-Seventies,* published by the American Cyanamid Company. The author is identified as Ken Sayers of the International Public Affairs section of Cyanamid.[6] Intended as an answer to the critics of multinational corporations, the work is a clear presentation of a free enterprise position; that is, it advocates no controls other than the forces of the free market and it assumes that making money in a society is naturally of benefit to the society.

The remaining materials come from articles and books of a more academic nature. They show quite differing opinions about MNCs. Four points of view are selected. The first, still representing a defense of multinationals comes from Raymond Vernon, an economist who directs Harvard's Center for International Affairs and who is actively researching the role of MNCs.[7]

Representing the critics, three sources were used showing the basic needs, dependency, and Marxist (or neo-Marxist) approaches. The basic needs approach argues that basic health and living needs should be the explicit goal of Third World governments, and that it should not be assumed that economic growth will explicitly provide these needs for the entire population. The major source material for this point of view comes from a book on multinationals by Paul Streeten and Sanjaya Lall, the former a British economist and the latter a research officer at the Oxford University Institute of Economics and Statistics.[8] Also used was an article by Streeten in which he relates the basic needs approach to development.[9]

One of the most widely accepted interpretations for Third World poverty, the "dependency" approach, is presented in three articles by Oswaldo Sunkel, a Chilean political economist.[10] Since Sunkel has been labeled a "moderate" by dependency thinkers ranging from virtual Marxists to individuals who are essentially pro-free enterprise,[11] he appeared to be the most logical source.

Finally, for the fourth view, it seemed appropriate to show a Marxist or neo-Marxist critic of multinational corporations. Again, there was the problem of finding a single author who typified the approach. We decided to map the 1978–1979 volume of *Monthly Review,* an independent socialist magazine that is the most widely read North American neo-Marxist journal of opinion. Assertions relating to the role of multinational corporations in the Third World occurred in five articles that showed considerable difference among the authors on various points.[12]

Some other critics of multinational corporations are not included in this study. For example, one logical critic would be the Christian religious groups which have been outspokenly negative about multinational corporation operations in Third World countries. However, not one single source provided a particularly coherent set of assertions. Also, much of the work was tied to specific incidents rather than presenting a world view from the Christian perspective.

It is of critical importance in judging this work to recognize that we *do not* attempt to verify the accuracy of the assertions or to substantiate the causal relationships of the arguments. In fact, the authors found some assertions to be rather poorly supported by empirical evidence. At times evidence was offered as if it were the final word when the evidence had little to do with the actual assertion. The overall goal for the study was to find the areas where the basic assertions (or attitudes) overlap either in terms of agreement or disagreement.

Four main sections of subject areas follow: (1) areas of disagreement (employment, technology, demand manipulation, and the influence of less-developed country (LDC) governments); (2) an area of agreement (diffusion of skills in LDCs); (3) a discussion of two areas valued by one side and ignored by another (codes of conduct, of concern to MNCs; and social class, of concern to MNC critics); and finally (4) a supplementary section on the use of capital and on the balance of payment rounds out the discussion of subject areas isolated by cognitive maps.

Employment Issues

Do MNCs raise or lower less-developed countries' employment levels and skills?

Perhaps the most consistent area of disagreement among the sources studied was the impact of multinational corporations on employment in less-developed countries. Most MNC supporters regard multinational corporations as benefiting LDC employment. Miller states that MNCs reduce inflation (which disrupts the economy), and thus raise employment. Morgan, too, claims that profits produced by MNCs directly lead to jobs and, in turn, to reinvestment—also raising employment. The Cyanamid study sees MNCs as raising employment directly (through their own hiring patterns) and also indirectly (by stimulating LDC firms to provide goods and services). The MNC capital intensive technology is also regarded as a positive factor in LDC employment.

On the other hand, reasoned disagreement with these arguments can be found in the works of Streeten and of Sunkel, two MNC critics. Streeten questions whether MNCs raise employment levels, listing factors detrimental to local firms while being advantageous to MNCs. These factors include (1) technology, (2) the MNC tendency to maintain the oligopolistic conditions of the home market in order to maintain a stable business environment (a factor that lowers LDC employment levels), and (3) the powerful advantage of MNCs' advertising abilities.

Sunkel, too, questions the multinational's ability to raise employment. The three positive factors which he relates to employment all have negative implications for MNCs: (1) the MNC domination of the industrial sector, which slows the growth of the locally owned industrial sector; (2) the MNC tendency to buy from its own sources, which hurts local suppliers; and (3) the general modernization process, which lessens demand and lowers employment.

On the side of the MNC critics, a quite different line of

reasoning prevails. The *Monthly Review* sees the multinationals as fostering patterns of unskilled employment, and hence, low wages, by using technologies that lessen the importance of geographical distances. This continuation of the low wage structure attracts further MNC investors. In addition, this journal sees the movement of MNCs into low wage areas as causing free trade zones and export platforms. Because many MNCs hire younger women to do meticulous work, *Monthly Review* contends that MNCs cause an imbalance in the employment structure in the less-developed countries.

Technology Issues

   Do high levels of MNC technology lead to high levels of employment and development in LDCs?

   Although some of the speeches of MNC supporters do not deal directly with the issue of technology's effects, the Cyanamid document offers a rather basic statement in favor of MNC technology, asserting that it promotes research and development, an increase in skills, industrialization, and scientific and manufacturing know-how in the host countries. Furthermore, Cyanamid argues that an effective patent system and a sufficient national market is needed in order for an effective research and development base to be generated.

   Vernon, concentrating on the political aspects of the question, sees the MNC ability to dry up or promote technology as a source of North-South tension, and he argues that higher levels of technology are necessary for increased interdependence.

   Streeten's complex and extensive analysis of MNC technology lists a number of factors which justify its advantages for multinationals: high research and development, exclusive marketing to sustain large markets, outside financing to support continued research and development, patent system protection, and complementary technological advances in related markets. Generally, he sees these technological advantages as lowering LDC employment as well as the LDC's research capacity and ability to compete, all of which discourage development in the host country. Streeten also states that the MNC tendency to transfer excessively sophisticated technology produces a bias toward production for a high income, sophisticated market with high product differentiation. This situation helps MNCs in their international operations, but it hurts the MNC in the degree to which it adjusts to the labor-capital in the LDC. Discussing a system of licensing technology as opposed to direct foreign investment, Streeten claims that licensing will lead to an unbundling of technology. This assists the host country, but the concomitant lower profits diminish the MNC's utility and its willingness to invest. An LDC's decision to opt out of the international patent system can also weaken that willingness. Finally, Streeten argues that the LDCs' lack of knowledge about the world technology market (reinforced by the absence of research and development facilities in host countries) hurts their ability to bargain with the corporation and thereby supports the continuation of the MNC's oligopolistic advantages.

As mentioned before, Sunkel directly disputes the Cyanamid assertion that high levels of technology lead to higher levels of employment. But his most interesting contention is that the concentration of research in the developed countries prevents the possible backwash or spread effects of technology which, if they existed, would help narrow the developed/less-developed technology gap. Additionally, he observes that the MNC's desire to offset its research and development costs leads to a failure to adapt the technology to local conditions and hence does not contribute to a narrowing of the gap.

The *Monthly Review* advocates efforts to develop LDC research capabilities, asserting that the MNC's technological advantages make it difficult for the LDCs to develop the technology to achieve autonomous successful industrialization. This journal also maintains that newer MNC technologies encourage corporations to exploit unskilled labor pools in low wage areas of less-developed countries.

Demand Manipulation Issues

Luxury goods or basic consumer goods? What is the role of MNC advertising and LDC free choice?

Related to the controversy about technology is the question of demand manipulation in LDCs. MNC supporters, such as Vernon, see the effective and constructive ability of being able to sell goods that people demand as a positive aspect of MNC operations, not as a source of tension. The Cyanamid analysis, too, sees the MNC's marketing abilities as a means of providing information to potential customers, and hence of leading to a freer choice of products.

The *Monthly Review*, on the other hand, argues that import substitution industrialization increases the demand of the small, middle, and upper classes in LDCs for luxury goods and retards the development of an LDC mass market for consumer goods. Other critics also dispute the economic wisdom of MNC demand manipulation. Sunkel, the Chilean economist, states that the MNC's ability to influence consumers increases demand for consumer goods and modern services. This demand produces a greater need for higher technology goods and therefore a higher demand for imports, which, in their turn, complicate balance of payments problems. Streeten and Lall suggest that the sophisticated, large-scale advertising abilities of the MNCs undermine the ability of smaller local firms to compete, which detracts from the existence of local competitive markets and the employment they engender.

Third World Government Issues

Can and should LDCs control MNC operations, or is a free enterprise system desirable?

When evaluating the role of the LDC government in the economy, not surprisingly, the MNC supporters propose variations of a free enterprise position while the critics regard the less-developed countries as unable to successfully control the powerful multinational corporations.

Miller believes that LDC nationalism and suspicion of MNCs lead to an excessive desire to control the entire means of MNC production. He sees LDC codes of conduct, legal restrictions, and other kinds of MNC restrictions, in a positive light, however. These latter can, he says, help the LDCs achieve national goals at the least cost, give the corporation forewarning and protection from quixotic government treatment, and help the host country to adjust to MNC-induced changes.

Morgan regards the LDC requirements for national conduct in manufacturing production as forcing multinationals to be guided simply by local laws and customs, a "situation ethics" syndrome. But, more importantly, according to Morgan the local requirements contribute to competition by assuring that international investment complies with national development goals. He advocates a free market as a means to identifying, producing, and distributing economic resources in a manner responsive to man's needs. This, he says, will help to bridge the trade gap between rich and poor nations.

Vernon, who writes more from the perspective of trying to understand the situation than to advocate policies, cites seventeen sources which create tensions responsible for the efforts by foreign leaders to control outside investors. These controlling efforts lead to disincentives to foreign investors, increased cooperation among industrial nations, attempts to balance MNC economic contribution with national control, and support for local public and private enterprises. Vernon is also particularly critical of the LDC state-owned enterprise system. He claims it leads to featherbedding, to the freezing of local prices, and to the use of status to cloak special privileges. He feels, however, that these unprofitable activities may be socially useful.

Streeten and Lall blame "complicated LDC government regulations" on domestic political problems. These regulations adversely affect competitive markets and the ability of local firms to compete in these markets. Also, they stimulate MNCs to use transfer pricing techniques. The presumption is that government regulation may be even more of a hindrance to local firms than to MNCs.

The relationship between the LDC government and the multinational corporation varies with perceptions about the LDC government's power and its wisdom to control or formulate policies. Deep differences of opinion exist on this issue. Pro-MNCs appear confident (if not fearful) of the state's power but not so confident of the state's wisdom. This is certainly true for Miller and Morgan. Cyanamid takes a slightly different position. In its view, the economic world is divided into two types of states: those that follow redistributive economic policies (restricting LDC utility, economic growth, and MNC operations), and those that produce policies that encourage the creation of a favorable investment climate (facilitating LDC utility). By representing the will of the people, Cyanamid argues, these policies help solidify the power of the LDC government. The need for international MNC controls is negated by the essential vulnerability of MNC operations. Furthermore, this vulnerability suggests that the multinationals are more likely to comply with LDC laws than the local companies.

Vernon, on the other hand, sees the MNC as uniquely able to avoid the restraints of LDCs, while recognizing, however, that this ability can lead to tension which is ultimately against the best interests of the MNCs. Streeten and Lall make a similar observation. The inability of any government to control or monitor the MNC's financial transactions leads to suspicions of the corporations and some obvious abuses by them —both factors negative to MNCs. It should be pointed out that this does not mean that the policy of monitoring might not be even more negative in its impact.

Sunkel sees the situation differently. The concentration of research and entrepreneurial decision-making in the home country, multinationals' political power in Third World countries, their ability to intrude in the host country's culture, and the ability he believes they have to escape LDC control, all serve to negate the LDC's ability to control the operations of foreign capital.

The *Monthly Review* presents a blanket assumption that, because of existing class structures, multinationals are not or cannot be limited by the less-developed countries.

AN AREA OF AGREEMENT

Diffusion of Skills Issues

Does MNC transfer of technology benefit the host country?

One important aspect of modernization, and one which nearly all sources in this study acknowledge, is the increase in skill levels of the population of less-developed countries. Five of the sources see an explicit link between the MNCs and the spread of skills within LDCs.

The Cyanamid pamphlet suggests that the MNC's transfer of technology produces both a higher level of local skills and an increase in the host government's scientific and manufacturing know-how. Vernon argues that the MNC's ability to

mobilize information, expertise, and money is one of the characteristics which enables the spread of risks over many markets and sources. This becomes useful to LDCs by encouraging economic efficiency, the promotion of exports, and the
training of workers.

Streeten and Lall deal with the topic of skill diffusion in
two places. First, they argue that the MNC marketing models
directly benefit local entrepreneurial development. Second,
they see acquisition of skills in Third World countries as an
indirect outgrowth of MNC employment.

Agreeing with that view, Sunkel states that the growth of
MNC-dominated industrialization spreads modern management techniques. He also feels that the development of a
modern industrial sector will increase demand for skilled labor
and decrease demand for unskilled labor. While he sees the
multinationals as ultimately harming employment levels, he
accepts the idea that skills are diffused to some limited sectors
by foreign-based operations.

Monthly Review argues that the MNCs import substitution
industrialization would not ultimately generate the local
craftsmen and technicians needed for the LDCs to control
their own industrialization. Presumably the free enterprise answer to this assertion is that the best industrializations are
those that are controlled the least.

"PARTISAN" CONCERNS

Social Class Issues

*Should the relationship of MNC to LDC be a matter of governmental
concern?*

The best example of an issue valued by one side and ignored by another is the one of social class and its relationship
to MNC–stimulated economic growth. MNC managers seem
to virtually ignore social class.

The *Monthly Review* views MNCs as polarizing the lower
classes on one side and the upper and middle classes on the
other. It sees import substitution strategy as producing both a
ruling structure with links to foreign investment and an increased demand for luxury goods among the relatively small

middle and upper classes in LDCs. This polarization, and the failure of MNCs to substantially improve the skill level of LDC populations, impedes successful industrialization and the possible development of a mass market for consumer goods in the LDC, which development might help prevent the risk of political tension. Adding to these tensions are the imbalance of employment structures and balance of payments difficulties. These tensions, in the *Monthly Review* opinion, increase the likelihood of the establishment of a multi-class popular government—a government that would socialize the means of production and produce a classless LDC society.

Monthly Review also discusses the MNC's effect on rural poverty in less-developed countries. It argues that import substitution industrialization leads to low agricultural productivity, and that this causes, in turn, rural poverty. Such poverty not only keeps wages low in LDCs, it also leads to limited agricultural reforms which create a new small landowning class in the country. The *Review* further contends that this small landowning group, which now believes it has something to protect, supports the continued oppression of the rural poor by the merchants and large landowners.

The Sunkel analysis, though similar, differs in at least one important respect: Sunkel accepts the idea that development through an emerging entrepreneurial class could lead to a legitimate national ruling class. However, he sees the continued growth of the MNC–dominated industrial sector as undermining the possible emergence of this local entrepreneurial class. He posits an additional undermining factor: The MNC's power to intrude in the politics and culture of the host country which, he claims, can inhibit the creation of a legitimate entrepreneurial class.

Sunkel believes that the MNC–dominated industrial sector has tended to divide the working class into privileged (hence unionized) and underprivileged (exploited) sectors. On balance this makes unionization in the lower class more difficult; and it contributes to low wages, which may benefit the prosperity of the middle and upper classes but harms the more numerous lower classes. Combined with racial, cultural, and political discrimination, these low wages tend to marginalize many LDC people, creating a resentful, frustrated lower class. This situation increases the probability of redistributive government policies.

Codes and Ethics Issue

Do MNCs compete responsibly? Are LDC codes, international codes, or internal MNC codes desirable?

Although ethical codes of conduct are discussed at considerable length by MNC managers, MNC critics gave this issue little attention. In the former group, Morgan rather flatly denies an MNC tendency to escape regulation and accountability, and he states that where bribery and kickbacks have existed they have detracted from the efficient operation of the free market. Miller neither affirms nor denies that MNCs have characteristically violated laws in order to compete, but he says that this possibility has contributed to suspicion in LDCs. Cyanamid appears to accept the free market as the regulator of behavior, a position which, somewhat ironically, Streeten and Sunkel also seem to accept as the determining factor in MNC behavior.

Among the MNC critics, Streeten and Lall see complicated LDC codes and regulations as the reason for MNC transfer pricing techniques, and they argue that the inability of any government to monitor financial transactions leads to some obvious MNC abuses. Sunkel regards the multinational's ability to bypass LDC controls as a fairly inescapable characteristic of the system.

At the level of public international organization a great deal of debate is directed toward setting standards of behavior for MNCs. Much of the furor in the North-South debate has come on that issue. One possible response has been to agree upon international codes of conduct for MNCs—perhaps simply as standards, but perhaps as the beginning of a system of enforcement. This issue, too, is ignored by MNC critics in our sources, and extensively discussed by MNC managers.

Although Cyanamid dismisses the need for such controls due to the ease with which the countries concerned can control the multinational corporations, both Miller and Morgan see possible advantages to international codes due to the suspicion which has been generated by four factors: (1) the efficiency of MNC production and distribution of services, (2) the belief that MNCs violate laws in the name of competition, (3) the MNC's allocation of tasks and resources according to an efficient equilibrium in terms of worldwide (rather than local) supply and demand, and (4) a geographical imbalance in production, location, and distribution of resources.

In Miller's analysis, two further factors account for the international codes: some past duplicity and shortsighted actions by MNCs, and the fact that many MNC activities seem unregulated by national laws. Miller doubts that codes would be effective or useful in regulating MNCs, and he feels they would probably lead to actions that would be opposed by most businessmen. However, he sees them as a valuable outlet for criticism and a basis for international standards of reporting and accounting.

Morgan is more favorably disposed toward international codes. He states that the conflict between the less-developed and the industrialized states arises from valid charges against MNCs and from problems of worldwide economic growth. Fair and effective international cooperation and scrutiny of MNCs can yield a continuing public audit which may be useful to them. Morgan also feels that the worldwide need for improved common management of economic problems should assist the operation of international forums which generally lead to better global understanding.

Vernon sees two factors affecting the United Nations actions regarding MNCs: tensions (included in his map of seventeen factors), and the efforts of LDC leaders. He believes that United Nations actions lessen the current inability of any agency to hold MNCs accountable for their actions. He cites seven outgrowths of UN actions: (1) the willingness of sovereign states to expose national economic policies to collective scrutiny, (2) the pursuit of goals which could not be sought separately, (3) stiffened national systems of administration and regulation, (4) demands by Third World states for capital, technology, and access to markets, (5) freedom to take measures to further national objectives, (6) disregard for differences in ideology and interest among LDCs, and (7) an "atmospheric effect" which will better the situation in which debate or disagreement has been taking place.

Although only Miller and Morgan discuss the idea (one presumes that the others believe outside factors such as the marketplace to be the primary limitation on MNC activities), there is also a possible third area of *internal* codes of conduct for corporations with foreign interests. Miller sees these company codes as resulting from general suspicion, the international efforts, and response to LDC efforts to control the conduct of MNCs. He lists five outcomes, or advantages, to the internal codes: (1) they provide standards against corruption, (2) they indicate that a company is not going into every country to which it is invited, (3) they commit the MNC to learning about any host country in which it operates, (4) they signify the MNC's concern for its impact on society, and (5) they show the MNC's determination to cooperate and compete.

Morgan views internal codes as resulting from doubts about business ethics and morality. These codes lead to five outcomes: (1) the use of morality as a criteria for choosing managers, (2) the providing of information for the staff concerning the corporation's views of responsible, ethical business practices, (3) increased reflective thought within management as to its proper role, (4) a way of registering beliefs and experiences about the reciprocal responsibility of host countries, and (5) the establishment of high goals for the corporate organization. Additionally, the code should lessen the tendency of the corporation to be guided only by local laws or customs—a tendency that Morgan, as mentioned previously, believes leads to "situational ethics."

ADDITIONAL SUBJECT AREAS

Capital Issues

Do MNCs export or import capital?

Quite appropriately, MNC defenders do not make a simplistic argument claiming that multinational corporations are major suppliers of capital. Somewhat surprisingly, however, the Cyanamid presentation acknowledges that older subsidiaries that export capital harm the LDC's balance of payments position, and that newer subsidiaries that import capital serve to alleviate that problem.

As mentioned in the section on employment, Morgan sees the MNC as a source of profits which leads both to investment and reinvestment, each producing more jobs. Vernon claims the international movement of capital mobilized by MNC action leads to higher levels of global interdependence—a situation he sees as a positive one. But he also acknowledges that the MNCs' ability to drain off capital causes tension in the LDCs.

Sunkel, speaking as a MNC critic, sees the capital needed for a modern industrial sector as dependent on a wage structure that keeps workers poorly paid. The *Monthly Review* sees the import substitution industrialization strategy as inhibiting the development of an indigenous LDC capital goods sector. It further claims that MNCs' debt repayment, shipping costs, insurance, banking service costs, royalties, interest, dividends, and management fees, all lead to capital outflows that cause balance of payments problems. From this perspective, then, more investment and loans are sought to alleviate the payments problem, but in the long run this makes the problem worse.

Balance of Payments Issue

What is the impact of MNC operations on balancing payments problems in LDCs?

Three sources specifically discuss the balance of payments problems in LDCs—two MNC critics and one MNC supporter. In the former category the *Monthly Review* argues that recent export gains are offset by LDC imports of raw materials. Transfer pricing of profits out of LDCs complicates the problem as does debt repayment, insurance, shipping costs, interest, etc. *Monthly Review* sees the LDC's tendency to welcome more loans and investments as counterproductive.

Sunkel sees balance-of-payments problems as partially caused by a demand for higher technology goods resulting from MNC advertising efforts and from the upper and middle class purchasing power. He also argues that import substitution industrialization leads directly to balance of payments difficulties (the problem here is, that production of goods locally often involves more importation of machinery, and ultimately a higher cost, than importing goods would produce), and to a decline in exports. This decline, of course, further hurts the LDC's balance of payments.

Cyanamid, on the other hand, argues that new subsidiaries provide capital that older subsidiaries cannot. Its analysis shows three other factors affecting the balance of payments situation. The host country's need to import is lessened due to MNC activities and the ability of the country to export is improved. Also, OPEC is blamed for some of the current problems. OPEC activities are one of the sources of

LDC food shortages. In following the free enterprise, specialization model the Cyanamid emphasis is on trade, and it does not assume that local agricultural production is the answer.

SUMMARY

What is clear from this review of opinions concerning the role of multinational corporations in less-developed countries is that points of view are often embedded in very different lines of reasoning. All the sources studied considered sound, productive economic growth as a positive means toward obtaining human well-being, but their definitions of constructive growth varied as did their ideas as to how this could be accomplished.

On the question of whether multinationals produce a diffusion of skills and technology in less-developed countries, each of the seven sources studied is in agreement. Some sources, such as *Monthly Review*, take issue with the particular effect that MNC–generated low level technologies have on LDC employment patterns. Others, such as Sunkel, see the increased demand for skilled labor and decreased demand for unskilled labor as a polarizing factor in LDC's social class structures. And Streeten and Lall see MNC high technology as ultimately producing low employment levels in their host countries.

But areas of direct disagreement among the sources included levels of employment, demand manipulation, and the influence of MNCs on local governments. Miller, Morgan, and Cyanamid all see the MNCs' employment impact positively — as raising employment by reducing inflation, stimulating economic growth, and furthering direct hiring policies. As mentioned above, however, Streeten attributes declining levels of employment in LDCs to MNC high technology, and Sunkel maintains that MNC industrial growth ultimately affects employment levels negatively.

Only Vernon and Cyanamid regard MNC marketing and advertising as a positive factor for less-developed countries; other MNC defenders do not discuss it. MNC critics (*Monthly Review*, Sunkel, and Streeten) see the LDC decreased demand for consumer goods, and increased level of imports as manipulated by MNC advertising advantages, which overpower LDC competitors.

Deep differences of opinion exist concerning the extent to which LDC governments should regulate MNCs and/or local enterprise. Morgan, Cyanamid, and Vernon advocate a free enterprise system in which local governments would hold few regulatory controls on either MNCs or LDC businesses. They regard regulations as adversely affecting both markets; however, perceptions about LDC's genuine ability to control LDCs seem to make this point a rather mute issue. Both Vernon, an MNC defender, and *Monthly Review*, an MNC critic, regard the LDC's power as finally too weak in this area to be effective.

Partisan concerns—valued by one side and disregarded by the other—include the MNC's effect on social class and on the matter of codes and ethics. Neo-Marxist MNC critics (e.g. *Monthly Review*) strongly base their larger critical concerns on the MNC's tendency to polarize the upper and middle classes on the one hand and the lower class on the other. Another MNC critic, Sunkel, while advocating the formation of an entrepreneurial class for the LDCs, sees the MNC influence on economic and political events as a serious deterrent to this possibility.

The last issue is not discussed by the MNC defenders in this study. An area of concern that *is* valued by MNC defenders, and is not mentioned by critics, is the need for international codes of conduct. Miller and Morgan see the advantages of such controls as bases for standards of reporting and accounting to ensure fair and effective international cooperation and scrutiny for multinationals. Vernon advocates UN actions in this area as a way of holding MNCs accountable for their actions in a nonpolitical arena for debate and disagreement.

A secondary level of controls proposed—internal controls generated from within multinationals—seems advantageous to both Morgan and Miller as a way of establishing high moral goals for corporate organizations and avoiding the subjective uncertainties of "situation ethics."

Finally, some topics in this study received only partial mention among the sources. Do MNCs import or export capital? Morgan and Vernon see MNC's profits and the international movement of capital generated by multinationals as economically positive for LDC investment, reinvestment, and increased employment.

MNC critics Sunkel and the *Monthly Review,* on the other hand, see the modern industrialized sector as causing both the capital outflows that upset the balance of payments and perpetuating an import substitution strategy that inhibits the LDC's indigenous economy. Among the three sources that expressly discuss this balance of payments issue, *Monthly Review* and Sunkel, respectively, see MNC's export gains as offsetting LDC's imports of raw materials—a situation resulting from MNCs' higher technologies and advertising efforts, and LDCs' cost factors for manufacturing. Cyanamid, however, sees new MNC subsidiaries as likely to become capital-producing sources which will ultimately improve the balance of payments situation for LDCs.

The analyses of those who are critical of the multinational role in development is often flawed in the sense that their criticisms are based on an ideal of painless development. Flaws or disadvantages via private investment may be quite real, and yet many states may have no alternative that is better or even as good in terms of income distribution and other measures. Judged as an ideal type, the operations of multinationals in a very disorderly real world may indeed fall far short of being a panacea for Third World ills. Realizing this, however, does not solve the gigantic problem confronting the developing world; that is, that all development strategies have high costs. Ironically, it may be the willingness of defenders of multinational corporations to see their operations as a painless solution that has allowed the discussion to drift onto an excessively abstract level. Hence there are aspects of the debate on both sides that fail to recognize the gap between the theoretical ideal and the untheoretical real world of comparative sacrifices and benefits.

NOTES

1. *Storm over the Multinationals* (Cambridge, Mass.: Harvard University Press, 1977), p. v.

2. An extended review of the findings of this study is available from Michael J. Francis, Chairman, Department of Government, University of Notre Dame, Notre Dame, Indiana 46556. It includes diagrams of the cognitive maps for each author or group cited as well as integrated maps of the comprehensive belief systems.

3. See Robert Axelrod, ed., *The Structure of Decision* (Princeton, N.J.: Princeton University Press, 1976).

4. Address to Conference Board Seminar, "Coping with Host Country Tensions," New York, 19 January 1977; Address to Inter-

national Management and Development Institute, "Future of the Multinationals," 1 March 1976; "What's Ahead for the Multinationals?" International Management and Development Institute, March 1976.

5. Address to American Chambers of Commerce of Switzerland and the United Kingdom, "Lowering the Walls," Autumn 1974; Address to the World Trade Conference, "Global Responsibility," Chicago, 30 April 1975; Address to the World Trade Dinner, 62nd National Foreign Trade Convention, "Worldwide Business Conduct," New York, 18 November 1975.

6. Publication used has no date; an earlier version is dated October 1976.

7. "Economic Sovereignty at Bay," *Foreign Affairs*, 52 (October 1968); "Does Society Also Profit?" *Foreign Policy*, No. 13 (Winter 1973–1974).

8. *Foreign Investment: Transnationals and Developing Countries* (Boulder, Colo.: Westview Press, 1977).

9. "A Basic Needs Approach to Economic Development," in Kenneth Jameson and Charles K. Wilber, eds., *Directions in Economic Development* (Notre Dame, Ind.: University of Notre Dame Press, 1979).

10. "Transnational Capitalism and National Disintegration in Latin America," *Social and Economic Studies*, 22 (March 1973); "External Economic Relationships and the Process of Development: Suggestions for an Alternative Analytical Framework," in Robert B. Williamson, William P. Glade, Jr., and Karl M. Schmitt, eds., *Latin American-U.S. Economic Interactions* (Washington, D.C.: American Enterprise Institute, 1974); and "Big Business and 'Dependencia': A Latin American View," *Foreign Affairs*, 50 (April 1972).

11. C. Richard Bath and Dilmus D. James, "Dependency Analysis of Latin America," *Latin American Research Review*, 11 (1976).

12. Harry Magdoff, "The Limits of International Reform," 30 (May 1978); James L. Dietz, "Imperialism and Puerto Rico," 30 (September 1978); Susan B. Kaplow and Frank T. Fitzgerald, "The African Working Class and the Labor Aristocracy Thesis," 30 (September 1978); Paul M. Sweezy, "Corporations, the State, and Imperialism," 30 (November 1978); Folker Frobel, Jurgen Heinrichs, and Otto Kreye, "Export-Oriented Industrialization of Underdeveloped Countries," 30 (November 1978).

13. In markets with excessively advanced technology, levels of employment decline, while in markets of low levels of production, technology employment levels increase.

PART II:
Roles and Responsibilities: Capabilities and Issues

PART II TURNS FROM an analysis of the nature of Third World poverty and the multinational environment to the capacity of multinationals to respond to that poverty within this complex and changing milieu. Four activities are reported.

The reflections by Father Hesburgh are a synthesis of his addresses to the workshop gatherings. Drawing on an unusually broad involvement with global development and multinationals, Father Hesburgh shares his views on the unique capability of multinationals to contribute to global development, a capability that stems from the corporation's drive for survival through the generation of adequate returns over the long term.

For the second activity a panel of three seminar participants comments on a potential role for multinationals. This panel describes multinationals as an inextricable component of the global economic system and is concerned with the limits that this broader environment imposes upon these firms. Glade sets forth three levels of "doubts and skepticism about whether multinational corporations have a constructive role to play in the alleviation of world poverty." Wilber points out that the multinational, like any other corporation, must function within the market in which it finds itself and sees multinationals as relatively unimportant in Third World development. Kelley discusses the potential for multinationals to make a contribution beyond the confines of the economic-political system and to lend their skills and funds on a special-projects basis outside of their normal operations.

The focus then shifts to the corporate decision-maker. Tavis and Powers explore the nature of the multinationals' obligation to contribute to the social and economic development of Third World countries and how they might approach this duty. Tavis argues that multinationals have a corporate developmental responsibility for the Third World. Powers places the corporate management issues in a moral context. He develops a "principle of moral action" and then goes on to demonstrate how multinational corporations might incorporate this principle into their Third World operations. In the last paper Doubet and Tavis identify areas in the corporate decision process that should be considered as managers attempt to meet their developmental responsibilities.

Two basic questions emerge in this section: (1) What are the limits on multinational corporate action, i.e., how free are multinationals to respond to poverty in the Third World? and (2) How should multinationals use their resources to enhance development in the countries where they operate?

The constraints on multinational corporate actions derive from economic markets, international and national laws, and national regulatory regimes. When financial, product, and labor markets are efficient and competitive, the economic choices for the corporate management are defined by the markets. When laws are clearly stated and enforced, and when regulation is effective, the manager has no real social choices to make. Under these conditions, the idea of social responsibility as a requirement either to do no damage or to pursue social good is really not relevant. Powers states the point well: "There is no 'responsibility' when the capability to respond is absent."

To the extent that markets are not efficient, laws are not exhaustive, and regulation is not effective, the manager's alternatives, as well as his or her ability to choose among them, increases. Given the great variety of multinational corporations and the uniqueness of national environments, the degree of freedom for multinational activity ranges across a broad spectrum. The choices for some multinationals in some countries are surely narrowly defined. For others, however, the burden of economic and social choice falls on the multinational manager. The seminar participants recognized this spectrum of flexibility, even though they placed the median for multinationals as a group at different points.

One form of response in which firms tend to have a good deal of freedom to participate consists in the use of information. The unique contributions outlined by Father Hesburgh were a result of the multinational ability to gather and use information. Doubet and Tavis make the general case for sharing this information with local regulators. Powers proposes a specific process for multinational participation in governmental planning.

In evaluating the Dolefil impact, which will be examined in the next section, Glade extends this notion of information use to a sharing of the process itself. Glade suggests that Dolefil should share its organizational efficiency as an "information gathering and information processing system" with local institutions. By sharing this capability with local groups, Glade concludes that one aspect of multinational vulnerability—the disparity between the multinational and other local institutions—would be reduced.

7. The Capability for Unique Contributions

REV. THEODORE M. HESBURGH, C.S.C.

THE ISSUE OF MULTINATIONAL managers and poverty in the Third World is surely a complex and controversial one. On the one hand there are people of good will and reasonable intelligence who are seized by the terrible aspects of world poverty and who see multinational corporations simply as obstacles to development. In their eyes, multinationals debilitate the economies of the countries in which they operate.

On the other hand, there are people working in multinational corporations who say, "Those do-gooders sit and talk about doing good, but they never do anything except talk, while we are out here facing the problems of the day and trying to do business in places where it is almost impossible to do business. And somehow we pull it off."

In many instances, the two sides cannot even agree on the facts. Each side tells a completely different story. It would not be so bad if the stories were as different as "M" and "N" were different, but the problem is that one is saying "A" and the other "Z".

But the complexity of the issue does not end even if you do your homework to get the facts straight about one situation. The international economy is so complex and varied that it is impossible to generalize about all companies on the basis of what is going on with any one of them. There are hundreds of multinationals; each does something different, and each often does it differently, depending on the part of the world it is operating in, the kind of activities it is involved in, and the kind of managers and policies each has, enlightened or unenlightened. I think that many of them try to act in a socially conscious and moral way. There are others—how many I do not know—who are not exactly seized by a concept of world justice. Still, it is impossible to generalize about the actions of them all. There is simply no way of passing judgment on what all multinationals are doing, let alone on what they should be doing. Moreover, there are no great, broad, or universally valid generalizations about poverty or about development. Thus, we must recognize that there are no simple, easy answers.

The very complexity of the issue and the impossibility of quick generalizations bring home to me the importance of this seminar group: a group that is informed; a group that has very strong ideas on the intellectual side regarding what development is and should be in the world; a group that includes practitioners who are in the field working, and who know the facts of the matter in their particular, concrete circumstances, and who are not perhaps as pressed ideologically as many people in academic life are pressed ideologically.

This seminar cannot do very much more than set down some general principles that would help us to understand what the role of multinationals might be as an engine of development in a world characterized by great poverty. In light of the dissatisfaction with multinationals and what I would almost call the war against them, evident in many quarters, I would suggest a theoretical framework or matrix within which the multinationals can be considered.

In a series of lectures called the Ditchley Lectures on Interdependence,[1] I laid out what I thought was a set of conditions under which multinationals could be considered prime engines for development. I applied these conditions to nations and pointed out that multinationals could do some things that most governmental entities cannot do. After all, when you look at the governments of the developed countries, there are not more than a dozen or a dozen and a half that could in the widest sense be considered helpers in the area of development. Most of the development funds, in fact about $12.5 million out of a possible $14 or $15 million, come out of the United States and the Western European community.

If one understands poverty, and if he understands the potency and capabilities of multinationals that can bear upon the situation, at least in theory, he can draw up a list of conditions or a list of possibilities that would establish for multinationals a significant role in development, which they should indeed have. Given these criteria, we can honestly look at multinationals one by one, and see to what extent the corporation fits the pattern or goes against it.

What are some of the things that multinationals can do in the area of development that could not be done quite so well by nations themselves?

The first thing they could do arises from the necessity for profit, without which a company cannot exist. Companies are forced to be realistic. They are not in business simply to do good; they are in business to make a profit, and if they do not make a profit, they go under. For that reason they have to make hard and tough decisions about where one manufactures what, or where one mines what, or where one sets up markets, or where one becomes involved in this or that application of science and technology for development within what countries.

These are all questions of priority, and there is no law that says you have to do your work in Zaire, or in Nepal, or in Indonesia. But when you consider that, to maintain a going concern in a Third World nation, a company must not only employ people and transfer technology but must also stay profitable, the whole exercise becomes a lot more realistic than a government exercise that can, because someone thinks it is a bright idea, invest $10 million or more, and really hurt the country in the process.

Since companies must take a very hard-nosed look at business situations—and this can involve any business, be it service, extraction, manufacturing, or whatever—they are likely to have the capability, which governments generally do not have, of looking at economic situations in a given country and making a judgment as to whether or not it is possible to support a successful business enterprise there. In other words, they are able to look at the economic potential, be it manpower, resources, lumber, minerals, or whatever, and say, "Yes, there is a market that can really use this product or service," or "This is a collection of manpower that can do this kind of manufacturing," or "This is a resource worth developing." The ability to make such judgments is something that I think is desperately needed throughout the world. It is especially important that we be able to look at difficult cases like

Niger and Bangladesh and have some realistic answer to the question, "What can they do to survive?" We could begin by asking, "What can they do to raise enough food to survive?" And there are companies that can be helpful in that regard.

The second thing that multinationals can contribute is something that many Third World governments and local companies cannot: capital. When we look at world entities, we generally think in terms of nations—there are about 150 of them now. Yet, over forty of the largest economic entities in the world are multinational corporations, not countries. This gives us some idea of how important they might be in this field of development.

Most governments—and especially most Third World governments—do not have that much flexibility in raising or providing capital, and in directing it toward specific tasks. But multinational corporations do have this flexibility. They have spent their lives in this activity. Thus, if a multinational does see a potential for a project in a Third World country, it can direct hundreds of millions of dollars, if need be, into making that project a reality.

The third thing that multinationals have to offer is their knowledge of world markets. Once something is produced, the multinationals have certainly learned how to identify and reach the appropriate market, wherever in the world it might be. They can produce something in Bangladesh and market it in New York City. It might be a jute bag, but they can do it. And not only can they identify markets, they can also utilize transportation systems in ways that many Third World countries cannot. They can gain access to these systems or can provide their own.

Fourth, multinationals also have an extraordinary capacity for transferring science and technology for development. Just as they can produce a jute bag in Bangladesh and market it in New York, they can take technology developed in New York—say for making computer chips—transfer it to Bangladesh and manufacture the chips there.

The issue of the transfer of technology is surely one of the most problematic—as well as most promising—aspects of multinational business activity facing us today. From the standpoint of those with the technology, there is a very complicated problem of proprietorship. There are two kinds of science and technology. There is the kind that speaks to basic human needs like hunger, health delivery, education, housing, and other basic concerns. This technology is public. Everybody knows what it is. There is no secret about the strains of rice coming out of the International Rice Research Institute in Los Banos in the Philippines, and there is no secret about the kinds of wheat or corn strains coming out of the International Corn and Wheat Improvement Center in Mexico City. But, when we get to very complicated points in industrial development, we are up against a proprietary technology which governments generally do not control. It belongs to the corporation that develops it. Most corporations will transfer such technology for a price, and very often they have paid a high price to develop it in the first place. One can argue about what a reasonable price is, but I do not think there is anybody in the world who says a company can spend a billion dollars creating something and then give it away. At that point companies would stop creating things.

There is also, from the standpoint of the developing countries, the problem of differing technological needs. What a multinational may have to offer may not be what the people living in the local economy of a Third World country may need. Developed countries create mostly capital-intensive technology, whereas underdeveloped countries, often with large numbers of marginally employed workers, need technology that is labor-intensive. Still, the development by multinationals of labor-intensive technology suited to Third World conditions is not an impossibility. It can be done, and I think that multinationals are more and more coming to understand this.

The issue of the adaptation of technology to local conditions brings us to the fifth way in which multinationals can encourage development: multinationals can make people self-sufficient. By adapting not only to local conditions but also to local needs, they can help people help themselves. In a sense, multinationals can put themselves out of business, or they can make a kind of ten- or twenty-year contract that says, if we have been good citizens of this country, and we have trained your people to help run this enterprise, and if your people are working at every level of management at the end of twenty years, because we are developing new science and technology continually, maybe it will be in your interest to keep us around for another twenty years.

Finally, I think that multinationals have understood interdependence perhaps better than any other entity in the world. They have certainly learned how to transfer funds; sometimes people say they do it too well and avoid all kinds of taxes. They have certainly learned how to transfer people to work across cultures. They have learned how to transfer technology in meaningful—and sometimes unmeaningful—ways. They have learned how to communicate across a whole world with a multitude of languages and cultures. They have learned to work with different political systems, and in many cases they have learned to do so without being immoral about it, without resorting to bribery, and without necessarily changing their own standards and values.

If these six points are true, then I would submit to you that multinationals can contribute more to development than can many governmental entities, either within the developing or the developed world. There is a realistic kind of Damocles sword hanging over their heads, in that they either perform well—which means economically soundly—or they are out of business. Moreover, we can say that multinationals are a kind of entity that is going to be necessary for the development needed in the years to come. Instead of writing them off as monsters, we should try to enlist their support in a task that needs all the intelligence, creativity, and resources it can muster.

We also need to look at the role that multinationals can potentially play in global terms, and that means in terms of the welfare of all the people on this planet. We all need to gain some of the multinationals' understanding of interrelatedness; we need to understand that the economic development of Third World countries that multinationals can help to bring about is no more a matter of charity for people in backward countries than it is one of unrestricted profits for the rest of us. Rather, the development of the Third World is something that benefits us all.

To take one aspect of this, there are now somewhere between three and one-half to six million undocumented or illegal aliens in the United States. There is a very simple explanation of why they are here: they have come for the same reasons that your and my grandparents and great-grandparents came. They are here because they live in places that have no economic hope. And if they can manage to negotiate a journey of a few hundred or a few thousand miles, they can have more hope than they could by staying where they were—even if it means working in a sweatshop, without eligibility for the Social Security benefits they pay for, without overtime, and with the constant threat of dismissal and deportation hanging over them.

I have been involved with a government commission that recently reported on its recommendations for reform of the laws on immigration and refugees. I think such reforms are necessary if we are to gain some control over this problem, but at best such changes in the laws are a stopgap measure. Ultimately, what we have to do is create jobs and foster conditions of economic expectation where the people are. If we do not want to live in a world in which fifteen or sixteen nations are economic magnets drawing people from everywhere else, we need to set up magnets of economic opportunity in all the other nations on the earth. What we have to do is to develop the world.

The problem is analogous with—and related to—the food problem. There is no way we are going to solve the food problem by growing more corn in Iowa, Indiana, or Illinois. The real answer is to grow food in the countries where people are hungry. Doing so eliminates the export cost of transportation, the cost of distribution, and the drain of the importing nations' foreign exchange. This can be done. Theoretically it is no problem at all. But if we are actually going to get around to doing it, we are going to have to see the practicability of a new vision of the world, a vision in which a billion people are no longer hungry and without hope, because we have used the vast panoply of resources we now have to grow food and create jobs where—and wherever—the people are.

If we are to achieve this goal of global development, I suggest that we need to employ the full capabilities of multinationals. Instead of holding them back, we would encourage them to do more, but to do it perhaps in certain times and certain places in a different context.

To work, this vision must come from within the firm, from its management, in conjunction with external groups. I recently was asked to review a company's statement of objectives. From a business standpoint, it was effective. The first five points had to do with efforts toward profitability, success, and the economic well-being of this particular enterprise. The sixth and final point faced the moral issue of what it is to be a good corporate citizen, what it is to understand the social and economic context in which one works both here and abroad. And also what one's responsibility is toward social justice, both internally within the company and externally. The first five points, as carefully prepared as they were, could apply to any business, including illegitimate ones. It is only when one comes to the sixth point that this company begins to have a character of its own which differentiates it from other organizations that do not have these concerns, do not have this kind of planning, do not have this kind of vision of the society in which it lives and to which it contributes, not as one that feeds on the society but as one that contributes and still makes enough profit to stay alive and to grow.

I think that is what I would like to see us moving toward—a society that is efficacious and efficient, a society that makes profit from what it does for profit, but can do this and still contribute to the well-being of those who are in desperate need. I honestly believe, because I have seen examples of it, that we can do all these things at once. There are people doing them today—and people who are not doing them. I believe that to have a good discussion we must distinguish between the ones doing something worthwhile and the ones not contributing. And I think we are rational enough to agree on a set of general principles—general enough to be applicable to the many varieties of multinationals, the many varieties of local situations—that would represent our own ideals for what a good society, or, if writ large, a good world, should be.

NOTE

1. Sponsored by the Ditchley Foundation; see *The Ditchley Journal,* Spring 1975.

8. A Role for Multinationals: Three Panel Presentations

I: Multinational Firms and National Economies

WILLIAM P. GLADE

ALL COLLEGE LECTURERS, irrespective of their academic orientations, seem to be pedagogical trinitarians. This probably comes about because three points are sufficient to demonstrate that a given subject is complex and not flatly two-dimensional; yet three points are not too many for listeners to keep in mind as an exposition moves forward. In line with this hallowed tradition, I should like to sketch out three levels of questions, three levels of analysis if you will, about the subject at hand today.

In a sense, the three levels at which issues might be considered constitute three grounds for the doubts of skeptics about whether multinational corporations have any constructive role to play in the alleviation of world poverty. By the same token, these are also the different evidentiary levels on which answers to that key question must be sought by those who seek to identify a socially constructive role for transnational enterprise.

THE ATOMISTIC LEVEL OF EVALUATION

The first concern arises at an atomistic level, the microeconomic level of the firm. We can, in other words, examine

---

A summary of the general discussion which followed presentation of these papers is contained in an Addendum to this chapter.

the operation of individual enterprises to see which ones further and which ones fail to further the kinds of economic growth that reduce mass poverty. This is in some ways the simplest level to deal with because the information we need to gather can be readily specified. At this level some multinational activities seem rather clearly to contribute to economic growth and, at least to an extent, to the alleviation of poverty. Others, just as clearly, do not. Let me offer two limiting cases to demonstrate the point.

In the early years of the Alliance for Progress, one of the several citizen involvement efforts that came into being was the "Partners of the Alliance" program. The aim of this effort was to establish people-to-people linkages that could promote development in the Americas, and also bring people in Latin America and the United States closer together in terms of mutual understanding. The structure of this grassroots type of program paired individual states in the United States with countries or regions in Latin America. Among these partnerships was that of Texas with Peru.[1] Astonishingly, one of the opening projects of this particular partnership involved an arrangement with a well-known luxury department store in Dallas to send down to Lima a style show displaying all the latest in *haute couture*. Only in Texas, perhaps, could such an undertaking be thought a contribution to development, especially in a country then experiencing the early rumblings of social revolution. The notion comes to mind that this must surely have been a development program designed by Marie Antoinette. In any case, the business of high fashion is rather unarguably one which is negative in its relation to the development process in most of the world, and by any reasonable standards one which is antithetical to the alleviation of poverty. Except insofar as they might be set up to earn foreign exchange through exporting, enterprise operations catering to luxury consumption have little place in any serious program for eradicating poverty in the Third World.

The other limiting case might be the Caterpillar Tractor Company. Admittedly, there are controversial issues here, involving relative factor prices and the substitutability of capital for labor. One could, for example, question the suitability of different kinds of earth-moving equipment and agricultural machinery for various jobs in labor-abundant economies. But leaving such technical issues aside, we would all likely agree that some Caterpillar products are, at least with appropriate modifications in product design, quite useful in the alleviation of poverty and that they do indeed contribute to the development process.[2]

Granted that a lot of intermediate situations stand somewhere between these two limiting cases, it should in principle be possible to judge these on a case-by-case basis, to determine which could, on balance, be valued for their contributions to development and which would be found wanting in one or more respects. Quite obviously, the percentage of cases that might be judged either unambiguously good or unambiguously bad would tend to be relatively small, given the multiplicity of impacts an operation of any size and complexity will have on the host society. Nevertheless, despite such ambiguities, in the long run this micro-level of analysis may well afford, for reasons that will become clear as we go along, the most convincing evidence of the potential role of multinational corporations in helping poor countries to overcome material backwardness. It is not, however, the grounds on which the arguments for a beneficent role for foreign investment most often rest.

THE CATEGORICAL LEVEL OF EVALUATION

The second level of questioning, which I shall call the categorical level, looks at the whole set of multinational corporations. Does this set of institutions, as a prominent organizational phenomenon of our times, contribute to or detract from the development process and in particular the alleviation of mass poverty? Or is it, possibly, neutral in its impact? With some frequency, the case for multinational companies having a constructive role to play is developed primarily at this categorical level.[3] This is understandable on two counts. For one thing, categorical analysis often seems more satisfying than the case-by-case approach and more useful as a basis for public policy formation; for another, the extensive data requirements of the case study approach make this approach seem less economical to all concerned than would reasoning from general principles. Where it works, deductive logic is certainly cheaper and more efficient than empirically grounded inductive analysis.

Here, however, the case becomes much more problematic, in part because of concerns centering on the bargaining relationships that obtain between multinational corporations and the less-developed countries. It is, of course, evident that there must be *some* mutual benefits accruing to both partners in these transactional relationships; otherwise, they would not occur in the first place. This is the point very often made by people in multinational business, not to mention those enamored of the "Chicago School" in economics. It overlooks, however, at least two considerations which tend to be paramount in the minds of social critics in less-developed countries. The first reservation regarding mutuality of benefit has to do with "disaggregating" one of the partners to the transaction, the host country. That a given relationship may be assessed positively by some groups in the host country—say, public officials or the politically favored—does not necessarily ensure that it be viewed as a benefit by others, or even by the majority of the population. The transition to post-Somoza Nicaragua makes this point plain. Beyond this, there is a preoccupation with the distribution of mutual benefits in a context of unequal exchange. While benefits may accrue to both multinationals and their host countries, these benefits may tend to be asymmetrically distributed for a variety of reasons.

Whenever we have what is, rightly or wrongly, perceived to be a lopsided distribution of benefits, we can assume that the bargaining agreement reached will tend to be an unstable one. Unless there is some perception of parity in the bargaining relationship, sooner or later one or the other of the partners to the transaction will surely attempt to renegotiate it, to redefine the terms of exchange. While it is often said that such efforts at renegotiation generate conflict, it is perhaps as accurate to state that these efforts result from conflict. Or rather, the episode which, from the point of view of the multinationals, *creates* conflicts, actually, in the view of the host country, *derives* from conflict.

A close examination of the context of the bargaining relationship should reveal the factors and circumstances that constrain this relationship in a lopsided way and help to identify some of the elements that might conceivably be modified to create a different distribution of benefits, one which would operate to make the relationship more stable over the longer

run. While this is not the occasion for such a searching examination, a few points merit at least brief reflection to indicate
the general nature of the misgivings that arise at the categorical level.

The multinational corporations, as is well known, are very
often much larger than the less-developed economies in which
they operate. Consequently, one of the sources of anxiety
could be described, simply, as an intimidation factor: very
large multinational corporations have, in their dealings with
small countries, sometimes been perceived as threats to national autonomy in several areas of policymaking. Rightly or
wrongly is beside the point: the perception exists. Some forty
years ago, for instance, such a perception came explicitly to
the surface in the historic confrontation of foreign capital and
national power in the Mexican petroleum nationalization; over
the years since, this particular kind of conflict has been
reenacted many times, perhaps with increasing frequency.
While such fears are probably no longer so rampant in countries as large or as economically developed as Brazil or Mexico,
one does find the perception of threat prevalent in many of
the smaller and weaker countries.

A second factor to consider in ascertaining the terms in
which the bargaining transaction is set is that the multinational
corporations tend on the whole to be far more stable, as
organizations, than are many less-developed-country governments. Despite stockholder militancy in the United States in
recent years, the governments of the less-developed countries
might often be considered to be much more vulnerable to
stockholder action, more vulnerable to their own constituencies, than are the managers of the multinational corporations.
For all the talk of oligarchic rule, it is the multinational corporations, rather than the less-developed countries, that appear
to be management controlled entities. From this derives yet
another element of asymmetry. Stable bargaining units on the
one side are counterposed against bargaining units that, on
the other side, are far from stable, that are much more pre-
cariously perched on the support of their shifting constituencies. The more sophisticated dependency analyses of recent
years reveal how the state apparatus in Third World countries
can, at least at times, transcend the constraints set by the structure of domestic class interests, in part by playing off alliances
with various groups in the fragmented domestic polity against

the external support that can be mobilized from foreign governments and corporations as well as from international agencies. Even so, this relative autonomy of the state, a phenomenon which has attracted so much discussion of late, seems to spring more from the ability of a political class to orchestrate a rather delicate balance of social forces both internal and foreign than from any pervasive and conscious delegation of authority to the public sector by an electorate acting in consensus. Under the circumstances, the equilibrium of power tends to be fragile, to the relative disadvantage of governments whose ability to inflict damage on multinationals through arbitrary and capricious policies may greatly exceed their ability to extract benefits from them in any consistent and coherent fashion.

A third element in the picture is the locational mobility of the multinational corporations, which mobility contrasts markedly with the geographical fixity of the governments of the less-developed countries. While the governments must ponder what can be done to optimize the use of resources in their particular locations, the multinational enterprise will want to optimize across a whole range of locations. *La donna é mobile,* Verdi tells us, but in the modern world of multinationals *il capitale é mobile* too. Except when there is a large sunk investment in fixed capital which can, in effect, be held hostage by the host country,[4] there will, in most cases, tend to be more bargaining options open to the multinational corporation than there are to its bargaining partner, the host government. Especially is this the case in the pre-entry negotiations, but even in post-entry bargaining in fields where technology is dynamic, the posture of governments may have to be moderated by a need to maintain access to the next generations of evolving technology.[5] To be sure, competition among multinationals will strengthen the hand of governments, but since most multinational companies will have access to a relatively wide array of options, this situation will ordinarily work to establish a higher reservation price on the resources the multinational corporations bring to the transaction as compared with resources brought to the bargaining table by the local firms and/or governments with which they are dealing.

A fourth factor concerns the basis of the formidable power of multinational business, which power is often said to rest on resources of money, organization, and access. Besides these, however, the strength of multinational concerns derives from the fact that as information processing systems they ordinarily hold a great advantage over the local governments with which they deal. Any organization can usefully be viewed as an information processing system: one which takes in information from the outside, transforms it, and utilizes it to produce various kinds of output. The overall efficiency of the system should be judged in terms of the efficacy of the external monitoring of the environment as well as the internal processing of information. One does not have to look at very many governments of less-developed countries in comparison with the organizational structures and management practices of multinational corporations to conclude that as information processing organizations the multinational corporations usually have it all over the governments, that they are much more effective both in scanning their environments for relevant information and in transforming it into various kinds of outputs.[6] While this characteristic may in fact identify one of the more positive contributions multinational firms typically bring to their host economies, it also helps to explain why governments, only too aware of this disparity and its bearing on the relative bargaining positions of the two parties, tend often to be so guarded in their dealings, and so prone to inappropriate courses of remedial action.

It is perfectly true, of course, that categorical evaluations of the development contributions of multinational enterprise can be, and have been, made for countries and regions, aggregating their impact in such forms as employment and income generation, tax payments, foreign exchange earnings (or savings), share of capital formation, contributions to good works, and the like. That something less than unqualified enthusiasm nevertheless characterizes the reception generally accorded the multinationals need not be ascribed simply to ideological bias or to the perversity of human nature. Rather, the contextual factors which appear to skew the terms of the exchange relationship so evidently toward the side of the multinational companies virtually ensure that doubts will continuously arise concerning the mutuality of the benefit. The question is not whether the terms of the sharing will be redrawn but when, and how frequently.

THE SYSTEMIC LEVEL OF EVALUATION

There is, finally, a third level of questioning, the systemic level, the level on which spokesmen for multinational enterprises seem most given to arguing in favor of their social contribution. Yet this may be precisely the level at which the most substantial misgivings arise and at which the least defensible evidentiary basis is available for the case. Unfortunately, there is, at this level, no Maimonides handy to offer a guide for the perplexed.

Various development specialists, in enumerating the difficulties that afflict the less-developed countries, have referred to market imperfections and areas of market failures. The implication is that if these economies had more efficient markets they would be better off. As standard economic theory instructs us, more nearly perfect markets would enthrone consumer sovereignty, enforce technical efficiency in resource use, and guide society's resources into economically efficient patterns. Tidy up the externalities and all will be well.[7]

We must ask, however, if more efficient markets would really improve the situation. Would they not, perhaps, even worsen the predicament? At this point we need to remind ourselves of what, after all, a market mechanism does. At this level of examination the problem comes to rest not so much on the multinationals as such, but on the larger institutional system in which they are embedded and of which they are the expressive agents. That larger institutional system is preeminently the market, organized on the basis of private ownership of the means of production and driven by utility-maximizing behavior. What does the market register? Very simply, the textbooks tell us, it registers relative scarcity. But in asking what relative scarcity means, it may be appropriate to invoke the principle of Thurber's wife. (To a friend who asked, "How is your wife?" James Thurber is said to have replied, "Compared with what?") Relative scarcity, as the term itself indicates, is scarcity in relation to something else: alternative uses as registered in the signals of the market place. What is scaled and expressed, in other words, is scarcity in relation to the preferences and the economic weight of those spending units (households, firms, and countries) that hold the purchasing power.

Thus, the social validity of market judgments, no matter how efficient the market, cannot transcend whatever degree of acceptability may attach to the underlying distribution of wealth and income. If this distribution be questioned, then objection will perforce be raised that what the world market registers is essentially the preferences of the wealthy countries, the wealthy spending units of the world economic system. In the social judgments rendered by the market, the wants of the poor are institutionally ignored. More efficient markets, presumably, would merely enhance the ease and rapidity with which resources could be organized on behalf of the major beneficiaries of the market process and diverted from meeting the clamant needs of the impoverished.[8]

In the normal course of events, social systems tend to reproduce themselves. As both Adam Smith and Karl Marx would have agreed, the world economic system, if left to operate on the basis of the market, would also tend to reproduce itself, with such modifications as might be gradually induced by the using up of old resources in some regions and the discovery and development of new resources in others. Historically, technical change has been pivotal in altering resource patterns and economic relationships, but it is far from established that this force operates in any automatic way to redress social and economic imbalances and to even out regional disparities.

With the market system favoring the well off and with the social effects of technical change so unpredictable, it is scarcely a source of wonder that a good many people in the world have come to believe that reliance on the market to alleviate poverty would seem to be ill-advised and that specific measures must be devised to deal with it. Investment codes, preferential tariffs, commodity support schemes, and massive international transfer payments in a variety of other guises have all come into the picture as surrogate allocational mechanisms thought, rightly or wrongly, to be more efficacious than the market in harnessing resources to the preferences of the lower-income countries. Multinational managers may decry these and other forms of intervention, and examples may abound of instances in which the policy instrumentation of poor countries is counterproductive in the light of their own professed objectives. Constructive dialogue is more likely to be furthered, however, if this third, most radical, level of skepticism be recognized as a reasonable basis for doubts and if unsupportable general claims for the social efficiency of the market be abandoned in favor of efforts to identify and specify the conditions under which particular multinational business operations may be useful in reducing poverty. In this connection, we do well to keep in mind the fact that the centrally planned economies, where hostility to market economics is presumably at the maximum, have nevertheless seen fit to invite the limited participation of multinational firms in their economic affairs. The particular benefits being sought in this highly selective welcome should yield some clues of value for the agenda of the present inquiry.

In his controversial novel of some years back, Roger Peyrefitte has a worldly-wise Italian prelate caution a zealous young priest to moderate his claims for religion.[9] Don't try to prove too much, he admonishes the eager cleric, lest you end by proving nothing. The same cautious wisdom, I suspect, should guide one in dealing with the question of what contributions multinational management can make to reduce world poverty.

Notes

1. It might also be noted that someone with a real sense of whimsy paired the progressive state of Wisconsin with Somoza's Nicaragua.

2. The Ralston Purina feeder programs for small-scale poultry and edible rodent operations would represent another example of poverty-reducing development technology.

3. So, too, are the indictments, as in Richard L. Barnet and Ronald E. Muller, *Global Reach: The Power of the Multinational Corporations* (New York: Simon and Schuster, 1974), or the work of the late Stephen Hymer.

4. Governmental control of access to an especially valuable economic opportunity (e.g., Arabian oil or the Brazilian home market) represents another trump card sometimes held by LDCs.

5. Multinational enterprises are often referred to as monopolies by Third World social scientists, a charge which may seem odd to those who are aware of the multiplicity of international firms involved in different lines of production. Such allegations of monopoly generally are used in a Schumpeterian sense to refer to temporary

innovation-based monopoly positions. Since MNCs as a group dominate the areas of advanced technology, it is not, therefore, altogether inappropriate to view them as possessing a categorical monopoly.

6. There are, of course, exceptions, particularly among such semideveloped or advanced developing countries as Brazil, Mexico, Argentina, or Taiwan.

7. In this connection it is interesting to consider the mindset revealed by those who decry government policies as "artificial" barriers to trade, "natural" (and therefore acceptable) barriers being, presumably, such things as the Himalayas and the Andes. The clamorous critics of artificiality overlook, of course, that the market itself is an artifact (even, some would say, an artifice), along with money, patents, copyrights, private property, and corporations. It is a curiously skewed vision that sees tariffs as "artificial" and two other barriers to trade, a lack of money and an enforced regard for patents, as somehow natural.

8. In economic terms, we might therefore conclude that the real opportunity costs of using resources to support the affluence of high income countries is widespread destitution in low-income countries.

9. *Knights of Malta* (Springfield, Mass.: Phillips Publishing Co., 1959).

II: Market Structures and Profits

CHARLES K. WILBER

As an academic economist, I tend to focus on macro-phenomena such as changing market structures and historical development patterns. This paper is directed toward these macro-phenomena with an attempt to incorporate the multinational corporation in that picture.

First of all, I think multinational corporations are like quarterbacks on football teams. They get far too much praise and far too much blame. They are not really that important for development in the Third World. Someone can correct me, but I think that there are very few examples of countries that have gone through major development where the primary source of aid was foreign investment unless accompanied by rather large-scale immigration such as that which occurred in Canada, the United States, New Zealand, and so forth. I contend that we should think small about what we can do or how much blame we should shoulder for the problems of the world.

Let me begin by establishing a framework for analysis. There is no doubt that capitalism, which is a system of more or less free markets, has been the most revolutionary phenomenon in history and has led to the development of what is now called the developed world. In other words, it has been the greatest engine of growth known to man. Or, in terms economists prefer, profit seeking within more or less free markets has led to an increase in the general welfare. It has been said that the world is run by self-interest, and a desirable goal is to see that the self-interests of cads and those of decent men coincide. Supposedly that is what the market tries to do through its various disciplinary forces. The question, therefore, is, "Why have those same market forces not generated development in Asia, Africa, and Latin America the way they have in Western Europe, the United States, Japan and a few other outlying spots?" An immediate answer is, "They will, give them time." That is a possible answer. Brazil has made considerable progress in most people's eyes; the same is true for Nigeria. Time will take care of the problem. The retort to that is: "It may be there is not that much time available; that is, people are restless, both leaders of Third World countries and people in those countries." Simply hoping that time will take care of it may not be enough.

A second answer is that massive government interference today may limit development in poor countries. That may be a contributing factor, but it is not going to change or go away. As William Glade has said, given the fact that we do not have highly competitive markets à la Adam Smith, freeing things up may not actually improve the situation. Another phenomenon at work has been at least a partial reason for the failure of full-scale development in Third World countries: when capitalism matured in the developed countries, it did so in an environment very different from the one within which poor countries are now trying to develop. For instance, early capitalism in Great Britain, the United States, and much of Europe developed, somewhat ironically perhaps, as a producer for the masses of the population. Production began in things like cheap textiles which was one of the major items of new production. That was where the technological gains were at the time, in automation of those kinds of processes. Today, technological gains have been made not only in textiles but in television sets, tractors, and so on. Items that are produced and sold in the Third World countries are not similar to those that were being produced and sold back in England in the early nineteenth century; they tend, instead, to be "luxury" consumer goods.

An influential factor in the industrialization of the developed countries was a rather sizable middle class with an income distribution that was quite equal compared to today's developing countries, such as Brazil where the top 1 percent of income earners receives about 18 percent of all income and the bottom 50 percent receives 14 percent. The demand that flows onto the market to buy things comes heavily from that top group, so we sell television sets and other such goods. The structure of the market is different because production is not for mass-produced textiles, but for "luxury" consumer goods.

Another difference is that when the West was developing, the technological processes for producing grew up indigenously. The kinds of technology that were put together reflected the relative scarcities of capital, labor, and natural resources.

Today, we are importing technology into Third World countries; it is not growing up indigenously. Instead, technologies are designed in different countries with very different structures of capital and labor. Thus, in many cases these technologies are capital intensive and labor saving.

A problem exists because of the transnational character of the corporation. Transnational corporations existed a hundred years ago but they are a different animal today and this relates to the aforementioned characteristics.

The multinational corporation, like any other corporation, functions within the market in which it finds itself. Therefore, the kinds of issues I would raise are these: When a corporation moves its production abroad it brings in advanced technology from its headquarters area which may be very inappropriate to the area where it is going and thus may worsen structural unemployment. For example, the data seem to indicate that in terms of dollar sales U.S. corporations generate fewer jobs than do local corporations in Latin America.

Second, the corporation brings with it a whole marketing apparatus that includes an advertising structure which, conditioned out of its environment in the United States, is very oriented toward generating demand for its products. Advertisements promoting white bread in Latin America or for baby formula in Africa appear, but what are the implications of these? Such issues must be raised.

Another point is that by being transnational, the concern is with maximizing global profits. The profits in any individual country are of less concern than those of the whole international enterprise. Thus a firm can engage in practices, such as transfer pricing in response to increased taxation in one country versus another country, all of which could be detrimental.

It is impossible to agree on what multinationals actually should do about these problems. We will never agree on what is good in a society, but we might agree about what is bad. How many are against hunger? All can agree to that one. Perhaps we can examine not what multinational corporations can do to eliminate poverty but some of the things they might do to keep from being obstacles in the elimination process.

Here are some suggestions. Corporations could investigate practices such as transfer pricing, or investigate the redesigning of technology to increase labor utilization in Third World states. For instance, at Caterpillar is it possible to get something smaller than a D-7 to utilize more labor and use less capital? Is it possible to redesign our technologies for better labor, but less capital, use?

Advertising campaigns that push "luxury" consumption could be monitored so that these campaigns might not have the effect of diverting savings to consumption, or necessary consumption to frivolous consumption. People may go without food to buy lipsticks or transistor radios.

Corporations could help poor countries develop codes of conduct which then become compulsory so corporations are all treated alike. One of the biggest problems is that poor countries do not have the expertise to negotiate with corporations.

These are a few of the areas in which corporations can use their expertise to play a significant role in helping the Third World. It is the responsibility of the corporations to develop and use their expertise to the benefit of the poor countries as well as the rich ones.

III: A Self-Help Project

ROGER T. KELLEY

THIS PAPER DESCRIBES a self-help program in Bolivia as evidence that positive things can be done by and for the poorest of the world to relieve their hunger and suffering.

In 1975 a citizen group of Peoria, Illinois, interested in trying to alleviate poverty in the Third World, learned of an agricultural cooperative located in the lowland jungles of Bolivia. Its name: Cooperativa Agricola Integral Mineros (CAIM). Dudley Conneely, a lay missionary and founder of CAIM, was invited to visit Peoria during his home leave early in 1976 to provide a firsthand account of the Cooperative's activities.

The Bolivian government had given each of 450 native Indian families a small parcel of land for farming. The problem was that the land could be farmed only if cleared of its jungle growth. Working by hand with machetes and occasionally chain saws, a farmer could partially clear and farm about one acre, barely enough to eke out an existence. So the native families pooled their resources, each investing 50 pesos ($2.50) and their labor to clear 40 hectares (99 acres) of this jungle land. Clearing was done by hand, the fields were then burned and raked, and finally corn or rice was planted among the stumps or roots. This was the CAIM's beginning.

Dudley Conneely's visit to Peoria confirmed that CAIM was indeed a project with high potential. But machinery was needed to achieve acceptable acreage yields—specifically, a D-7 Caterpillar tractor equipped with a Rome KG clearing blade.

Most Indian farmers of the Mineros region had never seen such a machine, much less dreamed of owning one. A few had seen mechanized farms owned by the rich farmers, but these operations were totally beyond their understanding. And even if they had known about such a machine, its cost was apparently out of their reach. A D-7 machine, equipped with a KG clearing blade and delivered in Bolivia, would cost as much as the total income of those 450 families for five years.

117

But realization of the dream was not so impossible. Through individual gifts and several special events, $50,000 was raised toward purchase of a new D7 tractor. And with $50,000 as leverage, things happened fast. A U.S. Caterpillar dealer offered the D-7 machine for sale at his cost. The Caterpillar dealer in Santa Cruz agreed to service the machine and help train its operators. The Maryknoll Missionary Order loaned the Cooperative $25,000, interest-free. Catholic Relief Service and the U.S. Agency for International Development paid for overseas shipping costs, and local Peoria sources absorbed the remaining balance of several thousand dollars. In March 1977 a D-7 machine from Caterpillar's East Peoria Plant and a KG clearing blade from Rome, Georgia, were on their way to the Port of New Orleans. Destination: Mineros, Bolivia.

In the first five months of operation, the D-7 cleared 350 acres for farming at the rate of about four to five acres a day—about twice as much land as one farmer could clear in a year. In addition to clearing land for farming, the machine pioneered about 20 kilometers of jungle road and repaired additional roads to make them passable. It takes about one hour to drive 12 miles on one of these so-called passable roads.

The Cooperative rents its D-7 to other cooperatives and to the town of Mineros for 550 pesos per hour ($27.50). Most of these rentals are for land-clearing projects.

The machine is being well cared for. A Maryknoll lay missionary in the area is an agronomist with experience in farming and machinery. He plans and supervises the land-clearing and farming operations. A Mennonite lay missionary from Santa Cruz, experienced in operating Caterpillar machines, was employed part-time to train CAIM employees in operating and maintaining the D-7. Senor Poppy and Senor José of CAIM soon became skilled operators, and they take great pride in the machine.

In the first five months of activity, the D7 machine "earned" about $12,000 after deducting the expense of fuel, operator wages, and other equipment costs. The machine works nine months of the year—December, January, and February are the rainy months—and so the earnings of the machine for the first full year of operation were about $25,000. The $25,000 loan was paid back after two years, and most of the remaining earnings were used to purchase additional equipment.

A Caterpillar agricultural engineer visited the project in 1977 to observe the work being done with the D-7. A bulldozer blade, rather than the KG clearing blade, was being used in land clearing. Unfortunately, this removed the rich organic top soil, along with trees and brush, and a continuation of that practice would have greatly reduced the productivity of the soil. Technical personnel of the Caterpillar dealership in Santa Cruz were consulted, and corrective measures involving use of the KG blade were taken, resulting in more efficient clearing and more favorable conservation practices. The KG blade shears tree trunks at ground level and clears away brush while leaving the soil in its natural state.

Additional tools were needed and have since been acquired. For example, the land, when cleared by the D-7, had to be plowed for use as pasture land and for cultivating crops. A late model Reme TRH 16 × 32 harrow, weighing over 9,000 pounds, was purchased for approximately $10,000. Now the D-7, equipped with KG blade and plowing harrow, leaves the jungle ready for pulverizing and planting before moving to another area. With the terrible road conditions in the jungle region of Mineros, the dual-tandem function of the clearing blade and the plowing harrow is a very important advantage.

The productivity of the D7 tractor, in contrast to the farming-by-hand methods it replaced, represented an obvious and substantial benefit to CAIM. The D7's presence resulted in a giant leap forward that could be measured in several ways:

(1) For the first time, the farmers could meet and exceed the survival requirements for their families, and their farm output was competitive in the commercial markets.

(2) The D7's startling productivity, and their ownership of it, generated great enthusiasm and "espirit" among farmers.

(3) It provided the leverage needed to back up CAIM's request for support in acquiring additional equipment and other assets.

(4) Ownership of the D7 made it relatively easy for the Cooperative to get short-term commercial loans.

Banks did not hesitate in making loans, and their confidence was reinforced by the fact that the Cooperative always met its financial obligations.

The Central Cooperative (CCAM) which replaced its smaller predecessor (CAIM) has six departments, all administered by the farmers themselves. The departments are:

(1) *Transportation* — four trucks, two tractors, and eight trailers which are used to transport corn, rice, and sugar cane to the market. Before this equipment was purchased, the small farmer was at the mercy of middle men who brought their trucks into the farming villages and paid miserably low prices for the farmer's annual production.

(2) *Caterpillar and heavy equipment* — one D7B Caterpillar tractor, equipped with Rome KG blade and plowing harrow, plus two Caterpillar motor graders, each about 15 years old, for repairing secondary jungle roads. The motor graders were purchased from Peoria Tractor and Equipment Co. with earnings from crops grown on land cleared by the D7G.

(3) *Consumer Store* — basic foods like salt, sugar, cooking oils, noodles, and wheat at prices the farmers can afford. This has protected the farmers from exorbitant prices charged at other stores.

(4) *Credit* — Facilities to deal with the Central Bank of Bolivia and make small loans to the farmers to help them cultivate and harvest their products. Without this line of credit, the small farmer (campesino) is forced to abandon work on his own land and work for the "patron" to support his family.

(5) *Rice Mill* — facilities to process the rice grown by Cooperative members and other local farmers. The mill's daily capacity is 600 sacks of 100 pounds each and finished product is sold on the national market. The rice mill and the Caterpillar department are the big income sources of the Cooperative.

(6) *Mechanical Shop* — professionally trained mechanics who repair the Cooperative's machinery/equipment and train the sons of Co-op members in machine maintenance.

Agricultural products of CCAM include rice, sugarcane, corn, yucca (manioca), tomatoes, pimentos, and potatoes.

The Cooperative has a quota of 13,000 tons of sugarcane annually from the nearby sugar mill. With a grant from *Bread for the World,* a West German organization, the Cooperative has been able to purchase an equity share in the sugar mill.

The Inter-American Foundation provided front-end funds for purchase of three 15,000 bushel silos for storage of rice and corn.

In addition to the above, each of the 450 families has a dairy cow and each of the 14 villages a swiss bull. The former were provided through a grant of *Bread for the World;* the latter through the U.S.A. Heifer project.

Since 1979, Dudley Conneely's wife, Mary, has directed an educational program with over 1,000 women in 25 villages. The women are taught how to read and write (the majority have no formal education), hygiene and child care, nutrition and diet, sanitation, sewing and knitting, and home improvements. CEMUR (Center for Rural Women) has recently completed construction of an educational center and dormitory building in Mineros. This was made possible through earnings of the Rice Mill.

The accomplishment of Dudley Conneely and his enthusiastic flock of 450 Indian farmers is indeed remarkable. By U.S. standards, these natives had nothing. Disease, malnutrition, and death have been their constant companions. Only two of every five children were surviving to school age, and the lucky ones among them *might* get the equivalent of a second-grade education. But with "nothing" they seem to have everything—love, trust, a capacity for hard work, a sharing spirit, and a remarkable sense of personal worth.

The Cooperative is on its way. Over 3,000 hectares (7,400 acres) are planted; health and sanitation have improved, and more natives are learning to read and write. The full scope of the Cooperative's business and farming activities are run by the farmers themselves, and they are upgrading their technical skills at vocational schools and through courses run by the Cooperative. Jungle-to-town roads are being built so that decent medical care, schools, and other basic needs are within reach.

Helping 450 Bolivian farmers rise above their poverty makes a small dent in the world's poverty. But this successful self-help program contains the elements of a model that can be repeated throughout the Third World. In fact Dudley Conneely, while continuing to consult with this project, is about to begin a similar program with 517 native Indian families in the same region of Bolivia.

Addendum

IN THE DISCUSSION following the three panel papers, the seminar participants attempted to clarify the potential for the corporate response from multinationals. The diverse opinions, ideologies, and suggestions can be divided into two categories: what the multinationals potentially could do, and their current impact. These two areas are further elaborated below. Few of these observations reflect a uniform view of the group. The participant discussion is summarized with no attempt to state the degree of support. Indeed, given the intensity of the discussion, weighting would be impossible.

WHAT THE MULTINATIONAL CORPORATION CAN DO

At the root level, can the multinational corporation contribute to development? How do the line managers in normal business decision-making realize ways to help the poor?

One set of participants stressed that MNCs should continue what they do best: honing and refining until they achieve the highest quality product. The market system has been regarded as a problem, as if there were an alternative. Yet, although far from perfect, the market system works fairly well, particularly in the absence of a viable alternative. The multinationals, by doing what they do best, have contributed to refining the system. Thus by advancing the quality of their product, they are contributing to an efficient international market system.

There is not necessarily a conflict between corporate products and national development. If MNCs make their best product they are going to sell it for what it is worth. It is possible to make a profit and still help the community: through investment in the development of the host country, the MNC is improving its profit.

In the process of investment MNCs examine the sociological and culturally different contents of the country in which they invest. As a result of this orientation, economic expertise and technology can be adapted appropriately to the specified region. Moreover, part of the business of a multinational is not only to supply the technology but also to teach the indigenous people how to use that technology to their advantage; an ongoing process. This knowledge would help to avoid the possibility of mismatching technology to the environment, which is likely to occur when transferring technology between different levels. One participant pointed out that in the case of Brazil, technical machines circa 1958 are comparable to Brazil's production needs today.

The discussion revealed that MNCs do not publicize the humanistic, day-to-day activities which are present. New buses for transporting employees are not cut from the corporate operating budget nor are medical facilities. Tennis courts are installed near the plants and, inevitably in Latin America, so are soccer fields. Not that discussants were advocating advertisement of these actions, but rather stating a factor that contributes to the negative attitude with which they are sometimes confronted.

"Perhaps, too," said one participant, "we are using the wrong terminology." Phrases such as "eliminating poverty" and "exonerating resentment" can be turned around. We need to talk of what to do about the development of roads; the amelioration of water supplies; agricultural improvements; that is, generally, in lieu of focusing on "alleviation of poverty," concentrate on "participation in the development objective of the host country."

Other recommendations are more obvious: scholarships for employees and offspring; food, housing, medical facilities; church-related groups could work side by side with the MNC; underutilized retirees could be responsive in the various micro projects. One participant noted the enthusiasm of college students, and indicated that the combination of their energy with older experience could lead to quite positive advancements. There certainly is no lack of human resources.

By positively influencing the environment, the MNC will enhance the economic performance of the company. Thus the narrowly construed viewpoint of profit can be expanded. No longer will profit be limited only to the product. The factors of "how to do it" and "what to do" can become just as important as "what to make."

CURRENT ACTIONS

In terms of the three concepts introduced by Glade: we cannot view the alleviation of poverty on either the atomized level or on the categorical level. Before the mini-problems can be solved the macro level, the synergy, must first be tackled. As one participant said, "Allow the synergy to occur and allow the dynamics of opportunities to happen, then we could do a lot of good in the world."

On the other hand, even if a macro answer is found, the micro conditions might not be right. This can discredit the elixir that through research and comprehension of the macro situations, a general antidote can be prescribed. Participants hypothesized that the macro environment considered in conjunction with an analysis on the micro level will produce the unique remedial solution.

The full impact of alternative courses of action are, however, difficult to anticipate. One case was presented in which an agribusiness planned an entry in close cooperation with the host government. Their operation advanced rapidly to a position of corporate profit, enhanced local employment, and made an apparent positive contribution to the local economy. Due to the increased acceptance of this product in the market place, however, local farmers were drawn into its production. Consequently, over-production occurred, causing a shakeout of local farmers since they did not have the financial reserves to weather a temporary market glut. In this case, the best intentioned international MNC action resulted in negative spill-over effects.

In addition to what seems to be infinite recommendations on what MNCs can do in the Third World, there are some meaningful projects already in progress as Mr. Kelley witnessed. Another participant, referring to citizens of host countries, said, "Their success is our success." If the farmer improves his yield then the MNC shares in this gain. Another participant recounted a project his company created in Honduras. They advanced money to the different members of a farm cooperative who in turn purchased and planted bananas which sold at market for cash. Consequently the farmers were able to diversify their production, not only advancing their standard of living but at the same time providing them with the capital to invest in and improve on the production of primary products for the MNC.

However laconically stated, the preceding examples footnote the fact that multinational corporations do have a potential to respond to social needs. As evidenced by the panel and the seminar participants, a kaleidoscope of projects awaits the initiative.

9. Developmental Responsibility

LEE A. TAVIS

THIS PAPER OUTLINES THE unique opportunity and responsibility associated with multinational corporate involvement in the economic and social development of Third World countries, and suggests ways that managers might begin to incorporate an awareness of this responsibility into the decision-making structure of their firms.

This developmental responsibility of multinationals derives from: (1) the leading role of these firms in allocating resources between the developed countries of the Northern Hemisphere and the less-developed ones in the Southern, as well as their position within Third World economies, (2) the desperate circumstances of the poor in the Third World, and (3) the lack of guidance to aid the multinational manager in deciding the "best" trade-off among the firm's various constituencies both within and among countries.

Multinationals are inextricably involved in the development process of the Third World. Not only do they affect the resource balance between countries through capital investments and profit repatriation, but they often dominate sectors within these economics. Thus, the results of multinational activities reach beyond the balance of resources between rich and poor countries, to the balance among groups of people within these countries. A wage decision in a rural area of the Philippines, for example, is a direct allocation between the Philippine laborer and the U.S. shareholder, with indirect connectors to other local constituencies such as the laborer's family, the community, and local and national governments.

More than economic resources are transmitted across national boundaries in the process. Social attitudes and values are also communicated. Take the example of a fruit packing facility. Modern equipment and production techniques introduced into a Third World location would bring increasing productivity to the operation. At the same time, cultural modernization takes place, with its social as well as its economic consequences. Not only are workers employed but, for many, this employment imposes a new regimentation of work hours and other requirements. When the multinational arrival is in a remote rural area, the overall social change is even greater, as structured, organized activities replace small, rural farming for the workers, and whole communities grow up around the multinational economic center. These social impacts are evidenced in the Dolefil case example.[1]

In making decisions that necessarily affect the social as well as the economic position of their various constituents, multinational managers are not provided the kind of guidance available to a corporation operating in a single developed country. A firm in the United States faces product and financial markets where prices tend to be set by competitive pressures, and management faces strong unions where wages are negotiated. These market conditions exist in an environment where laws and governmental regulators are continually directing corporate activities to serve society, or to represent the needs of groups that are injured by the workings of unfettered markets.

Such is simply not the case for multinational firms with operations in the Third World. Too often, markets in these countries are inefficient, unions irresponsible, and government regulations, however well-intentioned, are not effective. Moreover, as resources are moved across national boundaries they are caught up in a host of conflicting political pressures and confusion with few institutions other than multinationals committed to long-term ties among countries.

This international environment can be viewed by managers in one of two ways. On the one hand, it provides an opportunity to pursue profit at the expense of local Third World constituencies, i.e., push profit opportunities against the less well-defined, and less well-organized, limits on the freedom of corporate action. Alternatively, this environment can be viewed as one requiring management to establish its own constraints—to internally represent constituencies that cannot represent themselves.

The concept of developmental responsibility calls managers to the latter view. When a firm is in a position to contribute to the well-being of those in the Third World who are unable to change their own circumstances, the responsibility falls to the corporate management.

The internalization of economic and social guidelines adds a demanding new dimension to corporate decision structures. Managers are required to consider a full range of new social and economic parameters. Data on the local impacts must be collected and fed through the firm's information network. The nature of these data as well as the techniques for its transmission present new challenges.

THE PRODUCTIVE-SOCIAL ROLE OF CORPORATIONS

The allocation of corporate resources has a complex impact on any society. Factors are drawn from a number of constituencies—labor, management, suppliers, owners, lenders—and are combined synergistically into products that are sold to others—intermediate processors or consumers. The broader public is also included directly through unabsorbed externalities or indirectly through linkages with the firm's constituents. The managers charged with making these allocation decisions are responsible for the necessary trade offs among the various groups and for the full range of direct or indirect impacts.

In classic Western social theory we have focused our attention on the corporate role of enhancing productivity, and have separated it from a responsibility to the constituents, save the owners. Management is assigned the task of enhancing productivity by optimizing shareholder wealth in efficient financial and product markets. Responsibility for the welfare of the other constituencies lies with the law, regulatory structures, or public opinion. These representatives of social consensus impose minimum performance requirements, or constraints, that represent the interests of these other groups.

In most developed capitalistic countries, governmental regulation is based on the existence of relatively efficient markets. One part of regulation is directed to improving this efficiency. In the United States, the Federal Trade Commission and the Securities and Exchange Commission, for exam-

ple, regulate the information flowing to consumers and investors, thereby enhancing their ability to make rational choices.

Paralleling this market focus, other legislation is designed
to protect groups that may be injured by the workings of a
free market. This regulation, based on broader social goals, is
the role of the United States Consumer Product Safety Commission or the Occupational Safety and Health Administration.

Thus, in classical social theory, responsibility is separated—managers shoulder the productivity responsibility and
represent the shareholders, while regulators and the courts
bear the responsibility for the effect on other constituencies
through the imposition of what might be termed social constraints.

The classic notion of corporate responsibility represents a
conservative end of the spectrum. It is staunchly supported by
a number of theoreticians and many managers.[2] This position
should not be seen as irresponsible. In this view, managers do
not maximize short-run profits to the detriment of long-term
wealth for shareholders; they do not violate their firms'
enlightened self-interest; they would stay within the unen-
forceable limits of the law.

If this productivity-social separation of responsibilities is
to work, however, the constraints on corporate activity must be
clearly communicated to the decision-maker. This is the role
of efficient markets and effective regulation.

Beginning in the 1960s, there has been a growing focus
on non-owner constituents in the academic literature and in
managerial attitudes. The notion of "trusteeship" is gaining
support. In its statement *Social Responsibility of Business Corporations*, the Committee for Economic Development stated:

> The modern professional manager also regards himself not as
> an owner disposing of personal property as he sees fit, but as a
> trustee balancing the interests of many diverse participants and
> constituents in the enterprise, whose interests sometimes
> conflict with those of others.[3]

We should note that clear signals as to the societal limits
on corporate actions are necessary conditions for managers
who view their function as a trustee as well as those who hold
to the classic view. The role of the law or regulation in establishing the boundaries beyond which one constituency cannot

be traded off against another remains, regardless of a person's position on social responsibility.

The necessary clarity of signals from markets and regulators seldom exists for the multinational firm. Signals from inefficient markets carry little information about consumer preferences, and regulation that is confused, or itself socially irresponsible, can be destructive.

In Third World countries both regulators and managers must cope with inefficient markets. Governmental regulations tend to replace the free activities of efficient markets with sets of artificial market mechanisms such as price controls, quotas, and exchange requirements. The regulatory span becomes broader and regulations tend to overlap one another.

As the span is broader, the resources available for the regulatory process are narrower. In all of these countries there are well-trained and talented technocrats, but they are often too few relative to the task and have small staffs and inadequate information. The bureaucratic infrastructure can be seriously inadequate. In circumstances such as these, we find that the signals transmitted to the private sector are not very useful.

At the present time there are few clear signals emanating from the international sector. This is unfortunate since, as the world becomes more interdependent, fewer problems can be effectively treated in a national context. The development of codes of conduct by a number of international organizations such as the United Nations, the Organization for Economic Cooperation and Development, and the International Chamber of Commerce, holds promise. Although these codes are general, and often contain conflicting requirements, they do indicate a direction and suggest a role that multinationals can play in our changing society.

With inadequate market and regulatory signals coming from national and international sources, the productivity-social separation principle does not hold. Managers cannot responsibly ignore the social impact of their firms' presence. They have no alternative other than to be developmentally responsive. Rather than the pursuit of wealth maximization to the limits of the marketplace, regulation, or enforceable laws, self-regulation through internal, managerially imposed constraints is in order.

As managers approach this new requirement for participation in Third World patterns of development they are morally called to a concern for the poor in those countries. When one person or group is in critical need, another individual or group in proximity to the situation must act to alleviate the need if they can. This is particularly true when other sources of assistance are not available in time to avoid a crisis. On this principle, a multinational manager who is in a position to aid the poor who cannot help themselves, incurs that responsibility.[4] With the multinational direct and indirect links to the poor, managers would apply corporate resources where their firms could uniquely contribute to the relief of poverty, even though their firms were not involved in the cause.

Thus, the management of a multinational's activities in a Third World country is subject to a far different environment than is the case for a domestic American firm. The opportunities and the nature of the constraint set are derived from a fundamentally different context. While multinationals are powerful economic and social forces in Third World countries, managers seldom have the needed economic signals from efficient markets nor guidance as to social preferences necessary to allow the separation of the productive dimension of their decisions from their social impact. In exercising this involvement, managers are called to the responsibility of helping those who are in desperate need.

Executives who accept this expanded responsibility in the Third World will increasingly evaluate the social as well as the economic dimensions of their decisions. The action focus is transformed from externally imposed market and legal requirements to management-directed efforts. For example, a developmentally responsive multinational corporation would monitor the life style changes that it imposes upon its indigenous employees; it would be alert to the potentially damaging misuse of sophisticated products among technically backward peoples; it would measure its long-term impact on local suppliers and competitors; it might provide local housing, health, or transportation services; it would be concerned with the nutrition and health of employees and their families; it would anticipate the economic and social effects of a new production technology on the employees and the community. Whereas many or most managers would prefer to relinquish the social dimension of their decisions to other institutions, this is impossible in the multinational environment. Managerial social neutrality is simply not possible in much of the Third World.

Meeting Corporate Developmental Responsibility

If one recognizes the development cusp, particularly its poverty dimension, and accepts the argument that multinational managers need to address this concern, how do they get the job done?[5] A firm cannot be developmentally responsive to the exclusion of its assigned productivity role. It must meet both responsibilities in an environment where the interests of the constituencies are generally quite diverse.

The local activities of a multinational operation are simultaneously an element of two systems—the multinational corporate system and the national economy—with close linkages to both. The key to multinational productivity lies in the multinational system, while developmental responsibility is a part of the national system.

Multinational managers must attempt to integrate their subsidiaries in order to achieve the efficiency associated with the international arbitration of factors of production if they are to meet their productivity responsibilities. Moreover, the advantages that multinationals gain through their ability to penetrate national boundaries is necessary to offset the disadvantages they incur as a result of absentee control. Thus, some degree of systematic optimization is an economic necessity.

To be developmentally responsible, however, the local operations must fit the needs of the national system. These needs can often be in conflict with multinational optimization. This kind of conflict is to be expected in any situation where systems with divergent goals overlap. Unfortunately, this conflict is too frequently played out between the multinational corporation and national institutions on the basis of power, with little room left for considering the needs of the poor. The rancor makes it difficult, indeed, for the manager to respond to the needs of the poor in the Third World.

The managerial entry point for a balanced developmental

response is clearly the firm's planning and information system. This is true for the assurance of ethical performance by any institution. For multinational firms it is critical because of the complexity of their decision environment and the difficulty of the trade-offs that must be decided upon.

If an institution is to respond favorably to its environment, this impact is best anticipated and evaluated while the institution still has maximum flexibility—early in the planning process. Rigidity sets in at an alarming rate as managers proceed through the planning sequence to implementation. Once resources are committed to an alternative, the social as well as the economic die is cast. If, because of an early lack of concern, the social dimension is not properly anticipated, or if social impact information is filtered out of the system, unintentional and often unavoidable damage can result.

In order to effectively respond to the development needs of the Third World, multinational planning and information systems need to: (1) measure the full impact of the corporation's presence in host countries—both economic *and* social; (2) transmit the "soft" social impact data through the system to the decision-makers for both strategic and operations decisions, as well as to those who are judging the performance of the decision-makers; and (3) establish a specific policy as to what information management will share with its various constituencies.

Environmental Monitoring

The goal of environmental monitoring is to identify the full range of corporate involvement in the host country. It includes the identification of the firm's linkages with the economic and social aspects of development. Monitoring must be undertaken on a country-by-country basis. The nature of the linkages with local poor can be very different among operating locations. Local environments are unique and what may be "best" for one multinational operating site may not fit the needs of others. Development patterns are incredibly diverse.[6] And, social preferences in one location can be vastly different from those in others.

When monitoring is broadened to include the social dimension of developmental responsibility, the firm is extending its data collection into a much larger system with longer relevant planning horizons and more obscure linkages. The earlier developmental response examples of product use, employee life styles, family health, community development, and new technology reflect the firm's broader reach of information needs.

Even though we are suggesting an additional dimension to the firm's usual economic environmental measures, multinationals have access to the most sophisticated social monitoring techniques in history through market research methodology. Surely these skills could be applied to social measurement.

Internal Information Processing

Full environmental monitoring must be accompanied by an information system that transmits this expanded data to the relevant decision and performance measuring points. It must flow through very complex organizational structures. The general organizational pattern of multinationals has been one of decentralized decisions associated with increased reliance on financial reporting systems. In these structures more decisions are made locally with headquarters judging the decisions after the fact through the financial reporting network. This process can mask much of the developmental impact of resource allocation decisions. Local managers who are judged strictly on financial performance cannot be expected to be alert to the full impact of their activities. Moreover, top management, isolated from the local setting, cannot provide responsible guidelines to the operating executives. Thus, firms cannot simply feed locally monitored information to decentralized local decision-makers. It must be moved through the information system.

Information in multinational firms must span great geographic and cultural, as well as organizational, space. The tendency for "soft" social information to be filtered out in decentralized firms will be more prevalent in a multinational than in a firm operating in only one country.[7]

Cultural differences must be faced at some point in an information network. Many firms employ nationals at local levels as a means of increasing their sensitivity to the local environment. For integrated planning, however, this sensitivity must become information and flow up through the organization. Without strong cultural sensitivity at the headquarter's level, the filter is simply moved from local monitoring to the division headquarters. For those situations where local secrecy and mistrust have developed, as is the case for many acquired firms, the filter is impervious, and most of the social as well as much of the economic data does not flow.

For performance evaluation, it is essential that data on developmental performance move through the firm, since managerial performance is always monitored at organizational levels above the manager who is being evaluated. The fact that the social dimension of developmental responsibility tends to be slow to develop exacerbates the problem of attempting to measure a long-term phenomenon in short, segmented, quarterly or annual time periods.[8] We cannot expect the "soft" estimates of developmental impact that are slow to appear and hard to measure to readily pass through the geographic-organizational-cultural boundaries in typical information networks.

Sharing Information

Disclosure is an essential element of all planning and information systems. Through its disclosure policy, management decides the extent to which it will share its power. Clearly, multinationals must meet disclosure requirements imposed by both parent and host countries as well as those initiated through shareholder resolutions. Disclosure policy deals with the sharing of information in those all-too-frequent cases in which the requirements are not clear, or in sharing information which is beyond clearly stated minimums. Since information is power, disclosure becomes a particularly sensitive issue in conflict situations.

Multinationals that undertake expanded environmental monitoring will develop an in-depth understanding of the local environment. They have three options for the use of this information:

(1) as a base for independent action,
(2) to share with local governmental authorities,
(3) for voluntary disclosure to the public.

The first two alternatives relate to our earlier conclusions concerning social neutrality. Where a firm must monitor and control its own social impact due to the lack of clear signals from legal structures or efficient markets, management can either use the information to plan a responsible economic and social program for the allocation of resources to and within the host country, or it can share this information with host country officials to jointly work through the productivity-social trade-offs.

A clear example of information sharing that could improve the living conditions of the poor in host countries is in the selection of technology. The capital intensity of the technology being transferred by multinational enterprises is currently a source of friction between multinationals and host countries. Whereas multinational technology from the developed countries is capital intensive, development planners in the Third World are calling for a more simple, labor-intensive, "intermediate" technology tailored to their labor skills and employment needs.[9] The development planners have the power to control, but the multinational enterprise has the critical information. Managers know the technical limits of their production function—the limits on the substitutability of labor for capital and the related efficiency. Having worked with that technology, they understand how amenable it is to modification and are in a position to judge how it relates to the realities of production in that country. When confrontation can be minimized and information shared, development will be enhanced.

When managers opt for the first alternative (independent action), they incur the danger of paternalism and of imposing values from one national or managerial culture on host country peoples. Alternatively, only when governmental authorities represent the needs of the people and there is a basis of trust for meaningful multinational-host government interaction is information sharing in order.

To voluntarily disclose information to the general public beyond that which is required (alternative three) is a decision to be openly accountable for corporate actions. (This broad disclosure can, of course, occur as a result of sharing information with governmental officials in alternative two.) Disclosure relinquishes power to other groups in the community with no assurance that they will employ it effectively or responsibly.

SUMMARY

In this paper, I have shared my world view and preferred role for multinationals—that poverty in the Third World is the most serious cancer in our global society and that effective action by multinational firms is an important ingredient for progress toward its relief. I have argued for a multinational form of corporate social responsibility designated as a "developmental responsibility."

Developmental responsibility is imposed on multinational corporations by conditions in Third World countries. Markets and regulatory regimes do not signal the requirements of a social consensus. In these conditions, multinationals must impose a form of self-regulation on their Third World activities. They are called to internalize a social responsibility. An extra dimension is added to corporate decision-making in what is already a complex and high-risk international environment.

The beginning point in implementing a policy of developmental responsibility is with the poor in Third World operating locations. This is the group universally in the greatest need, a need that should be recognized by all segments of society. Contributions to this group provide the most important measure of accomplishment for the developmentally responsive multinational corporation.

The managerial entry point for meeting developmental responsibility is with the firm's planning system. The extended planning horizons associated with this new dimension of the corporate role and the "soft" nature of its measured performance pose a real challenge to the multinational manager.

NOTES

1. See below, Part III.

2. Milton Friedman, *Capitalism and Freedom* (Chicago: University of Chicago Press, 1962).

3. Committee for Economic Development, *Social Responsibility of Business Corporations* (New York: Committee for Economic Development, 1971), p. 22.

4. In Catholic social teaching, this requirement is based upon human dignity and justice. "The discussion of justice in terms of

relative rights and mutual duties is characteristic of the entire modern Catholic tradition. . . . Respect for freedom and dignity, therefore, involves more than not interfering with the activities of persons. Obligations of justice include positive duties to aid persons in need." David Hollenbach, S.J., "Modern Catholic Teachings Concerning Justice" in *The Faith That Does Justice,* John C. Haughey, S.J., ed. (New York: Paulist Press, 1977), pp. 210–211.

A principal termed the "Kew Garden Principle" applies this same requirement to help those in need who cannot help themselves as the basis of corporate social responsibility. John G. Simon, Charles W. Powers, and John P. Gunnemann, *The Ethical Investor: Universities and Corporate Responsibility* (New Haven, Conn.: Yale University Press, 1972), p. 22.

5. A number of multinational managers recognize and accept their social role in the Third World. In a recent statement, Lee Morgan, President of Caterpillar Tractor, stressed the relationship between multinationals and human rights. In response to his question, "What contribution can a multinational like Caterpillar make to human rights?" he answered, "First, it can recognize it is unavoidably involved in the question—and hopefully, in the answer." Lee L. Morgan, *Improving the Human Condition and What Role for the Multinational?* (Peoria, Ill.: Public Affairs Department, Caterpillar Tractor Co., 1978), p. 10.

6. Two seminar participants found that national development patterns defied classification. "There are no general paths to development just as there is no general definition of development. Each people must write its own history." See Charles K. Wilber and Kenneth P. Jameson, "Paradigms of Economic Development and Beyond," in Jameson and Wilber, eds., *Directions in Economic Development* (Notre Dame, Ind.: University of Notre Dame Press, 1979), p. 35.

7. For a discussion of the problems involved with the transmission of soft information see Robert W. Ackerman and Raymond A. Bauer, *Corporate Social Responsiveness* (Reston, Va.: Reston Publishing Company, 1976).

8. Kenneth Milani, "It Doesn't Add Up: The Role of Human Resource Accounting in Effecting Work Humanization" in W. J. Heisler and John W. Houck, *A Matter of Dignity* (Notre Dame, Ind.: University of Notre Dame Press, 1977).

9. E. F. Schumacher, *Small Is Beautiful: Economics As If People Mattered* (New York: Harper & Row, 1973).

10. Seeking the Lowest Total Social Cost

CHARLES W. POWERS

CAN MULTINATIONAL FIRMS, especially those operating in poverty-gripped Third World countries, help alleviate the conditions that create material poverty and degrade the human spirit? And if so, how?

The suggestion that multinational firms should self-consciously examine the impact of their activities in Third World nations and should shape those activities according to ethical precepts encounters a variety of objections. These objections can be reduced to two basic themes:

(1) that using the only ethical categories available will result in moral or cultural imperialism and thus either cannot be justified or will do more harm than good.
(2) that the intense concern for protecting available sovereignty exhibited by many, if not most, Third World country governments has resulted in policies, official attitudes, and regulations that leave the corporate manager no room for discretion. Hence, even if a multinational corporation could justify self-consciously ethical policies, it would not be able to implement them.

My task is to consider these objections in an effort to chart approaches multinationals could take. My purpose is to be concrete; my starting point must be theoretical.

A summary of the general discussion following presentation of this paper is contained in the Addendum to this chapter.

A SEARCH FOR THE APPROPRIATE MORAL CATEGORIES

How do we find moral principles that take into account radically different cultural patterns, economic circumstances, life expectations, and political traditions without slipping into a bottomless pit of moral relativism? I think there is a way.

I begin with the premise that, to guide the evaluation of social impacts, we should look for a moral principle that embraces the richness and diversity of the people whose lives are affected by our actions.

The evolution of industrial and technological development in any culture has always brought rapid change and has tended to cause the deterioration of traditional life patterns. It has also, through increased communication and travel, exposed the fact that much of the world's population lacks adequate material resources and is today—as it has always been—incredibly vulnerable to disease, weather, food shortages, and other vicissitudes. Equally important, however, is that "development" has regularly provided immediate benefits primarily to a small portion of the population.

Deterioration of traditional meaning-giving patterns, awareness of the sheer extent of malnutrition, and radically unequal distribution of the benefits of rapid change: this is a recipe for moral outrage among all morally sensitive people. It gives rise to efforts to quantify the extent of the hurt experienced and the anomalies created, according to a host of indicators: wage differentials between developed country and Third World country workers; distorted consumption patterns within Third World countries; severe disparities between the average incomes of urban and rural families or the economically least advantaged 50 percent or 20 percent; urban immigration figures; figures relating to the dissolution of family life.

These statistics help us to think we have solidified our rationale for moral criticism of technological development. But, in fact, figures usually do little to help us determine appropriate remedial action. They do not help us to focus on what would constitute acceptable living conditions for people whose societies are in transition. Whenever a social indicator abstracts from real lives and collects data concerning only an *element* of a disturbing social phenomenon, it leads us toward single-

faceted social policies or social action which often exacerbate
other morally serious differences or problems.

As an example, multinational corporations frequently are
criticized for not paying Third World workers wages equivalent to those paid their developed country counterparts. But
Constantine Vaitsos, a development scholar and adviser to
many Third World country governments, sharply criticizes the
fact that multinationals, by paying wages substantially higher
than the wages paid by indigenous enterprises, create social
instability and syphon off the most able work force.[1] It is easy
to find oneself saying "aha" when the average U.S.–Third World
factory worker pay scales are compared, and then turn around
and say "aha" when multinationals' wage scales distort local
economies. The appropriate "aha" in this case, may, I suggest,
be an awareness that neither an international "equal pay for
equal work" wage principle, nor a simple "when in Lima pay
as the Limans pay" rule, provides a morally satisfactory guide
to action.

Second, we should look for a moral principle that tempers
the application of moral ideals with a realization that our first
responsibility is to help attain for those whom we affect the
minimum conditions of a life we would call human. I shall try
to state those conditions and then try to state a principle that
helps convert these conditions into a guide for actions—
individual and institutional.

In my view, all persons need to *have available both the material and other social security prerequisites to a healthful and safe existence. They need to have sufficient freedom of choice and continuity of
culture to have the opportunity to develop an identity in their community.* And they must be able to use that identity to contribute to
the development of others. If, and only if, these conditions
have been afforded to people have we accorded them the
dignity and respect to which, by being human, they have a
right.

With what sorts of things are we concerned if I have cor-
rectly identified the minimally ethical?

First, the economic systems or policies or corporate activities must bring about as rapidly as possible a distribution of
goods and services that will make available the basic necessities
of a healthy and safe existence. The concern here involves
adequate and appropriate caloric intake, access to health care,
the means to control temperature within a certain range, etc.

Some thinkers, including Abraham Maslow, have considered provision of such goods and services to be the base on which the hierarchy of human needs is built.[2]

Many people are attempting to determine precisely what these physical minimums are. Some say that soybeans, lard, orange juice, and beef liver constitute the cheapest medically balanced diet, and in the United States it would cost about $150 per person per year in retail markets. One completely misunderstands what I have said about minimum needs, however, if he attempts to break out the material minimums in this way. The material requirements of human beings cannot be distinguished from their psychological or spiritual ones—and these other needs are importantly contingent upon, though not wholly relative to, the community in which a person grows up and lives.

When confronted with these purportedly more ephemeral aspects of human dignity, many policymakers have been prepared to throw out the concept of "needs" and adopt in its stead a completely relative definition of "wants." An expression of desire then becomes the indicator of what is deserved.

I understand the logic of this conclusion. It proceeds from the argument that if one abstracts from the warp and woof of lives lived in particular places and communities and begins to speak in general terms about "human rights" or "freedoms," then the patterns of choice that are alive and real in specific communities of people disappear.

In the culture of our own homes, we continually attend to the psychological possibilities and limitations of children, spouse, and other loved ones. The choices we encourage are always shaped by a concern for the psychological and spiritual coherence of the lives we know well. The same range of possibilities exists for the mail clerk newly arrived in Mexico City from a tiny mountain village, for the production worker in Manila struggling to reconcile her Catholicism with the life styles of her fellow workers, or for the Indian maintenance man who believes his job is inherently unworthy because it is below what the caste system says is his birthright.

We know that a concern for human dignity can never be abstracted from the identity of the person who is shaped by, and is shaping, the lives around him. In fact, however, most institutional policies are inherently less sensitive to these nuances. Institutional activities, including those of corpora-

tions operating in the Third World, can never fully grasp—
nor make just the appropriate room for—the multiplicity and
fecundity of these choices in any certain way, especially as the
effect of an action ripples out from the local community to the
state, national, and international levels. That is why we do
need generalizations such as work rules, human rights claims,
management policies, even government regulations. And yet,
if we allow any generalization to replace or even to obscure the
range of concrete concerns on which the statement of minimum conditions focuses, we begin to lose our moral bearings.

To some, my statement of minimum conditions has
seemed conservative or relativistic; to others, quite radical.
Egalitarians, for example, would attack it on the grounds that
it clearly does not make distributive equality a constitutive
element. In fact, I think, it has inherent tendencies which
drive it toward greater equality.

Studies of relative deprivation make it clear that there are
strong inhibitions to identity development if incomes—or better, consumptive capabilities—are too disparate within a
community. The point at which this happens differs among
cultures. And what counts as a justification for material differences—for example, the view that people should be rewarded
in proportion to the contributions they make—will depend on
what is valued in a culture or how it is organized. The central
point here is that both "material equality" and "contribution"
are relative to the criterion of need.

Can this concern for minimum conditions be turned into
the principle for moral action? Let me try:

An action is ethical which is *successful in establishing the material and social security prerequisites for a healthy and safe existence
for those it affects while preserving sufficient freedom of choice and
continuity of culture to allow them to develop an identity in their
community—so long as it does not deprive or undermine those conditions for those who already have them.*

Several new factors must now be explained. First, this
principle is responsive to the elemental moral concern—John
Rawls in his *Theory of Justice* calls it a natural duty—not to do
harm. And yet, it relates the definition of harm to the
minimum conditions. No one wants to be deprived of what he
has or values or would like to choose; but to be deprived of
what is more than a minimum condition is not unethical if it
helps establish the minimum conditions for those who do not

have them. Hence, the justification for a progressive income tax and other redistributive programs if the other minimum conditions tests are passed.

A second point about this principle is that it insists that we be radically attentive and alert to the full scope of moral concerns. It asks us to see, listen, ask about, explain, find out, notice, heed what is happening in the places where we undertake our actions. And it never permits us to say: *If only* (and fill in the blanks: the government would wait; "these people" were more literate; the union was not politically motivated), *then we would* (and again fill the gaps: get the technology transferred; be able to train better; be able to bargain for both better productivity and protection of worker safety). The principle allows us to link the full welfare of the people we affect with the possibilities which, however limited, are available in a given situation. When the "if" clause is a significant deterrent to meeting the minimum conditions, then that constraint becomes the object of a moral action and not an excusing condition for ignoring the moral factor.

A third point, perhaps the most important, is that this principle does not depend upon rules for its application. Instead, it is one by which rules and mores and actions and policies may be tested. It tends, indeed, to be a solvent for our moral preconceptions. I call this point the most important because of the concern that self-conscious efforts by multinationals to monitor or regulate their Third World impacts would inevitably subject them to criticisms of moral or cultural imperialism.

The minimum conditions principle keeps the moral impulse alive in such a way that moral categories are held at bay until we can determine their relevance. Such concepts as "self-determination," "property rights," the "right to organize," the "sanctity of contracts," and the "right to privacy" contribute to human dignity if they are understood in the appropriate context. But if these concepts are seen as concrete realties, equally important and appropriate in all circumstances, they will skew the moral concern.

The question to be asked is, "When and in what form do these concepts come alive and build the fabric of social interactions which preserve or help establish the minimum conditions?" Then we will be beyond the debate over whether economic rights precede civil liberties or whether political rights are inconsistent with distributional ones. These debates take place only on a conceptual battleground, not where people live, breathe, love, eat, sweat, or cry.

OPPORTUNITIES TO ESTABLISH MINIMUM CONDITIONS

The impatient manager or corporate critic may well be saying, "The author still hasn't told me what I should do," or "I still have nothing concrete for which to hold the corporation accountable." There are two reasons why that is so: First, there is no responsibility before the *context* of action is known. If human need is complicated, we must know its complexity before we do something about it. The minimum conditions principle helps us to see the point of moral action steadily and wholly. Second, there is no responsibility when there is no capability to respond. An enormous literature is developing which describes the power of the multinational; it has generated an equally impressive volume of responses which deny that the corporation can make concern for minimum conditions integral to corporate policy or practice.

I think we must demythologize the issue of corporate capability.

The sphere of autonomous corporate action in Third World countries has diminished during the past decade. It probably will get even smaller. Governments no longer see themselves as pawns on chessboards located in New York, Washington, London, Paris, or Rome. Most have developed the technical capability to enforce their view of their industrial destiny. Moreover, when their domestic markets are too small to interest or support multinational activity, countries are joining together and laying down strong regional guidelines for multinational entry and activity. On this, sources as different as Ronald Muller in his most recent writings and *The New Yorker* magazine seem to agree. However, it is an important mistake to assume that less opportunity for corporate *autonomy* means corporations now lack the *capability* to participate in the development of policies, or to implement practices, which have the pursuit of minimum conditions as an important purpose.

To illustrate, I want to look at the various levels on which corporations have choices in developing countries—beginning with the level of least opportunity and moving toward those where opportunity is greatest.

(1) Export of products

(2) Promotion of exported products

(3) Choice of distributors or service organizations for exported products

(4) Sale of technical assistance to an indigenous firm or agency

(5) Employment of people by, and the sales and service practices of, sales subsidiaries for exported products

(6) Licensing of technology to an indigenous firm or agency

(7) Employment and other activities associated with the partial assembly of products for domestic consumption or for re-export

(8) Development of manufacturing or sales and distribution capability in a commercial or industrial sector where production rights are not restricted

(9) Bidding for the right to extract or manufacture in countries which restrict markets (by tariff or import controls)

(10) Development of extraction or manufacturing capability in a sector where multinational access is limited to one or a few firms

(11) Governmental requests for comments on, or for information necessary to, the formulation of public policies related to market access, product, or production data

(12) Governmental requests for help in defining general development policies for a particular commercial or industrial sector

This list, although not all-inclusive, represents the various levels of involvement a corporation can have in a foreign economy. In general, the impact is more pervasive as the level of involvement increases. Another phenomenon rarely noticed by those outside of corporations is that as involvement increases, so also does the interdependence of country and company. Each begins to have a greater stake in the activities or policies of the other. If, for example, the developing government adopts reprehensible policies, an exporter may have to scramble for new markets if it decides to stop the sale of products it fears will be used reprehensibly; but for a mining company located in that country, the costs—moral or financial—are very high.

As the industrialization process evolves in a country—as an economy moves from the importation of consumer goods toward the manufacture of capital goods—the country's stake in the company begins to grow. Interdependence becomes the rule, rather than the exception.

The most complex questions regarding the opportunity of multinationals to affect minimum conditions arise where companies have, or are contemplating, a substantial involvement in a foreign economy, as manufacturers and thus as employers, creditors, borrowers, landowners, technology transferrers, taxpayers, shippers, investors. In Third World countries, there are generally two characteristics of such ventures: (1) The country is trying to incorporate within its own economy technological capabilities which its infrastructure and existing markets would not yet support without governmental sponsorship, and hence, (2) the government is offering protections which impair normal market indicators. For example, they require measures to screen out imports and to limit free access of firms into the industrial sector.

Multinational corporation involvement invariably represents a foreign element in an economy, not primarily because of the company's country of origin, but because the venture would not exist in a world where comparative advantage, private enterprise, and free markets characterized international economic activity. Nevertheless, such a world does not exist. Nor is it clear to me that Third World countries would benefit if it did. The terrible price of major technological change has already been paid by developed economies. There is no reason why every society should pay it again. Also, the technological infrastructure of a developed economy gives it an unbeatable head start over less-developed ones unless the technology is transferred.

Hence, the price of bringing a "foreign" element into an economy is not *inherently* a price not worth paying. The questions are, What is the price? How can it be lowered? To answer, we must look at the consequences of "foreignness." First, the life patterns of those most directly affected usually change substantially. Assuming that the *product* is needed and is appropriately modified to local conditions, the major impact of this sort is on the employees and on the surrounding communities. Second, the distortions in the economic infrastructure usually are paid for by the public sector. For example, most new multinational projects are supported either directly by government financing dollars or subsidies, or by foregone taxes. And, especially for capital goods, the price paid by the customer is usually higher, at least initially, than if the product were bought at international prices. I want to relate each of these consequences to the minimum conditions principle and to suggest ways in which corporations could minimize them.

Foreignness, Minimum Conditions,
and the Change of Life Patterns

The minimum conditions principle does not say that change is bad; rather, it rules out actions that result in changes with which an individual cannot cope. We know some factors that determine whether a person can cope with the speed of change—for example, the extent to which the change causes him to abandon rather than modify the beliefs, habits, and attitudes that give life meaning.

We know this abandonment when we see it in the faces of rural people who stream into major Latin American cities to find that not only is there no work (and thus no prerequisites to a healthy and safe existence), but also there is no substitute for their rural relationships and institutions. Another aspect is that the sudden imposition of the rigid work schedules, speed, and precision necessarily associated with a viable capital-intensive enterprise on a small community of artisans, labor-intensive farmers, and small shopkeepers may bring instant prosperity—but may also bring about the collapse of the fabric of a community. Alienation and anomie, the inability to cope, often result.

It is too late, after an ill-planned production process is established, to start training programs, provide counseling, or develop drug abuse prevention facilities. The time to examine whether the dose of foreignness a multinational venture brings is too big to be absorbed by the community, is at the start, not after the damage has begun. A company that makes such a preliminary examination will not, I think, find its ethics being attacked as imperialistic by any government with which it can otherwise make an acceptable agreement.

Foreignness, Minimum Conditions,
and Economic Distortion

The complicated set of assumptions and factors that development planners in a Third World country must take into account is mind boggling. In trying to play catch-up, they must attempt to measure the future in a way U.S. officials are never forced to do. Many of these planners are incredibly good at it, and they are getting better. But when Third World country planners reach for a technology they do not know well but suspect the country will need, and when the lead time is almost gone, they have little chance of staying within the margins of error that will mean success or failure for the country's economy. The foreignness is too great; and, though they know they need help, they do not know where to turn for it.

While corporations frequently have the information and the skills to help developing countries sort through their options, at the moment these two interdependent entities — Third World governments and multinational corporations — rarely trust each other enough to allow their complementary skills to come to bear on making decisions. Yet, if made poorly, these decisions will have social consequences that dwarf *any* other cost of multinational activity.

Cost is the key term in most Third World countries. The wrong price tag for industrial development translates directly (much more directly than in more market-oriented economies) into a sewer not built, running water not installed, irrigation ditches not dug, clinics not built. The principle that should be tested against the minimum conditions principle in the area of industrial development is *appropriate increase in industrial capability at the lowest total social cost.* "Appropriate" here refers to whether the benefits derived from the increased capability are synergistic with the development process as a whole. "Lowest total social cost" relates to whether the increase can be accomplished (1) without undermining the minimums for those affected, and (2) with the least drain on those resources which would be used to establish the minimum material conditions for those who do not have them.

How might governments and corporations work together to make sure a principle will work, without sacrificing the essential characteristics, responsibilities, and strengths of each?

The issues that really count must be explored at the conception of a plan for development. Some of these are:

(1) What are the economies of scale for this product? How are they changed with more or less volume?

(2) What are the key bottlenecks in supply lines and how much would a delay in integration schedules help reduce price premiums?

(3) What are the market trends for the product in similar countries? How important is it to pay an extra price for technology which can later be modified in order to avoid retooling?

(4) What is the difference in both employment levels and cost for using more or less capital-intensive technology?

(5) What are the key elements of the needed infrastructure for plant support?

(6) What technological developments are likely to occur? How do they influence a decision to start now or wait?

(7) How does this industry or sector fit into the country's overall development needs?

These and similar questions, if developed in consultation with interested multinationals before regulations are set in concrete, would help the government sharpen the focus of the conditions of competition set forth in the tender.

Once the plan and policy are developed and the tender drawn, the two entities would return to their bargaining positions. But those corporations competing for the tender could still exercise responsibility. A company has responsibility to look at a tender, compare the conditions to its own capabilities, standards, and structures,[4] and honestly say, "Yes, we can make a contribution" or "No, we can't." At this point an autonomous decision can preclude negative interdependence. If a company decides to go ahead, the bid would try to demonstrate that, within the parameters set by the tender, a company could achieve the result at the lowest total cost.

If policies were developed in this way, and more tenders were issued after this kind of consultation, the temptation to promise more than could be delivered would be reduced. Then a company would enter into a complex relationship in which, as with any interdependent relationship, there would be ups and downs, periods of harmony, and periods of effort to maintain mutual understanding. The relationship probably would change over time as the needs of both parties change, but the constant concern would be building the minimum conditions for those affected at the lowest total social cost.

In a world where angry voices still dominate the rhetorical debate about codes of conduct and technology transfer in most international forums, a vision of cooperation in pursuit of a lowest-total-social-cost result may seem as probable as the Biblical rapprochement between the lion and the lamb. The debate about codes of conduct is like the debate about human rights: The issue has been reified; the concepts are abstracted from the realties; the differences, exacerbated.

I suspect that a record of solid performance focused on the real issues where multinational corporations affect Third World countries would allow us to see the problems more steadily and completely. Then we could figure out how to work as institutions—public and private—toward that which we should value above anything else in the world: the dignity of the persons whose lives we affect.

Addendum

FOLLOWING THE POWERS' presentation the discussion unfolded in three phases. The first issue was whether corporations have the freedom to be socially responsible in an ethical sense. If a corporation is to incorporate ethical considerations into its decisions, it must have decision-making freedom; that is, corporations must have alternative courses of action available and the flexibility to choose among them. If a firm is totally encumbered by the rules and regulations of the host country, it cannot be socially responsible—or, indeed, irresponsible. An area where most of the participants believed that firms have a wide range of options open to them was in their marketing activities. Thus, the second issue was the extent to which multinationals should attempt to create wants in the Third World. Finally, the group turned to a philosophical issue raised by Powers—the relevance of ethical concepts to the issue of social responsibility.

GOVERNMENTAL CONTROL

Local governments obviously have a great deal of control over the private sector. It is in negotiations with local agencies, that the multinational corporation can participate in defining its environment. A manager's social concerns can be brought to bear most effectively in the initial interaction between the firm and the government.

When determining the marketability of a new product, for example, the MNC often must rely on the host country for a sense of the product's acceptability. Frequently, the information is ambivalent. Even though managers would like to rely on elected government officials to help set priorities on exactly what products could go into the market, the signals are too frequently insufficient or inappropriate. In some cases, the governmental officials themselves have abdicated office. This

implies that the key to endurance through anticipated decidu-
ous governments is to pursue basic investigations rather than
accept solely the superficial indicators provided by temporary
officials.

It was generally agreed that the government decision affecting the investment of the multinational could be a good
deal stronger and clearer, if the dialogue concerning what the
corporation has to offer and what the government wants was
entered into at a much earlier stage.

Advertising and Culture

Participants noted that local consumption patterns are affected strongly by the alien influence of MNC marketing procedures. On the other hand, through their purchases, local
nationals demonstrate their desire to adapt to a way of life or a
level of expenditure similar to that of the developed world,
even though these may well exceed the available resources.
These consumers are not forced to buy the product. Or are
they? MNCs have been accused of advertising techniques designed to cause a stampede to the market for their product
with little regard to the cultural side effects of this rush.

Most companies take a careful look at the people before
introducing a product. Once a product reaches the advertising
stage it has been thoroughly researched. Companies go to
great lengths by running test panels and conducting other
forms of market analysis on the current indigenous market.
Nevertheless, some participants cited examples in which companies' advertising campaigns created false wants. There were
allegations at both extremes: (1) that insufficient information
passed between supplier and user of the product, and (2) that
a passing of too much information creates pressure to change
cultural identities. The correct balance between the extremes
may be difficult to assess.

This is a moral judgment. Individuals and institutions
face the same issue: To what extent should we try to change
concepts, ideas, and cultures to fit our own value system? A
number of participants believe that ultimately the decision
should lie with the host country. As one member stated, "We
cannot, here in the United States, divine the social and economic priorities of the various countries. When we make an

investment in another country it has to be compatible with what that country wants."

The problems of transmitting this kind of cultural impact information to the organization was stressed by one of the participants. He noted that when a manager out in the boondocks is told to "make that bottom line," he may well be blinded to the primary and secondary cultural impact of his actions. Moreover, when information is transmitted from headquarters across great geographic and cultural distances, it is likely to become garbled along the way.

APPLICABILITY OF ETHICS

No society in the world is a static community: within the next 50 years all will be changing. This underlying fact brings even more pressure on the need for understanding from one culture to another. Because what we do affects that change, our concern must center around a discussion of ethics. Business is an integral element in any society. For this reason, businesses, and especially MNC businesses, are not going to succeed unless they are approached from an ethical viewpoint. Yet ethical thinking as we have learned it is not easily applicable today.

NOTES

1. Constantine V. Vaitsos, "The Role of Transnational Enterprises in Latin American Economic Integration Efforts: Who Integrated and with Whom, How, and for Whose Benefit?" Main Conclusions of Report prepared for UNCTAD.

2. A.H. Maslow, *Motivation and Personality* (New York: Harper & Row, 1954).

3. For Muller's view see Michael Maccoby and Ronald Muller, "Human and Economic Development," prepared for the Consultation on Human Values and the Economic Order, National Council of Churches, October 1978. *The New Yorker* of 30 October 1978, in the column "Notes and Comments," states: "In our present day world, people are taking over their own countries. . . . People seem to prefer almost any native regime, no matter how monstrous, to foreign domination" (pp. 31, 32).

4. Companies that have thought through these issues sufficiently clearly to be able to issue company codes of international conduct are to be commended. Such codes are important indicators to a government of what it will be getting if it decides it wants a particular enterprise.

11. Managing the Social Response

EARL W. DOUBET AND LEE A. TAVIS

THE INTERNATIONAL ENVIRONMENT provides an unprecedented managerial challenge. The multinational setting is characterized by intricate, complex, and difficult-to-identify relationships both within and among countries. The uncertainties of continually moving people, funds, goods, and information across national boundaries are exacerbated by the unsettled economic and political conditions so common in the underdeveloped world. Managers are doing a remarkable job in coping with these complexities and uncertainties. A good deal has been written on the technical competence employed in meeting these challenges.

What has not been adequately treated is how managers should approach the social aspects of their developmental responsibility. This responsibility has been defined earlier as a requirement to respond to the social as well as the economic needs of Third World peoples. It derives from the opportunity to contribute rather than from a complicity in some past wrongdoing. Indeed, other papers in this volume are unique in that they express the need for this kind of multinational involvement.[1]

Recognition of a developmental responsibility adds a whole new dimension to the multinational decision process. As a first step in defining the nature of this need, we interviewed a number of executives from firms participating in the seminar. Three areas emerged as meriting early attention: (1) statements of purpose, (2) local decision flexibility, and (3) regulatory internalization and participation. These three areas are discussed in this paper. In each case, we present a statement of our position, the reasoning behind that statement, and a summary of our interview findings.

Statement of Purpose

Premise

Statements of purpose such as credos or codes of conduct enhance a firm's ability to meet its developmental responsibility.

Reasoning Behind the Statement

Many factors influence the value orientation of a firm's decisions. Basically, the ethos comes from the values and attitudes of those promoted to positions of responsibility. Organizationally, these values must be translated into objectives and reflected in corporate actions. Corporations approach this task through overall statements of purpose, policy guidelines, and finally as an input into objectives at all levels of corporate activity. Through this process, the firm as an institution takes on a values commitment.

Interview Findings

In this part of our study, we concentrated on two firms: Johnson & Johnson and Caterpillar Tractor. Johnson & Johnson relies on a credo intially written by General Robert W. Johnson in 1944 and supported by a limited number of policy statements, while Caterpillar employs a detailed code of conduct to achieve the same purpose.

These firms differ greatly in their capital intensity, product lines, and production facilities. Johnson & Johnson produces and sells a vast array of health care products to a broad range of consumers on a global basis. Organized into 140 operating companies, the firm is a highly decentralized organization. Management stresses its corporate philosophy as presented by the Credo (Exhibit A). Policy guidelines beyond the Credo are intentionally kept to a minimum.

Caterpillar produces a narrow line of globally standardized components and products distributed through over 250 independent dealers across the world. In a production-oriented, capital-intensive industry, Caterpillar is highly centralized. Its Code of Conduct (Exhibit B) was developed in the early 1970s as a means of dealing with corporate–host country relationships. Details of the Code were thrashed out between headquarters and operating managers in order to ensure a final document that could stress the highest possible standards and still be operationally feasible. Each year, managers are asked to sign a statement that they have fully met all of the Code requirements.

While the Credo of Johnson & Johnson and Caterpillar's Code of Conduct differ substantially in detail, each addresses many of the concerns that are found in all corporations. It is clear that each company believes that its statement acts as policy guidelines to company management, and that it is expected that the managers will conduct their affairs in accordance with those guidelines.

These statements of purpose do have a substantial impact on the operations mode of these companies. They provide a philosophy as well as a value-oriented guide to management, and set the tone for the company's dealings throughout the world. The value of such a code to a multinational company is to orient all managers with different cultural and ethnic backgrounds to a common mode of doing business which reflects the beliefs of the men who direct the corporation. It is also clear that a basic understanding of the content is not easily imparted to the management of a company. Words mean different things to different people, and this is especially true when people are communicating in other than their mother tongue. Meetings must be held at which senior management explain fully what is meant by the statements.

Implementation of the policy which these statements either stand for or represent is also a difficult process. More than assuring understanding what a statement of purpose calls for in daily operations, it means operational changes within a company are also required. These changes could involve any facet of business activity, but certainly will affect the financial and accounting practices of most firms. As an example, the Foreign Corrupt Practices Act has forced accounting changes upon all U.S. companies that did not previously have adequate accounting systems to detect illicit payments. While in this instance there is a legal requirement to comply with U.S. law, a code of conduct could require changes in all activities of a business to conform with the requirements of senior management.

The degree to which a credo or a code of conduct is detailed in its direction to an organization depends upon the personality and individual feelings of top management or, in any case, the top man. It is very likely that there would be a difference in the policies of each company and the amount of detail required for clarity.

In the case of the two companies studied, the statements of purpose have become an integral part of the business philosophy and activity of each. We conclude that a credo or code of conduct is beneficial to the management of a company by formally instructing all management on the basic level of conduct that is expected of each manager. It removes many of the questions raised by different social, cultural, and ethnic backgrounds and permits the management of the company to act in the same manner anywhere in the world. It appears that this creates a comfortable environment because it gives each manager a firm set of guidelines.

Based upon the discussions with the managers, we believe that the establishment of a statement of purpose would be propitious for any multinational company, and that it could be a vehicle to enhance the ability of a firm to meet its developmental responsibility.

LOCAL DECISION FLEXIBILITY

Premise

Flexibility in adapting to the unique cultural and social dimensions of host country environments is a necessary condition if firms are to meet their developmental responsibility. Financial control systems work against this needed flexibility.

Reasoning Behind the Statement

The balance between the need for global coordination of multinational activities and the firm's ability to respond in an informed manner to the needs of the local environment is a basic issue for all multinational organizations. On the one hand, coordination of international activities is both an economic necessity and a requirement if the firm is to contribute to Third World development. Alternatively, if multinationals cannot react to the uniqueness of local needs, they cannot meet the specific requirements of their developmental responsibility. The coordination-flexibility trade-off is an important dimension of multinational planning.

In competitive economic terms, multinationals must take advantage of their simultaneous presence in a number of countries if they are to gain the associated economic benefits and remain competitive with other multinationals as well as with indigenous entrepreneurs. Still, at the local level, products must serve the demands of the domestic market and production techniques must be modified to fit available labor skills, component quality, and existing cost structures.

The need for a coordination-flexibility balance is also an element in the multinational developmental response. The contribution of these firms to Third World productivity derives from their ability to inject needed managerial skills, technology, and capital drawn from the developed world into less-developed host countries and, further, to direct these factors to productive uses within those countries. Yet, the infusion of standardized factors of production or products may not admit to the uniqueness of the developing country experience. The Third World is not simply the Western World of a century ago. Nor, as indicated earlier, are patterns of economic development among these countries very similar. What is "best" for local situations is not uniform across all operating sites. The tension between returns to the corporations and the needs of local constituents cannot be solved on an over-all basis. This introduces an organizational need for local planning flexibility tied to over-all accountability.

In order to cope with the operational complexities of diverse local environments, there has been a major tendency among U.S. multinationals to decentralize their decision-making process. In general, most decentralized firms are those producing and selling a broad range of products requiring different technologies serving different kinds of end users.

Decentralization, however, does not necessarily enhance a firm's capability of meeting the full developmental needs of local societies. Even though production and marketing decisions may be moved down into the organization, when they are associated with tightened financial controls local managers are not, in fact, given the flexibility to include the social and cultural considerations in their decision process. They are free only to choose those alternatives which maximize periodic profits.

Interview Findings

Corporate decision processes naturally fall into two classifications: (1) the allocation of resources to long-term uses, and (2) the more routine operating decisions.

As firms commit their resources in the long term, they structure the nature of their host country participation and define the local constituencies with whom they will deal. In this decision process, the strategic dimension tends to dominate the more traditional capital budgeting analysis. In most cases, the decision to enter a new market, to expand existing facilities in a major way, or to shut down a production facility is made on the basis of strategic considerations, with the capital budgeting analysis relegated to the guidance of selecting among alternative approaches to increasing or decreasing capacity.

This priority serves well the needs of the developmental response. Strategic planning processes are generally amenable to the inclusion of soft cultural or social data, whereas capital investment procedures tend to strip away all considerations other than cash flows and criterion rates.[2] Moreover, in high risk situations, present value analysis tends to stress the short run at the expense of the long run.

Although the decision process for long-term resource commitments tends to be highly centralized, the data collected on the local economies appear to be extensive and the response to the uniqueness of local environments appears to be great. Thus, our exploratory interviews suggest that the data collected and the evaluation procedures conducted by multinationals relative to these long-term commitments support Father Hesburgh's statement that multinationals "are likely to have the capability, which governments generally do not have, of looking at economic situations in a given country and making a judgment as to whether or not it is possible to support a successful business enterprise there."[3]

So far, we have insufficient evidence to judge the extent to which long-term commitment decisions incorporate the non-economic data deemed necessary for an informed developmental response, although we did uncover a number of situations where cultural considerations dominated. In any case, the organizational mechanisms are there, and it is a matter of ensuring that the social and cultural data relative to Third World development can continue to be weighted among the firm's objectives. The typical centralization of these decisions does not seem to detract from their sensitivity in the local environment.

The advances made in operations planning over the past few years have been surprising, particularly in the area of financial control systems. These developments are a result of added disclosure requirements by the Security and Exchange Commission and the accounting profession, advances in computer technology, and the move among U.S. multinationals toward the decentralization of non-financial operating decisions.

Disclosure requirements increase the amount of information and the frequency of reporting by corporate subsidiaries. The requirement of the Foreign Corrupt Practices Act to guarantee that control systems are capable of identifying illegal payments will lead to further tightening of financial controls.

Developments in computer hardware and software have dramatically increased the speed of internal information flows. In one case, performance information flowed to the headquarters with such speed that the headquarters reaction was received by the subsidiary manager before he had seen the original data. Associated with the enhanced quantity and transmission speeds, bottlenecks can develop at headquarters with the summarization and interpretation of data.

In most firms, the emphasis on control systems has been closely associated with organizational decentralization. As decisions have been moved down into the organization, headquarters tend to monitor performance more closely in order to discern the first sign of a problem.

The net result of these advances in operational planning and control systems is a tendency to work against the firm's ability to respond to the full range of developmental needs of the Third World. These systems are geared to measure and reward short-term financial performance, whereas the contribution to local development is measured only in the long term and includes many non-economic, difficult to measure variables. When managers are being compared to a return-on-investment yardstick, their focus will be on the events of the immediate accounting period that will be captured by this ratio. Developmental concerns that do not enhance profits or that reduce assets will be bypassed, particularly when a financial target ratio is not being met. Indeed, in many cases these control systems have become so oppressive that even long-term financial considerations tend to be washed away.

The overemphasis on short-term financial results, which can occur in operational control systems, exists in domestic as well as multinational firms. For the multinational, however, the problem is exacerbated. Even though developments in information processing are bridging the geographic span between subsidiaries and parent companies, a linguistic-cultural gap remains. With operations spread across the world, informal networks do not develop to cross this cultural-linguistic barrier. To suggest that headquarters people spend more time in the field is not practical. Executive travel schedules are already overextended.

This issue demands major attention. The thrust of advances in operational control systems is headed in the wrong direction.[4]

Regulatory Internalization and Participation

Premise

In those cases where host country regulation is inadequate, multinational firms must impose internal constraints on their local activities and participate in the regulatory process. This involves information sharing for entry or major expansion decisions and working to improve the regulatory process for industrial operating decisions.

Reasoning Behind the Statement

The interface between multinational firms and national or international regulatory agencies is where the freedom of action available to multinational managers is defined. In this interaction lies the answer to part of the question as to whether multinationals can contribute to the amelioration of poverty within the confines of the present economic system. Even though the multinational is a key actor in the local economy, it is only one element in the development system. Ideally, Third World governments, national and local, should structure the response.

When conditions are less than ideal, when product and financial markets are inefficient and local regulation is ineffective, multinationals can find themselves in the position of an unregulated monopoly. When this occurs, and there are no clear signals from either efficient markets or effective regulation, the firm must internalize the trade-offs among its various constituencies. This process is fraught with problems as multinational managers find themselves in the position of deciding what is best for society in a culture that may be foreign to them. Even the best advised and intended balancing can result in paternalism. Still, in many situations, managers simply have no other choice.

While internal constraints may serve for the short run, the long-run solution calls for an improvement in the regulatory environment, an activity that may be enhanced by multinational participation. Firms can participate in the regulatory process by sharing information with governmental officials. For example, the multi-country intelligence networks of multinationals and their ongoing research into many local markets generates information often not available to national governments and seldom, if ever, to local officials. Moreover, the typical shallowness of regulatory staffs often prevents the collection and evaluation of data to which they do have access. The sharing of information about the capital-labor ratio of transferred technology was outlined in chapter 9. In chapter 10 Powers has outlined specific kinds of information that multinationals could share with local officials relative to the entry decision.

Sharing information with host country regulators involves a shift in corporate policy from an adversarial negotiating stance to one of participation. And, of course, information is shared with no assurance that it will not be used against the firm.

When the regulatory process itself is inadequate, managers must proceed with great caution. Attempts to change flawed governmental practices incur the danger of political meddling.

Interview Findings

In general, we found that the host country regulation of multinational corporate entry was quite sophisticated for industrial firms, whereas the post-entry operational regulation was inadequate. For banks, the reverse held: Entry was more a function of political decisions than potential contributions, while operational regulation was highly sophisticated.

In the industrial sector, regulators are using the multinational competition for entry to provide information not available to the host country, such as, for example, the potential for local products to compete on the world market, or data that could have been collected by the host country such as capabilities of local suppliers. In the situations that we encountered, the balance of power in entry negotiations had clearly shifted to the potential host countries. This is probably also the case for major expansion decisions. We did not identify any abandonment situations.

Once assets are in place in a host country, host governments have more power to impose their will on the corporation. But, they do not seem to be using this post-investment power effectively. Regulatory signals are difficult to interpret or appear to be confused, and the rules of the game are in a state of flux in many countries. These kinds of regulatory regimes add to the perceived risk on the part of multinational managers and encourage them to push for higher returns as a means of compensating for this risk. In these cases, it is the process that needs revision. As indicated, multinational participation in modifying regulatory processes is a more tenuous undertaking than sharing information.

An organizational issue is the level at which discussions with host country regulators should take place. For entry decisions, since there is not local management, these discussions must clearly be at the headquarters level. For expansion and operating decisions, most firms rely on their local managers for the direct interaction. Headquarters staffs are available to assist in these endeavors, but they generally become involved only at the request of the local manager.

In contrast to the generally ineffective regulation of industrial operations, central bank regulation has often been more creative than that existing in the developed countries. As an example, the Central Bank of Brazil invited private banks, primarily multinationals, to participate in a program of financing agricultural cooperatives. Executives of the Central Bank asked the private banking system to undertake the training of cooperative financial officers as well as to participate in supplying credit. The net result was a remarkable improvement of the credit worthiness of many cooperatives, to the point where they became good credit risks and profitable accounts for the private banking sector.

SUMMARY

Managing the social aspects of developmental responsibility is central to the effective response of multinational corporations to the needs of the Third World. The literature is replete with statements as to how multinational firms should be controlled by various national and international bodies. What is missing is the crucial other side of the issue: How can well-intentioned firms respond to conditions encountered in the Third World, and how do executives position their firms to most effectively manage this response?

This paper has addressed three components of the task: (1) the usefulness of statements of purpose, such as credos or internal codes of conduct, in creating a managerial culture and directing actions toward the needs of local peoples; (2) the need for, and problems associated with, meeting the unique requirements of each operating site; and (3) the need for creative policies in dealing with local regulatory regimes.

These three points serve only as a beginning thrust in a vital area of concern. The issues and problems associated with managing multinational responsibilities are the subject of continuing research on the part of our seminar.

NOTES

1. See especially chapters 9 and 10.
2. It should be noted that the dominance of strategic factors over capital investment analysis, while serving developmental needs, runs counter to the thrust of academic research in finance. Over the past two decades, academicians have concentrated on the determination of criterion rates to the exclusion of other considerations in capital investment decisions.

3. See chapter 7.

4. In the seminar discussion this statement caused the greatest controversy among the participants. Although most of the executives agreed with the first part of the statement, and indicated that their firms stressed decentralization as a management objective, many disagreed with the statement that financial controls tend to reduce flexibility at the local levels.

EXHIBIT A
Our Credo
JOHNSON & JOHNSON

We believe our first responsibility is to the doctors, nurses and patients, to mothers and all others who use our products and services. In meeting their needs everything we do must be of high quality. We must constantly strive to reduce our costs in order to maintain reasonable prices. Customers' orders must be serviced promptly and accurately. Our suppliers and distributors must have an opportunity to make a fair profit.

We are responsible to our employees, the men and women who work with us throughout the world. Everyone must be considered as an individual. We must respect their dignity and recognize their merit. They must have a sense of security in their jobs. Compensation must be fair and adequate, and working conditions clean, orderly and safe. Employees must feel free to make suggestions and complaints. There must be equal opportunity for employment, development and advancement for those qualified. We must provide competent management, and their actions must be just and ethical.

We are responsible to the communities in which we live and work and to the world community as well. We must be good citizens—support good works and charities and bear our fair share of taxes. We must encourage civic improvements and better health and education. We must maintain in good order the property we are privileged to use, protecting the environment and natural resources.

Our final responsibility is to our stockholders. Business must make a sound profit. We must experiment with new ideas. Research must be carried on, innovative programs developed and mistakes paid for. New equipment must be purchased, new facilities provided and new products launched. Reserves must be created to provide for adverse times. When we operate according to these principles, the stockholders should realize a fair return.

A Code of Worldwide Business Conduct
CATERPILLAR TRACTOR CO.

To Caterpillar People:

Large corporations are receiving more and more public scrutiny.

This is understandable. A sizable economic enterprise is a matter of justifiable public interest—sometimes concern—in the community and country where it's located. And when substantial amounts of goods, services and capital flow across national boundaries, the public's interest is, logically, even greater.

Not surprisingly then, growth of multinational corporations has led to increasing public calls for standards, rules, and codes of conduct for such firms.

Three years ago, we concluded it was timely for Caterpillar to set forth *its own beliefs,* based on ethical convictions and international business dating back to the turn of the century.

Experience since then has demonstrated the practical utility of this document—particularly as a means of confirming, for Caterpillar people, the company's operating principles and philosophies.

This revised "Code of Worldwide Business Conduct" is offered under the several headings that follow. Its purpose continues to be to guide us, in a broad and ethical sense, in all aspects of our worldwide business activities.

Of course, this code isn't an attempt to prescribe actions for every business encounter. It *is* an attempt to capture basic, general principles to be observed by Caterpillar people everywhere.

To the extent our actions match these high standards, such can be a source of pride. To the extent they don't (and we're by no means ready to claim perfection), these standards should be a challenge to each of us.

No document issued by Caterpillar is more important than this one. I trust my successors will cause it to be updated as events may merit. And I also ask that you give these principles your strong support in the way you carry out your daily responsibilities.

W. L. Naumann
Chairman of the Board
Issued October 1, 1974
Revised September 1, 1977

OWNERSHIP AND INVESTMENT

In the case of business investment in any country, the principle of mutual benefit to investor and country should prevail.

We affirm that Caterpillar investment must be compatible with social and economic priorities of host countries, and with local customs, tradition and sovereignty. We intend to conduct our business in a way that will earn acceptance and respect for Caterpillar, and allay concerns — by host country governments — about multinational corporations.

In turn, we are entitled to ask that such countries give consideration to our need for stability, business success and growth; that they avoid discrimination against multinational corporations; and that they honor their agreements, including those relating to rights and properties of citizens of other nations.

Law and logic support the notion that boards of directors are constituted to represent shareholders, the owners of the enterprise. We have long held the view that Caterpillar board members can best meet their responsibilities of stewardship to shareholders if they are appointed solely by them — and not by governments, labor unions or other non-owner groups.

Board composition and board deliberations should be highly reflective of the public interest. We believe that is a basic, inseparable part of stewardship to shareholders.

We recognize the existence of arguments favoring joint ventures and other forms of local sharing in the ownership of a business enterprise.

Good arguments also exist for full ownership of operations by the parent company: the high degree of control necessary to maintain product uniformity and protect patents and trademarks, and the fact that a single facility's profitability may not be as important (or as attractive to local investors) as its long-term significance to the integrated, corporate whole.

Caterpillar's experience inclines toward the latter view — full ownership — but with the goal of worldwide ownership of the total enterprise being encouraged through listing of parent company stock on many of the world's major stock exchanges.

Since defensible arguments exist on both sides of the issue, we believe there should be freedom and flexibility — for negotiating whatever investment arrangements and corporate forms best suit the long-term interests of the host country and the investing business, in each case.

CORPORATE FACILITIES

Caterpillar facilities are to be located wherever in the world it is most economically advantageous to do so, from a long-term standpoint.

Decisions as to location of facilities will, of course, consider such conventional factors as proximity to sources of supply and sales opportunities, possibilities for volume production and resulting economies of scale, and availability of a trained or trainable work force. Also considered will be political and fiscal stability, demonstrated governmental attitudes, and other factors normally included in defining the local investment or business "climate."

We don't seek special treatment in the sense of extraordinary investment incentives, assurances that competition from new manufacturers in the same area will be limited, or protection against import competition. However, where incentives have been offered to make local investment viable, they should be applied as offered in a timely, equitable manner.

We desire to build functional, safe, attractive facilities to the same high standard worldwide, but with whatever modifications are appropriate to make them harmonious with national modes. They are to be located so as to complement public planning, and be compatible with local environmental considerations.

Facility operations should be planned with the long-term view in mind, in order to minimize the impact of sudden change on the local work force and economy. Other things being equal, preference will be given to local sources of supply.

RELATIONSHIPS WITH EMPLOYEES

We aspire to a single, worldwide standard of fair treatment of employees. Specifically, we intend:

(1) To select and place employees on the basis of qualifications for the work to be performed—without discrimination in terms of race, religion, national origin, color, sex, age or handicap unrelated to the task at hand.

(2) To protect the health and lives of employees. This includes maintaining a clean, safe work environment free from recognized health hazards.

(3) To maintain uniform, reasonable work standards, worldwide, and strive to provide work that challenges the individual—so that he or she may feel a sense of satisfaction resulting from it.

(4) To make employment stabilization a major factor in corporate decisions. We shall, among other things, attempt to provide continuous employment, and avoid capricious hiring practices.

(5) To compensate people fairly, according to their contributions to the company, within the framework of national and local practices.

(6) To foster self-development, and assist employees in improving and broadening their job skills.

(7) To promote from within the organization—in the absence of factors that persuasively argue otherwise.

(8) To encourage expression by individuals about their work, including ideas for improving the work result.

(9) To inform employees about company matters affecting them.

(10) To accept without prejudice the decision of employees on matters pertaining to union membership and union representation; and where a group of employees is lawfully represented by a union, to build a company-union relationship based upon mutual respect and trust.

(11) To refrain from hiring persons closely related to members of the board of directors, administrative officers and department heads. If other employees' relatives are hired, this must be solely the result of their qualifications for jobs to be filled. No employee is to be placed in the direct line of authority of relatives. We believe that nepotism—or the appearance of nepotism—is neither fair to employees, nor in the long-term interests of the business.

PRODUCT QUALITY

A major Caterpillar objective is to design, manufacture and market products of superior quality. We aim at a level of quality which offers special superiority on demanding applications.

We define quality as the sum of product characteristics and product support which provides optimum return on investment to both the customer and Caterpillar.

Caterpillar products are designed to the same exacting standards, and manufactured to uniformly high levels of quality, throughout the world. Maximum interchangeability of components and parts is maintained—wherever they are manufactured.

We strive to assure users of timely after-sale parts and service availability at fair prices. From our experience, these goals are best achieved through locally based, financially strong, independently owned dealers committed to service. We back availability of parts from dealers with a worldwide network of corporate parts facilities.

We believe pursuit of quality also includes providing products responsive to the need for lower equipment noise levels, compliance with reasonable emissions standards, and safe operating characteristics. We continually monitor the impact of Caterpillar products on the environment—striving to minimize any potentially harmful aspects, and maximize their substantial capability for beneficial contributions.

SHARING OF TECHNOLOGY

Caterpillar takes a worldwide view of technology. We view technology transfer in a broad context—as sharing information, from many varied business functions, aimed at improved company operations everywhere.

We therefore provide design and manufacturing data, and marketing and management know-how, to all Caterpillar facilities, while observing national restrictions on the transfer of information. Managers are encouraged to participate in professional and trade societies. Managers are provided access, on a worldwide basis, to corporate technical competence which is appropriate to their jobs.

We seek the highest level of engineering technology, regardless of origin, applicable to our products and manufacturing processes. We locate engineering facilities in accordance with need, on a global basis. We encourage equitable relationships with inventors, consultants, and research and development laboratories that have technical capabilities compatible with our needs.

We believe the principal threat to future relationships among nations has to do with the widening gap between living standards in industrial and developing countries. Intelligent transfer of technology is a major means by which developing countries can be helped to do what they must ultimately do—help themselves.

However, technology transfer is dependent not only on the ability of people in one nation to offer it, but also on the ability of people in other nations to utilize it. We therefore encourage developing countries to create an environment of law and custom that will maximize such utilization. We support effective industrial property laws, reasonable licensing regulations, and other governmental initiatives which encourage sharing of existing technology with such countries.

Technology is property; it requires time, effort and money to create, and has value. We believe governments can foster the spread of technology by permitting a reasonable return for its transfer.

Finance

The main purpose of money is to facilitate trade. Any company involved in international trade is, therefore, involved in dealing in several of the world's currencies, and in exchanging currencies on the basis of their relative values.

Our policy is to conduct such currency transactions only to the extent they may be necessary to operate the business and protect our interests.

We buy and sell currencies in amounts large enough to cover requirements for the business, and to protect our financial positions in those currencies whose relative values may change in foreign exchange markets. We manage currencies the way we manage materials inventories—attempting to have on hand the right amounts of the various kinds and specifications used in the business. We don't buy unneeded materials or currencies for the purpose of holding them for speculative resale.

Intercompany Pricing

Our intercompany pricing philosophy is that prices between Caterpillar companies are established at levels equivalent to those which would prevail in arm's length transactions. Frequently, such transactions are between Caterpillar companies in different countries. Caterpillar's intercompany pricing philosophy assures to each country a fair valuation of goods and services transferred—for tariff and income tax purposes.

Accounting and Financial Records

Accounting is called the "universal language" of business. Therefore, those who rely on the company's records—investors, creditors, and other decision makers and interested parties—have a right to information that is timely and true.

The integrity of Caterpillar accounting and financial records is based on validity, accuracy, and completeness of basic information supporting entries to the company's books of account. All employees involved in creating, processing, or recording such information are held responsible for its integrity.

Every accounting or financial entry should reflect exactly that which is described by the supporting information. There must be no concealment of information from (or by) management, or from the company's independent auditors.

Employees who become aware of possible omission, falsification, or inaccuracy of accounting and financial entries, or basic data supporting such entries, are held responsible for reporting such information. These reports are to be made as specified by corporate procedure.

DIFFERING BUSINESS PRACTICES

While there are business differences from country to country that merit preservation, there are others which are sources of continuing dispute and which tend to distort and inhibit—rather than promote—competition. Such differences deserve more discussion and resolution. Among these are varying views regarding competitive practices, boycotts, information disclosure, international mergers, accounting procedures, tax systems, transfer pricing, product labeling, labor standards, repatriation of profit, securities transactions, and industrial property and trademark protection laws. We favor more nearly uniform practices among countries. Where necessary, we favor multilateral action aimed at harmonization of differences of this nature.

COMPETITIVE CONDUCT

Fair competition is fundamental to continuation of the free enterprise system. We support laws prohibiting restraints of trade, unfair practices, or abuse of economic power. And we avoid such practices everywhere—including areas of the world where laws do not prohibit them.

In large companies like Caterpillar, particular care must be exercised to avoid practices which seek to increase sales by any means other than fair merchandising efforts based on quality, design features, productivity, price and product support.

In relationships with competitors, dealers, suppliers and users, Caterpillar employees are directed to avoid arrangements restricting our ability to compete with others—or the ability of any other business organization to compete freely and fairly with us, and with others.

There must be no arrangements or understandings, with competitors, affecting prices, terms upon which products are sold, or the number and type of products manufactured or sold—or which might be construed as dividing customers or sales territories with a competitor.

Suppliers aren't required to forgo trade with our competitors in order to merit Caterpillar purchases. Caterpillar personnel shall avoid arrangements or understandings prohibiting a supplier from selling products in competition with us, except where: (1) the supplier makes the product with tooling or materials owned by Caterpillar; or (2) the product is one in which the company has a proprietary interest which has been determined to be legally protectable. Such an interest might arise from an important contribution by Caterpillar to the concept, design, or manufacturing process.

No supplier is asked to buy Caterpillar products in order to continue as a supplier. The purchase of supplies and services is determined by evaluations of quality, price, service, and the maintenance of adequate sources of supply—and not by whether the supplier uses Caterpillar products.

Relationships with dealers are established in the Caterpillar dealership agreements. These embody our commitment to fair competitive practices, and reflect customs and laws of various countries where Caterpillar products are sold. Our obligations under these agreements are to be scrupulously observed.

OBSERVANCE OF LOCAL LAWS

A basic requirement levied against any business enterprise is that it know and obey the law. This is rightfully required by those who govern; and it is well understood by business managers.

However, a corporation operating on a global scale will inevitably encounter laws which vary widely from country to country. They may even conflict with each other.

And laws in some countries may encourage or require business practices which—based on experience elsewhere in the world—we believe to be wasteful or unfair. Under such conditions it scarcely seems sufficient for a business manager to merely say: we obey the law, whatever it may be!

We are guided by the belief that the law is not an end but a means to an end—the end presumably being order, justice, and, not infrequently, strengthening of the governmental unit involved. If it is to achieve these ends in changing times and circumstances, law itself cannot be insusceptible to change or free of criticism. The law can benefit from both.

Therefore, in a world characterized by a multiplicity of divergent laws at international, national, state and local levels, Caterpillar's intentions fall in two parts: (1) to obey the law; and (2) to offer, where appropriate, constructive ideas for change in the law.

BUSINESS ETHICS

The law is a floor. Ethical business conduct should normally exist at a level well above the minimum required by law.

One of a company's most valuable assets is a reputation for integrity. If that be tarnished, customers, investors and employees will seek affiliation with other, more attractive companies. We intend to hold to a single high standard of integrity everywhere. We will keep our word. We will not promise more than we can reasonably expect to deliver; nor will we make commitments we don't intend to keep.

In our advertising and other public communications, we will avoid not only untruths, but also exaggeration, overstatement and boastfulness.

Caterpillar employees shall not accept costly entertainment or gifts (excepting mementos and novelties of nominal value) from dealers, suppliers, and others with whom we do business. And we will not tolerate circumstances that produce, or reasonably appear to produce, conflict between personal interests of an employee and interests of the company.

We seek long-lasting relationships—based on integrity—with employees, dealers, customers, suppliers and all whose activities touch upon our own.

Relationships with Public Officials

In dealing with public officials, as with private business associates, Caterpillar will utilize only ethical commercial practices. We won't seek to influence sales of our products (or other events impacting on the company) by payments of bribes, kickbacks or other questionable payments.

Caterpillar employees will take care to avoid involving the company in any such activities engaged in by others. We won't advise or assist any purchaser of Caterpillar products, including dealers, in making or arranging such payments. We will actively discourage dealers from engaging in such practices.

Payments of any size to induce public officials to fail to perform their duties—or to perform them in an incorrect manner—are prohibited. Company employees are also required to make good faith efforts to avoid payment of gratuities or "tips" to certain public officials, even where such practices are customary. Where these payments are as a practical matter unavoidable, they must be limited to customary amounts; and may be made only to facilitate correct performance of the officials' duties.

Public Responsibility

We believe there are three basic categories of possible social impact by business:

(1) First is the straightforward pursuit of daily business affairs. This involves the conventional (but often misunderstood) dynamics of private enterprise: developing desired goods and services, providing jobs and training, investing in manufacturing and technical facilities, dealing with suppliers, paying taxes, attracting customers, earning a profit.

(2) The second category has to do with conducting business affairs in a *way* that is socially responsible. It isn't enough to design, manufacture and sell useful products. A business enterprise should, for example, employ people without discrimination, see to their job safety and the safety of its products, help protect the

quality of the environment, and conserve energy and other valuable resources.

(3) The third category relates to initiatives beyond our operations, such as helping solve community problems. To the extent our resources permit—and if a host country or community wishes—we will participate selectively in such matters, especially where our facilities are located. Each corporate facility is an integral part of the community in which it operates. Like individuals, it benefits from character building, health, welfare, educational and cultural activities. And like individuals, it also has citizen responsibilities to support such activities.

All Caterpillar employees are encouraged to take part in public matters of their individual choice. Further, it is recognized that employee participation in political processes—or in organizations that may be termed "controversial"—can be public service of a high order.

But partisan political activity is a matter for individual determination and action. While Caterpillar may support efforts to encourage political contributions by individual employees, the company won't make contributions to political parties and candidates—even where local law may permit such practices.

Where its experience can be helpful, Caterpillar will offer recommendations to governments concerning legislation and regulation being considered. Further, the company will selectively analyze and take public positions on *issues* that have a relationship to operations, when our experience can add to the understanding of such issues.

DISCLOSURE OF INFORMATION

The basic reason for existence of any company is to serve the needs of people. In a free society, institutions flourish and businesses prosper only by customer acceptance of their products and services, and by public acceptance of their conduct.

Therefore, the public is entitled to a reasonable explanation of operations of a business, especially as those operations bear on the public interest. Larger economic size logically begets an increased responsibility for such public communication.

In pursuit of these beliefs, the company will:

(1) Respond to reasonable public inquiries — including those from the press and from governments — with answers that are prompt, informative and courteous.

(2) Keep investors and securities trading markets informed about Caterpillar on a timely, impartial basis.

INTERNATIONAL BUSINESS

We believe the pursuit of business excellence and profit — in a climate of fair, free competition — is the best means yet found for efficient development and distribution of goods and services. Further, the international exchange of goods and services promotes human understanding, and thus harmony and peace.

These are not unproven theories. The enormous rise in post-World War II gross national product and living standards in countries participating significantly in international commerce has demonstrated the benefits to such countries. And it has also shown their ability to mutually develop and live by common rules, among them the gradual dismantling of trade barriers.

One of the world's first priorities is to find more effective ways of bringing similar improvement to those developing countries whose participation in the international exchange of goods and services is relatively limited.

As a company that manufactures and distributes on a global scale, Caterpillar recognizes the world is an admixture of differing races, religions, cultures, customs, political philosophies, languages, economic resources and geography. We respect these differences. Human pluralism can be a strength, not a weakness; no nation has a monopoly on wisdom.

It is not our aim to attempt to remake the world in the image of any one country. Rather, we hope to help improve the quality of life, wherever we do business, by serving as a means of transmission and application of knowledge that has been found useful elsewhere. We intend to learn and benefit from human diversity.

We ask all governments to permit us to compete on equal

terms with competitors. This goes beyond the influence a country can exert on our competitiveness within its national boundaries. It also applies to the substantial way a government can control or impact on our business in *other* lands — through domestic taxes and regulations affecting the price of products to be exported, and through "host country" laws affecting our operations outside that country.

We aim to compete successfully in terms of design, manufacture and sale of our products, not in terms of artificial barriers and incentives.

REPORTING CODE COMPLIANCE

Each officer, subsidiary head, plant or parts department manager, and department head shall prepare a memorandum by the close of each year: (1) affirming a full knowledge and understanding of this Code; and (2) reporting any events or activities which might cause an impartial observer to conclude that the Code hasn't been fully followed. These reports should be sent directly to the company's General Counsel, General Offices; Peoria, Illinois.

Multinational Social and Economic Influence: A Case Study

PART III CONTAINS A report and critiques of the main research activity undertaken by the seminar: an evaluation of the Castle & Cooke pineapple growing operation in the southern Philippines—its Dolefil subsidiary. Two dimensions of the research activity are reported: the evidence collected by the research team, and evaluations of that evidence by three seminar participants.

The study of Dolefil was initiated as a means of moving the seminar from the general conceptual level to a more specific discussion of how multinationals might respond to poverty in the Third World. The present report is the result of a two-year study by a team of executives and academics attempting to analyze as objectively as possible the results of the Dolefil presence in the southern tip of the island of Mindanao in the Philippines. Over the two-year period, six seminar participants actually visited the site for brief studies of one to four weeks.

The project focused on the local community in an attempt to clarify how the people's lives changed as a result of the Dolefil presence. The report is the result of extensive interviewing of local managers, Dolefil headquarters personnel, and among church groups that have taken issue with Dolefil over its Philippine activities. The team believes its report presents an objective picture of the situation.

For the seminar dialogue, three participants who had not been involved in the study were invited to serve as "issue focusers." They were asked to review the data from their own perspective and to evaluate the impact of Dolefil's presence. Their comments are included in chapter 13.

The Dolefil study contributed an important focus for the

seminar. On the one hand, it provided specific examples for the various issues under consideration. On the other hand, participants found that the understanding drawn from the study could be meaningful for multinationals other than agribusinesses or firms producing for export. Furthermore, debate over the Dolefil impact and whether it could, in fact, be judged in the restricted context of the southern Philippines, or whether it should be evaluated as a fractional part of the global system, greatly enhanced the group's understanding of the nature of the conflict over multinational corporate presence in the Third World.

12. The Dolefil Operation in the Philippine Islands

YUSAKU FURUHASHI, REV. DONALD McNEILL, C.S.C., AND JOHN P. THORP

THE DOLEFIL STUDY WAS undertaken as a means of filling the perceived gaps in the comprehensive studies and published materials in the areas of our concern, as well as supporting the continuing dialogue of the seminar. From seminar discussions it emerged that the subject of multinational corporate impact on Third World peoples should be one of the specific areas of the group's concern for research. It was therefore agreed that an exploratory case study of a multinational business firm in a Third World society would be undertaken in order to establish as objective a data base as possible, the reliability of which can be broadly agreed upon by all seminar participants. In other words, the case study was intended to be: (1) a presentation of objective information and data relevant to the discussion of major issues involved in a multinational business firm in a Third World society, and (2) a medium for the discussion and interpretation of concrete data about issues by persons with diverse world views.

The case selected was the pineapple operation of Castle & Cooke, Inc., on the island of Mindanao, the Philippines. Dole Philippines, Inc. (Dolefil) was not singled out as typical of all multinational business or even multinational agribusiness. Rather, there had been criticism of Castle & Cooke, both in this country and in the Philippines (by groups represented in the seminar), so it seemed to offer a good case for study. Most importantly, the management of Castle & Cooke consented to cooperate in our effort to develop the study.

Major issues that emerged in the course of the study are presented without making specific evaluations. Although some issues may include contradictory perspectives or implications, and some may be refuted on some "obvious" ground by groups closely associated to the case situation, most of the major issues are presented so that they can be discussed and evaluated from the different world views of the seminar participants.

By design the study is limited in scope. A case study can be posited on four different levels of analysis:

1. *At the global, or macro, level,* a case could be written to examine Dolefil as an integral part of the multinational corporate system, representing a form of large-scale economic organization operating predominantly in the market-directed economies (vis-à-vis other forms of the politico-socio-economic system). At this level of analysis, a variety of philosophical and conceptual issues on multinational business corporations may be raised and debated — multinational corporations as a "sinful structure" in "savage capitalism," versus a "good, efficient institution"; the power of multinationals; their ownership and control; the issue of human rights as it relates to Third World economic development; the United Nations New International Economic Order (NIEO) declaration; and so forth.

2. *At an intermediate categorical level,* a case could be written to examine various dimensions and issues surrounding the multinational corporations operating in the Third World, as a group.

3. *At the firm level,* a comprehensive case could be developed to examine Castle & Cooke as a large, integrated, multinational agribusiness operation, covering all geographic locations, functions, etc.

4. *At the atomistic level,* a case could be developed to describe Dolefil operations in the Philippines, in the South Cotabato Province in particular.

This study is basically confined to the fourth level of analysis. It is recognized that a comprehensive evaluation of Dolefil operations in South Cotabato Province can be made only in the context of the larger, more comprehensive issues of the multinational corporate system. Nevertheless, for the sake of manageability and compactness within the limitations of the project, it has been decided that the case would be limited primarily to an atomistic level analysis of Castle & Cooke's operations present in South Cotabato.

An important aspect of the complicated issues that emerged and were considered here is what may be called a *micro-macro dilemma*. Stated succinctly, the micro-macro dilemma refers to the difficulties encountered in establishing the direct linkage between micro (business firm) level and macro (nation or society) systemic level problems and solutions for the reason that what seems desirable from the point of view of individual business firms or consumers (acting in their own best self-interests) often appears to turn out to be undesirable for the whole society. Each of the micro-level operations (producers and consumers) may be engaged in some activity which contributes to the operation of the whole system, i.e., to the macro system; however, the aggregate of the individual efforts may fall considerably short of what the society feels it ought to accomplish. In other words, Adam Smith's "invisible hand" may not work as well as some or all of the members of the society would like. Further, proposed remedies for a "bad" situation may help that particular situation, but they may or may not improve the overall operation of the macro-level system.

Many of the questions raised in this study involve this micro-macro dilemma. In a modern society composed of a complex interrelated web of micro operators, each one's seemingly "good" actions (from the viewpoint of self-interest), may or may not benefit the macro system. There may be no "absolutely" right answers to micro-macro problems, and seemingly good answers to micro problems may be bad for the macro system. Thus, before actions to remedy some problems of this kind are undertaken, it is extremely important that we understand both the micro- and the macro-level consequences, if the proposed actions are to be "socially responsible."

The primary objective of the Dolefil Exploratory Case Study has been to examine a number of specific issues that have been raised about the operations of multinational corporations in less-developed countries. The central question, and the one that has been the central guidepost throughout this study, was: "Has the multinational corporation had a positive or a negative effect on the host community in which it operates?" More specifically, this question was: "Has Dolefil's presence in South Cotabato Province had a positive or a negative effect upon the local community, or upon larger segments of Philippine society?"

A further objective was to explore how a positive or negative effect could be related specifically to "poverty" as experienced by persons in the community surrounding the Dolefil operation. In examining this question, we indicate some issues raised about the Dolefil operation by various critics, such as the Passionist Fathers, the Disciples of Christ, the United Church Board of World Ministries. In some instances, the executives from Dolefil had comprehensive answers to these negative statements about their operations. Also, some individual members of these religious groups expressed their personal feelings that Dolefil is doing a fairly good job in some areas in improving the economic lot of its employees.

It is not the purpose of this case study to take a stand on these various criticisms or to provide a comprehensive resolution of the issues for either the company or the company's critics. Rather, the authors hope that the reader will gain some sense of the kind and the scope of the issues that need to be dealt with in the specific context of the Dolefil operation, and will come to appreciate the different world views of company managers, company critics, and local Filipinos. The value dimension of these issues is left to the reader and to the three commentators in the following section.

Three major areas of concern are involved in addressing the central question of the study. They have been elaborated into three series of questions.

First, To what extent can or should a multinational corporation, a profit-seeking institution, be expected to promote human rights and alleviate poverty in the less-developed country in which it is operating? What are an MNC's responsibilities to its stockholders, to its employees, and to the local communities where it operates? What priorities should there be among these responsibilities? and, How can the adversary nature of the argument between MNC executives and activist stockholders be changed into constructive dialogue?

Second, When a multinational is operating in a less-developed country whose government sets the rules for the company, for labor unions, and for other social institutions, how can the MNC contribute to the increase of basic human rights and freedoms, and to the lessening of the extent of poverty in the host country? Also, To what extent should an MNC tailor its operating procedures to traditional customs and values within the culture of the host country? and How are "codes of conduct" or "statements of principles" such as that issued by Castle & Cooke (Exhibit A) to be empirically implemented cross-culturally?

Third, What concrete policy choices are available to an MNC to upgrade the living standards and working conditions of its employees? What policy choices are available to an MNC so that it can contribute to the overall socio-economic development of the local communities where it operates? Also, Are basic changes in corporate structure, day-to-day business practices, and community relations programs of the MNC called for? and How should the multinational corporation relate to other, local social institutions concerned with promoting socio-economic development?

These three areas of concern proceed from the more general to the more specific and localized issues, for which the Dolefil case study provides a focal point for discussion. For this purpose, a number of very specific issues about Dolefil's operations are raised in the main part of the study so that the more generalized issue of corporate economic, social, and possibly political, responsibility for social justice may be seen in concrete terms.

DATA: THE COMPANY, THE PEOPLE, THE WORK

Dole Philippines, Incorporated (Dolefil) is a Philippine subsidiary of Castle & Cooke, a corporation headquartered in Honolulu, Hawaii. It has most of its Philippine operations in South Cotabato Province on Mindanao Island, the second largest of the more than 7,000 islands in the Philippine archipelago (figure 1). The Dolefil operation consists of raising pineapples, which are either shipped fresh to Japan or processed in the cannery to be shipped to many parts of the world. Its plantation is located mainly in the municipality of Polomolok, with some fields in Tupi Municipality and General Santos (figure 2). Canning and other related activities, as well as Dolefil staff headquarters, are located at the Cannery Site, Polomolok.

Compared to the largest of the islands, Luzon, in the north where the capital city of Manila is located, the southern-most island of Mindanao is comparatively underdeveloped economically. South Cotabato was only sparsely populated until about 1939 when General Paulino Santos brought

Figure 1
The Philippine Islands

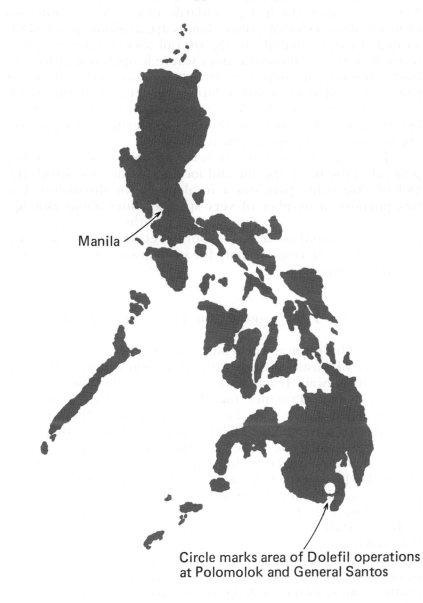

Manila

Circle marks area of Dolefil operations
at Polomolok and General Santos

new settlers, who had been carefully recruited from Luzon and from the Visayan Sea group of islands in the central Philippines, to the settlement in the Koronadal Valley, where there were 97,000 hectares of idle land. Each family was given a home lot and 12 hectares (one hectare is approximately 2.5 acres) of land to till and, eventually, to own. At first the project was subsidized by the government, but gradually the settlers were helped to become more and more self-reliant. Within two years several settlement communities—including Koronadal, Polomolok, and Tupi—developed into organized, thriving, political units, which eventually became part of the new province of South Cotabato with Koronadal as the capital. For the population growth of the province from the immigration of 1939 to 1960, just prior to the start of the Dolefil operation, see table 1. By 1975 the total population of the province was almost 600,000, and at the time this study was made the population just at Dolefil's main site at Polomolok was 59,200, an increase of almost 44,000 people in less than 20 years.

Before Dolefil came into operation in the Polomolok-Tupi area, the area was inhabited by some of the original homesteaders and/or their children who cultivated their 12-hectare

Figure 2

Province of South Cotabato, 1975

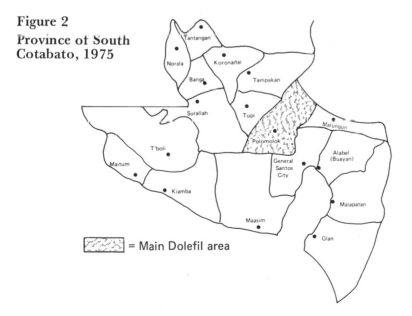

= Main Dolefil area

lots (or lots subdivided among children), raising mainly rice, corn, and sorghum. The uncultivated areas were covered with cogon grass. Apparently, agricultural productivity was considered comparatively low, so that the original 12-hectare lot (before subdividing it among children) was now only adequate to sustain a family with its one carabao (water buffalo). On the hillsides above the homesteaders' areas lived (and still live) "slash-and-burn" cultivators who are descendents of the original inhabitants of this area of Mindanao.

The Land: Ownership and Use

Dolefil began its operation in 1963, and in the ensuing 18 years has become one of the largest plantation-processing operations in the world. It has approximately 10,000 hectares (about 25,000 acres) of land under its control. Of these, 8,000 hectares are leased from the National Development Corporation (NDC), a Philippine government agency, for a 25-year period, subject to renegotiation for lease renewal. Under the rental arrangement, Dolefil pays NDC a rent based on production amount, with a minimum guarantee; the amount of this minimum guarantee is reviewed periodically. Recently, a

Table 1

South Cotabato Province, Pre-Dolefil Population Growth

| Municipality | *Selected Years* | | |
	1939	*1948*	*1960*
Polomolok	na	na	15,536
Tupi	na	na	22,945
General Santos City	14,115	32,019	84,988
Glan	9,364	na	31,320
Kiamba	14,687	15,824	32,358
Maitum	na	na	9,484
Norala	na	na	19,579
Koronadal	19,651	53,563	32,437
Banga	na	na	36,468
Total	57,817	101,406	285,115

Source: Compiled from various population statistics.
na = not available.

modification to the original rental fee has been negotiated, and the new rental fees have been pending, awaiting the Philippine National Executive Office's approval.

The remaining 2,000 hectares have been obtained through Farm Management Contract arrangements with individual owners. Under these contracts, Dolefil can use the land for ten years and has a renewal option. In exchange, individual landowners receive a set annual rent amount (varying among the owners, depending on location and soil condition) per acre, plus a premium based on the quantity of pineapples produced.

Fields are carefully plotted with soil erosion in mind. Blocks of fields are normally laid out across the slopes to reduce the erosion potential. Contours are installed at regular intervals and at a given slope to carry away excess water to natural waterways traversing the plantation.

When the field is prepared, it is planted with crowns or slips. The maturation of pineapples can be chemically controlled so that the first crop is ready to be picked between fourteen and seventeen months after planting. About a year later, the plant will produce a second crop called first ratoon. Then the old pineapple plants are knocked down, dried, and turned under. After a two- or three-month fallow period, a field can once again be properly tilled and a smooth seedbed prepared for replanting. When the fields are prepared, pineapple trash from the cannery also is incorporated back into the soil, thus gradually increasing the organic content of the soil and its fertility. Thus, fields are put into production for three-year periods during which two crops are obtained.

The Dolefil agricultural operations contain different degrees of labor intensity. Planting and harvesting are labor intensive, whereas the rest of the agricultural operations is more mechanized—from bulldozer and tractor operations for soil preparation to spraying mechanisms for insect control and fertilizing.

The company started and continues to maintain its own comprehensive training programs to teach its Filipino employees to use these various machines, thus enabling them to move upward in the company organization. Furthermore, working out the daily logistics for transporting fresh pineapples to the cannery, and for transporting agricultural workers to and from the areas where they live and to and from the different fields for planting and harvesting, requires good planning and

well-coordinated efforts among various departments within
the Dolefil organization.

From the early stages of Dolefil's development, questions
have been raised about the constitutionality and legality of
Dolefil's sublease agreement with the government-owned National Development Corporation for the use of land in Mindanao. The constitutionality issue refers to the 1,024 hectares
(2,530 acres) limitation imposed by the Philippine Constitution
on foreign corporate land holdings. The legality issue refers to
the fact that the NDC was not empowered by law to sublease
public agricultural lands, much less those in excess of the
aforementioned constitutional limitation.

The Dolefil–NDC agreement has also been criticized as
being a heavy blow to the much-heralded land reform program of the government, the declared purpose of which was
to establish owner-cultivatorship and economic family-size
farms as the basis of Philippine agriculture. It is felt that the
incursion of giant plantation companies, both Filipino and
American, into land reform areas like Mindanao has the undesirable effect of reconcentrating land ownership into a few
hands.

In addition, critics of Dolefil question the fairness of the
way the NDC acquired the farmers' plots, which were to be
used eventually by Dolefil, and the low rentals Dolefil allegedly
pays to NDC for the leased lands. Critics point out that
Dolefil's cheap rental arrangements stem not so much from a
comparison with prevailing rates as with its long-term feature,
which greatly favors Dolefil because of currency devaluations
in these periods of inflation. More recently, to meet its expansion requirement, Dolefil has been leasing directly from local
landholders through the aforementioned farm management
contracts. Critics of Dolefil also question the fairness of these
long-term fixed-fee arrangements, again, in an inflationary
period.

Dolefil agronomists have responded that the land is mar-
ginal at best and is, therefore, incapable of producing decent
indigenous food crops, such as corn or highland rice, using
current methods. The social history of Polomolok seems to
support the marginality of this area. Before Dolefil's arrival in
Polomolok, immigrants to South Cotabato for the most part
bypassed Polomolok for areas of South Cotabato further in-
land in the Koronadal Valley. Furthermore, numerous

informants in Polomolok point out that many of those who had attempted to farm the area had abandoned the attempt before Dolefil arrived. Some of these informants also recount with obvious relief their own "sale of land" to Dolefil after having attempted to farm the sandy, rocky, water-deficient soils of the area. Some of the original settlers whose land was more arable and tillable, however, have been successful in their efforts to farm, and they have not felt any need or desire to "sell" to Dolefil.

Given this information about the 10,000 hectares now planted to raise pineapples, questions have often been raised as to whether Dolefil's export-oriented use of this land is more beneficial to the local residents and to the Philippine nation than would be the use of this land for the traditional Filipino family farming.

Finally, critics express their skepticism regarding the announced size of Dolefil's pineapple plantation. While the company's officially announced plantation size has been fairly stable in recent years, they allege that the company has been adding a substantial amount of land at the same time, resulting in a considerably larger area of operation than 10,000 hectares.

Along with the size of Dolefil's land holdings, questions arise about the use, or abuse, of the land. Land erosion, for example, is a serious problem throughout the Polomolok area, and sometimes has been attributed to Dolefil's operations. Floods due to erosion have not only damaged surrounding farms, but have hit Dolefil's operations as well. It is claimed that Dolefil is responsible for the occasional damaging floods and that the floods have become worse since Dolefil's operations started. It is also claimed that such floods are caused by the changed terrain resulting from the process of preparing fields for pineapples, and that fields of pineapple plants do not retain water as well as the wild cogan grass and trees that used to cover much of the uncultivated areas. It is alleged that Dolefil has not paid sufficient attention to this problem, has not done an adequate job of improving the situation, and has not compensated the farmers for the damages caused by the floods.

Dolefil agriculturalists, not surprisingly, will not accept total responsibility for all of the erosion problems. However, they do realize that their procedures within the plantation efficiently channel water out of the plantation where it is a serious problem. Dolefil engages in a number of erosion control procedures such as contouring fields, reorganizing and reshaping the dry creeks, and extensive planting of ipil-ipil trees on creek banks.

Because of these measures, erosion within the plantation has been controlled to some extent. Outside the plantation, however, erosion remains a serious and widely recognized and discussed problem. This is especially true of those areas below the plantation. The widespread local feeling in Polomolok is that Dolefil is entirely responsible for all the erosion problems.

Dolefil representatives, on their side, point out that local farmers have not adopted any control procedures. Instead, their farming practices, such as planting in dry creek beds or on the banks of the creeks after clearing these areas of permanent plants like trees and grasses, increase the likelihood of continued and increasing erosion. They contend that without changes in indigenous methods of farming, erosion cannot be controlled.

What other local social institutions would have to be mobilized besides Dolefil, if these practices were to be changed? Do these institutions have the necessary resources of capital, know-how, and will? Who should have the main responsibility?

As a modern agricultural operation, Dolefil uses substantial amounts of chemicals such as various fertilizers, insecticides, and herbicides, all of which are approved by the U.S. Food and Drug Administration and the Environmental Protection Agency. Also, given a similarity of operations, workers' exposure to these chemicals are substantially the same in the Philippine and Hawaiian operations. People in the Dolefil operational area are allegedly concerned over the increasing amount of fertilizer used, due, presumably, to the continuous deterioration of the soil. They fear that it may one day become unproductive and would lead to Dolefil's pull-out. In case of such an event, it is alleged that the soil would not be fit to raise such local staple crops as rice, corn, and sorghum. It is further alleged that these chemicals are pollutants, and Dolefil is criticized for not taking adequate precautionary measures against skin rashes and the like in the short run. Exposing workers to these chemicals is also seen as a long-term health hazard.

Still another criticism arises from Dolefil's use of modern

equipment to work the land. It is claimed that, although Dolefil employs a large number of people in its agricultural operations, it could do more to alleviate the labor surplus situation by switching to more labor-intensive technology. It is alleged that methods of operation and the degree of mechanization in agricultural operations in the Philippines and in Hawaii are substantially similar, despite very different manpower and capital availability and cost structures in the two areas.

Facilities

In addition to pineapple plantations in the Polomolok-Tupi areas (most of the 10,000 hectares mentioned above are currently under cultivation), Dolefil has various canning and other industrial operating facilities in the area. While little criticism is directed exclusively at these facilities, the issues and criticism can be understood and discussed more intelligently with some knowledge of the operational facilities.

The cannery, a modern, large, mechanized pineapple processing plant, is considered to be the best pineapple cannery in the world. It is located at the Cannery Site, Polomolok, about eight kilometers from downtown Polomolok. Here pineapples from the fields are processed into cans and boxed, and then loaded onto trucks for shipping. Every part of the pineapple is used for something, including the shells, which are either made into cattle feed or processed for field emulsion. Its operation is both capital intensive and labor intensive at various stages.

Several fresh pineapple-packing plants are strategically located throughout the plantation. Fresh pineapples are packed into cardboard boxes according to size, loaded onto trucks, and taken to the dock for loading and shipment to Japan (all the fresh pineapples exported are sent to Japan). The operation at the packing plants is very labor intensive.

Adjacent to the cannery is a modern manufacturing plant which produces cans of various sizes from imported tin plates. The operation here is not as labor intensive as many phases of the canning operation.

Also at the Cannery Site, adjacent to the cannery and the can-making plant, are facilities for the supporting service activities: electric generation, repairs, maintenance, and engineering. Due to the rather remote location of the Dolefil operation, these support services and activities are of the utmost importance. All of the electricity used is generated here; and most of the repair and maintenance of machinery, motorized vehicles, and equipment is completed by Dolefil's own locally trained Filipino personnel. All personnel training is carried out in Dolefil's own training department. A huge inventory of replacement parts is necessary to ensure the smooth and uninterrupted operation of the mechanized processing operations.

Dolefil's staff headquarters is located in the same building as the cannery and can-making plant. Most of the offices are here.

All the water used in the Dolefil facilities in Polomolok is treated at the company's own water treatment plant, which is located several miles away from the cannery. Water comes from a spring-fed stream near the treatment plant.

The paper cartons used for packing are made by Dolefil in its plant at the Calumpang Wharf. It is a highly mechanized plant, utilizing both domestic and imported paper products to make corrugated paper board for a variety of carton boxes.

Calumpang Wharf is the shipping dock for Dolefil and for Stanfilco, another Castle & Cooke Philippine subsidiary. The latter produces bananas in the Davao area primarily and on a smaller scale in the General Santos area. From this modern wharf the two companies ship pineapples (fresh and canned), bananas, and frozen tuna to the United States, Japan, and other parts of the world.

Adjacent to the shipping dock is a large warehouse for storage of canned pineapples without air conditioning. There is also a refrigerated area for the fish and pineapple concentrate. The electric power for the warehouse comes from generators which service the whole Dolefil compound in the wharf area.

Dolefil builds and maintains hundreds of kilometers of dirt roads throughout the plantation. It also maintains many of the provincial roads running through the plantation. Many of the field and service roads are extremely difficult for buses to travel on, thus buses are not used to transport field workers; the same transport method is used in pineapple operations in Hawaii and Thailand.

Employment and Working Conditions

There are approximately 9,000 Dolefil employees now in South Cotabato Province.* This is more than double the number of Dolefil employees of a few years ago, indicating the rapidly expanded operations since the opening of the plantation in 1963. Of this labor force, about one-half are in agricultural operations, about one-third in industrial operations and services, and the rest in administrative and general services activities. Of the 9,000 employees, there are fewer than ten permanent non-Filipino executives, all of whom are in top management.

The General Santos-Polomolok-Tupi area was first settled in the late 1930s, as explained earlier. Even in 1963 when Dolefil began its operations, the area was sparsely populated. The population of Polomolok was 15,500 at that time and has increased in the intervening years to about 37,500 in 1970 and 59,200 in 1980, due largely to the Dolefil operation and to expanding employment opportunities made available, not only to the local population, but also to people from the north. Today, over 60 percent of Dolefil employees are not local people, and people continue to migrate into the area seeking employment opportunities at Dolefil. This migration of people to the area from other islands has been necessitated by the unavailability of a sufficient number of local people, as well as by the need for a more varied skill mix than was locally available for the operation of a huge pineapple plant.

Issues in the area of employment and working conditions seem to center around the general subjects of the role of labor unions, casual workers, and working conditions.

As for the role of labor unions, a well-established tradition of unionization of labor exists in Polomolok, and all permanent employees of Dolefil are members of unions. However, the functioning of the unions as truly representative of their membership and the effectiveness of the collective bargaining power of the unions are frequently questioned by different informants in Polomolok, both because of the often prolonged infighting among the local unions and because of what is perceived to be a paternalistic attitude of the Dolefil management

---

*For Castle & Cooke's "Statement of Principles" on employer-employee relationships see Exhibit A.

in the area of industrial relations. Furthermore, strikes in "vital industries" are banned under martial law, which has been in effect since 1972, and vital industries include companies engaged in foreign exports under which Dolefil is classified.

Dolefil currently has collective bargaining agreements (CBA) with two unions: one representing the technical and office workers, and the other, the Polomolok Labor Union (PLU) representing the industrial and agricultural employees. Other union organizations exist, but they are not unions of record. One union organization, Dole Philippines, Inc. Employees Association (DPIEA), which until recently had the bargaining agreement with Dolefil for the agricultural and industrial workers, is very vocal at the Cannery Site in its opposition to the current CBA holder, PLU. During July 1980 DPIEA broadcast anti-PLU and anti-Dole speeches over loudspeakers in the Cannery Site at the workers' entrance to the cannery complex.

Union officials are regularly presumed to be using their positions to further their own personal financial and political interests, rather than the interests of the union membership. In the case of PLU, the officials representing the agricultural and industrial workers are not themselves currently part of the work force. Only a few seem ever to have been. The unions as social institutions give the impression of having been organized by non-employees or ex-employees who expect to earn their livings as paid intermediaries for the workers. The primary mediatory function of the union officials is seen to be the negotiation of the collective bargaining agreement every three years. Once this has been accomplished, union officials are expected to mediate individual grievances and to politick to ensure their union will be certified when the next agreement has to be negotiated.

The workers themselves are said to have very little understanding that they can and should have input in this process, and to have little awareness of what services and benefits the unions offer. The union members are thought of as dependent upon their officials, as being the persons with the proper skills and prestige to engage Dolefil management. There is little indication that these union officials have any interest in making the workers more involved in their function as intermediaries.

Persons not involved with labor unions in Polomolok generally consider the unions to leave a great deal to be desired when it comes to representing their members' interests. Persons with criticisms of Dolefil's employment practices do not even consider bringing these criticisms to the unions for their consideration and action. Dolefil, on the other hand, regularly interacts with union officials about labor-related issues.

The issue here is whether more participatory and representative labor unions would be in everyone's best interests, and it raises other questions: How can unions become more effective agents of social development? Should a multinational corporation be expected to encourage representative and participatory unions which will then enter into adversary relationships with it? Are churches, perhaps, as social institutions, in a position to promote more participatory unions? Should churches be involved in labor-management issues?

Another issue has been raised with regard to the Dolefil practice of hiring so-called casual workers "for the peak seasons and temporary needs." These workers are ineligible to join the union or to receive a variety of fringe benefits that Dolefil provides to the regular employees. In Dolefil's classification of workers, a "casual" is a probationary employee, a person who remains at the lowest step for a short period of time. By Dolefil's own accounting, few of its workers are at this lowest level. Two-thirds of the work year had been completed in July 1980, and the company had experienced only a 3 percent turnover in its work force. The employment picture in Polomolok by all indications is rapidly becoming very stable. Is it, then, a valid issue?

In regard to working conditions, some complaints stem from the transportation of workers to and from the fields, and others from the allegedly disproportionate working conditions between operations in the Philippines and those in Hawaii.

Transportation to and from the fields is provided by the company. Workers are picked up at certain key locations in Polomolok and other neighboring areas around 5 a.m. by uncovered cargo trucks. The time differential between getting up and the actual start of work is considered extremely long. Furthermore, the uncovered cargo trucks do not provide the workers with protection against sun or rain. Also, male and female workers are transported in the same truck on these trips.

With regard to the working conditions in Hawaii as compared to the conditions in the Philippines, it is alleged that at the Philippine operations there are no covered areas in the fields; safety precautions are less stringent; there are no locker facilities; and there are no buses, only trucks, for transportation.

In addition to these complaints, there is mention of 12-hour cannery shifts and of *de facto* mandatory Sunday work during peak periods as perceived by the employees. Critics of the company find objectionable the company's desire to maximize the use of their machinery by requiring 10- and 12-hour shifts of both cannery and agricultural workers. Given the more relaxed pace of agricultural labor when growing indigenous crops, is it valid to question the company's demands on its workers for so much of their time, even if they receive overtime bonuses? Of major concern to church personnel is the fact that people frequently work on Sundays, and therefore are unable to attend church services. They feel that even optional double-time work on Sundays should not be expected of employees.

Housing and Living Conditions

A larger concentration of persons live in Polomolok Town and at the Cannery Site under urbanlike conditions than live in other towns in South Cotabato Province (figures 3 and 4). Housing is scarce, and conditions are crowded.

Kalsangi, the housing area for top management people of Dolefil, is about five kilometers north of the Cannery Site and 1,000 meters higher on the mountain slope. It is a beautiful, and exclusive, suburban-type housing development. An invitation is required for entrance into the complex. The area has about 55 executive homes, its own school (elementary through high school), a well-manicured nine-hole golf course, a swimming pool, tennis courts, and a clubhouse which serves as the center of various community activities. The vast majority of families living there are Filipino.

At the Cannery Site, there is a residential compound for middle-level managers with several sports and recreational facilities. All of these Cannery Site housing facilities are subsidized by Dolefil.

Housing for hourly workers, also subsidized by Dolefil, is available for 2 percent of the workers. This housing was originally built when Castle & Cooke started their Philippine operations. Dolefil also has two housing development schemes underway whereby two 12-hectare plots, which it controls through a real estate company, are being subdivided and improved so that employees who wish may purchase the land and build their own homes. Dolefil is subsidizing the loans necessary for the implementation of this project, thereby controlling the quality of the structures erected.

The ordinary workers who cannot be accommodated in the subsidized housing must seek housing where they can, often at the exorbitant rates charged by the local inhabitants who take full advantage of the tight housing situation. Housing for these workers generally means no electricity, limited water supply and/or accessibility, and, usually, lower quality housing than that subsidized by Dolefil.

Rents in Kalsangi for executives' families amount to about

Figure 3
Polomolok Municipality, with Subdivisions

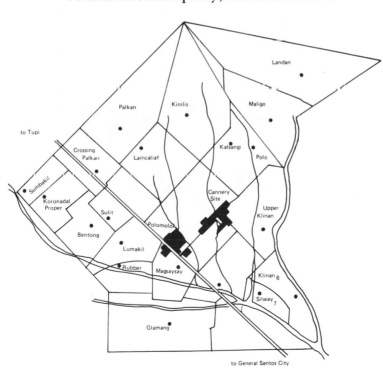

to General Santos City

$18 per month and include water and electricity. The Cannery Site subsidized housing is provided at about $8.50 per month, which includes water and electricity. Housing in Polomolok Town and at the Cannery Site that is not subsidized by Dolefil seems to run from $4 to $7 per month for one small room in a structure composed of many such "rooms."

A smaller but significant number of people do have their own homes, but for the most part they must pay rent for use of the land on which they have constructed their homes. People residing on one 12-hectare plot immediately to the south of the cannery have refused to pay rent to the absentee owner. Technically, they are squatters, but in the Philippines even squatters have certain occupancy rights, which may eventuate in these people becoming the owners of their home sites.

Figure 4
Polomolok Municipality,
The Cannery Site

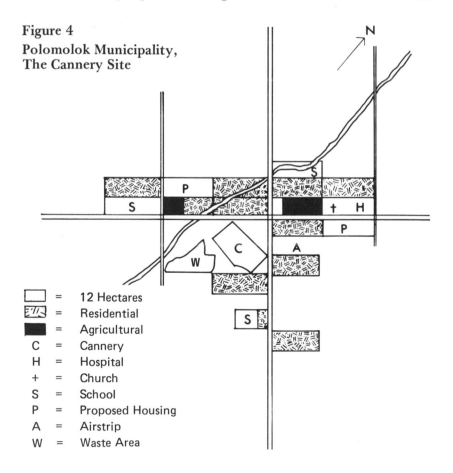

☐	=	12 Hectares
▨	=	Residential
■	=	Agricultural
C	=	Cannery
H	=	Hospital
+	=	Church
S	=	School
P	=	Proposed Housing
A	=	Airstrip
W	=	Waste Area

The tight housing situation in the Polomolok area is only one aspect of the living conditions. Due partly to the rapid increase in population and economic expansion in the last eighteen years since Dolefil came into the area, many of the expected public utility and sanitation facilities have not yet been constructed. Few houses of any size with electricity and modern water and sewer facilities are available in the Polomolok area. As explained later, Dolefil has been helping to expand some of these water and sewer (sealed water toilet) facilities.

Nevertheless, when compared to other communities which apparently are of about the same size and stage of development as Polomolok was before Dolefil started its operation, Polomolok is now much larger, and looks more prosperous. Polomolok seems to have at least comparable or even better public services and housing facilities than such cities as Malungon, which is located about the same distance from General Santos City on the national highway connecting General Santos City and Davao.

Housing and living conditions are, of course, affected by the rise in prices caused by the high rates of inflation which the Philippine economy has experienced in recent years. The high inflation rates of the early 1970s reflected marked increases in the price of fuel, light and water, clothing and food.

Table 2

Consumer Price Index, Southern Mindanao
(All Families, 1972=100)

Items	1973	1975	1977	August 1978
All Items	126.9	170.5	212.1	225.6
Food, Beverages, Tobacco	133.9	168.4	209.2	219.4
Clothing	114.2	188.2	216.7	228.6
Housing	114.4	145.6	216.1	232.4
Fuel, Light, Water	104.0	202.1	221.4	269.7
Services	115.4	160.6	206.1	216.4
Miscellaneous	120.5	190.7	229.8	225.8

Source: National Economic and Development Authority, *1978 Philippine Statistical Yearbook* (Manila, 1979). p. 588.

The situation was exacerbated by a domestic food shortage in the period of 1970 to 1973 which resulted in part from a series of bad harvests. Table 2 shows the rise in the consumer price index from 1973 to August 1978.

Housing is only one example of the relatively high cost of living in the area, and it is taken to be particularly so if it is not subsidized by Dolefil. This higher cost of living is said to be attributable to Dolefil's presence in the area and the subsequent tight market conditions it has created through employment. Housing is also an area where poverty conditions and inequities are seen by the Dolefil critics to be self-evident. One of the questions often raised is: Why do those who seem to need the least receive the largest amount of the company subsidy to substantially reduce the cost of living in order to enable them to maintain disproportionately higher and better living?

Interestingly, many Filipinos living in these conditions do not think of themselves as "living in poverty." Filipinos do not place the same kind of emphasis on housing conditions as Americans do. The Filipino sees himself as being in the process of gradually improving his overall lot in life as he becomes able to take advantage of a variety of productive "opportunities." Dolefil provides a number of such opportunities for employment and entrepreneurship. Renting one room is a first step, but a step to be followed by other steps that will include, eventually, the multiple step process of constructing a home of his own.

For this step-by-step process to occur in the future with any frequency, a great deal more land in Polomolok Town and the Cannery Site will have to be devoted to residential use than is now so used. Where provided with access to land, the Philippine worker will construct adequate and pleasant housing. Who can be expected to provide this land (especially since Dolefil does not own sufficient land) and under what conditions? Which land could best be used, that in the town or the Cannery Sites, or land somewhere else in the municipality? What other social institutions inside and outside of Polomolok will have to be involved in such an undertaking?

The issue of housing and living conditions involves a complex of economic, social, and cultural factors that cannot be simply stated nor easily comprehended by non-Filipinos. Certainly one consideration is the extent to which it is the place or the responsibility of a multinational corporation to organize, or initiate, or even participate in, such housing development schemes.

Similar criticism and problems are also said to apply to food. The complaint seems to be focused on the transportation cost between Polomolok and General Santos City, where food prices are lower. It is claimed that residents of Kalsangi are provided free transportation, while Cannery Site residents must pay half fare. Hourly workers must take public transportation, which would be prohibitive, since these households have no means of storing food and must make the trips often.

In the overall context of living conditions, then, a question most often raised is: Should not the company take direct, specific steps to neutralize the effect of the higher cost of living of its workers and the people living in the community, inasmuch as the very presence of Dolefil has been partly responsible for that comparatively higher cost of living?

Community Services, Welfare, and Development

Inextricably bound up with housing and living conditions is the more generalized question of the overall development of the quality of life in the local community of Polomolok. Dolefil has undertaken a variety of programs in this area.

At the time of the study, Dolefil had just completed a major addition to its 77-bed hospital, enlarging it to a 99-bed capacity. Utilizing corridors and other usable space in case of urgency, the hospital can now accommodate some 120 beds. Eight doctors and one dentist serve the Dolefil employees and their families.

In recent years Dolefil has gradually expanded its community programs intended to aid in improving the quality of life in the communities from which Dolefil draws its employees. The programs are in such areas as water availability, health, sanitation, education, and recreational facilities. Major programs either completed or in the process of completion are presented in table 3 in summary form. From 1973 to 1979 aid to community funding by Dole Philippines, Inc., and Standard Fruit Charities, Inc., amounted to $754,666 (table 4).

Some of the issues raised in connection with these quality of life areas are often inseparable from those raised about housing and living conditions. Some general questions are:

Since the presence and operations of Dolefil have created (or have contributed to the acceleration or aggravation of) these problems, should Dolefil not only remedy the situation but also take specific steps to ensure the continuity of improvement in the living and working conditions and the quality of life of its employees and the community? Is Dolefil doing enough in community affairs, even though it has built new roads, schools, and water systems?

Table 3

Dolefil Community Programs (as of Spring 1979)

WATER AVAILABILITY

Deep-well source with 20,000 gallon storage tank
13 complete outlets around Cannery Site
3 water outlets to be installed

HEALTH

Anti-polio and de-worming of children
Free treatment by foreign specialists; e.g., cosmetic surgery for deformed children
Implementation of Public Health Nursing Program: 3 nurses to be hired in first period of 1979. Program to include home visits, immunization, nutrition, hygiene program

SANITATION

Expansion and implementation of sanitation programs; e.g., garbage disposal, water-sealed toilets, insect spraying

EDUCATION

Summer School Upgrading Program, for elementary school teachers at the Cannery Site
3 classrooms under construction
3 classrooms projected for 1980, along with a high school building.

Table 3 (Cont'd)

Dolefil Community Programs (as of Spring 1979)

RECREATION

Sports: Community basketball courts, tennis courts, bowling alleys; tournaments for employees

Construction of covered basketball court and a Community Recreation Center scheduled for 1980

Entertainment: Movies, amateur singing contests, beauty contests

OTHER

Donation of construction materials, pineapple products

Assistance to civic, religious organizations

Grading purok roads and plazas, school athletic grounds

Source: Dolefil, Company Records

Table 4

Aid to Community Funding, 1973–1979

Year	Amount
1973	$ 41,648
1974	44,496
1975	78,769
1976	95,616
1977	114,480
1978	162,810
1979	216,847
Total	$754,666

Source: Dolefil, Company Records

Another factor to be noted here is that, besides the Dolefil Corporation, three local social institutions are associated with community development issues: the local government, the labor unions, and the churches, especially the Roman Catholic Church. Of these four institutions, whose responsibility is community development?

Some politically active Filipinos in Polomolok clearly hold the local government to be primarily responsible for such development. They point out that Dolefil has contributed millions of pesos in taxes to local government coffers over the years, but past administrations have not used these revenues for any significant community development. As one informant put it, "There is not one inch of paved road in Polomolok Town, not one street light." Nor are there adequate health care delivery systems or garbage and waste disposal systems. Much of the infrastructure that would make possible a higher quality life are absent in Polomolok Town.

This is especially true of the Cannery Site. What infrastructure that exists there has been constructed by Dolefil with the cooperation of community members. Many other local communities approach Dolefil for their assistance in similar community development projects.

Some residents of Cannery Site are trying to establish it as a formal governmental unit separate from Polomolok Town with control over some of the locally raised tax revenues, as one way of rectifying what they consider to be the failure of the local government to respond effectively to their needs.

To what extent can Dolefil go on providing services that are conceived to be local government's responsibility? The central issue here is not so much how one can determine Dolefil's responsibility for the conditions in this community which its presence has contributed to, as it is how can (should) Dolefil contribute to making the local government's administration of its resources more responsive to felt community needs. The same may also be asked of the other two major social institutions in Polomolok: Can (or, how can) the labor unions and the Roman Catholic Church be expected to contribute to encouraging the local political institutions to take increasing responsibility for community development?

Economic Development

The wide variety of the criticisms and questions about the role and effect of Dolefil on the local economy and society notwithstanding, as noted above, Dolefil's presence in Polomolok is often viewed by Filipinos in Polomolok as presenting them with opportunities for their economic advancement. Dolefil operations in Polomolok have expanded substantially since its beginning in 1963, both to its own benefit and to the benefit of the residents of the area.

Dolefil's sales have increased almost fivefold in the last ten years, with sales for the fiscal year 1979 amounting to about U.S. $48 million. Less than 10 percent of sales are for the domestic market. Its products are exported: about two-thirds to the United States, about one-fifth to Japan, and the rest to Europe.

With the substantial amount of salaries and wages paid to local Dolefil employees, and a substantial amount of business done in the procurement of supplies and services with the local businesses as presented in table 5, Dolefil (with Stanfilco in General Santos City) has been a core business around which various local suppliers and service businesses have grown. As mentioned previously, Dolefil has developed extensive training programs in various fields of management as well as in mechanics and engineering, programs conducted by its own training department. Many local nationals who have thus acquired new skills have left the company to start their own businesses or find other employment capitalizing on these salable new skills.

For Dolefil's first ten years the company operated at a loss, a much longer period of loss than was originally projected, and thus the company's capital was seriously eroded. It was not until 1975 that the capital was recovered and a profit shown in the books; since that time most of the profit has been retained internally for expansion or repayment of debts. No dividend payments have been made.

Workers are paid considerably more than the legally required minimum of ₱22.47 per day for agricultural workers and ₱26.12 per day for industrial workers—as of June 1980 approximately 40 percent and 55 percent more, respectively. (The prevailing foreign exchange rate is about 7.4 pesos (₱)

Table 5

Local Purchases and Services Cost, 1978 (Amounts in $000s)

Items (by class)	South Cotabato		Davao		Manila, Others		Tot. Philippine		Imported	Total
	Suppliers	Amount	Suppliers	Amount	Suppliers	Amount	Suppliers	Amount	Amount	Amount
Purchases										
Fuel & Lubricants	2	2,484	1	71	—	—	3	2,555	—	2,555
Fertilizers & Chemicals	2	857	6	760	6	67	14	1,684	1,186	2,870
Materials & Supplies	57	1,814	47	1,451	108	1,510	212	4,775	1,200	5,975
Sugar	—	—	—	—	1	875	1	875	—	875
Machineries & Equipment	2	21	6	66	3	415	11	502	1,275	1,777
Drugs & Medicine	4	196	6	290	3	8	13	494	—	494
Other	7	657	4	94	11	357	22	1,108	—	1,108
Total	74	6,029	70	2,732	132	3,232	276	11,993	3,661	15,654
Percent of total purchases		39		17		21		77	23	100
Services										
Private Trucks	19	595	1	259	—	—	20	854	—	854
Construction	6	1,515	—	—	1	3	7	1,518	—	1,518
Freight & Stevedoring	8	502	—	—	9	121	17	623	—	623
Pilotage Services	1	56	—	—	—	—	1	56	—	56
Medical Services	2	66	—	—	1	22	3	88	—	88
Total	36	2,734	1	259	11	146	48	3,139	—	3,139
Percent of total services		87		8		5		100	—	100

Source: Dolefil, Company Records.

per one U.S. dollar.) Also, the industrial workers' pay is approximately 30 percent higher than that of agricultural workers. Workers also receive a variety of fringe benefits. The average annual take-home pay of both agricultural and industrial workers, including overtime pay, was ₱10,170 in 1980.

The distribution of families by annual household income for 1975 in the South Mindanao Region is as shown in table 6. While more recent statistics are not available, a considerable nominal increase in family income has been made, reflecting the inflation in recent years as discussed in the preceding section. Also, these statistics are "household income" and not "average take-home pay of individual workers."

A major economic issue is, of course, wages. It is certain that Dolefil pays higher wages than its Filipino counterparts and that Dolefil provides more fringe benefits, such as hospital

Table 6

Family Income Distribution, 1975
(Preliminary) South Mindanao Region
(Total families: 301,000)

Pesos Per Year[1]	Percent of Total Families
Less than 1,000	0.1
1,000 — 1,999	9.5
2,000 — 2,999	25.0
3,000 — 3,999	14.0
4,000 — 4,999	14.6
5,000 — 5,999	10.4
6,000 — 7,999	11.8
8,000 — 9,999	6.0
10,000 —14,999	5.9
15,000 —19,999	1.8
20,000 —29,999	0.7
30,000 and over	0.2

Source: Republic of the Philippines, National Census and Statistical Office, *Philippine Yearbook 1979* (Manila, Republic of the Philippines, 1979), p. 597.

1. Rate: U.S. $1= ₱7.28.

and recreational facilities. It is claimed, however, that even such "high" wages are inadequate to provide the average family with the basic necessities of life. Further, it is claimed that, with the profitability of its Philippine operations, workers are entitled to reap "just" benefits for their labor. In terms of labor costs, a huge differential exists between Hawaii and the Philippines, even without taking into account the relative lack of benefits and other incentives for Filipino workers. If a comparable pineapple plantation can be operated profitably in Hawaii, even with such high wages and fringe benefits, Dolefil must reap substantial profit from taking advantage of the lower labor cost, even with a higher cost of shipping the merchandise to the United States.

Are these comparisons and this reasoning valid? Reasonable? Relevant? What would be some of the factual results of dramatic pay increases for Dolefil employees? To begin with, non-Dolefil employees, such as teachers and government employees, already receive less money than employment with Dole brings. Costs are already high and burdensome for these people. Would it be just to further burden them? Would a dramatic increase in Dolefil salaries prompt an equally dramatic increase in prices of a variety of foods and other necessities?

It is claimed that Dolefil's Philippine operations are extremely profitable. The common figure often quoted by outside groups is its extremely high return on equity of 174.3 percent and 76.77 percent in 1970 and 1971, respectively— years when the original capital had not yet been fully recovered. The criticism here seems to boil down to three interrelated questions: (1) Is the profitability officially reported, the "true" profitability of Dolefil? (2) Does not the use of "transfer pricing" mechanisms result in some or most of Dolefil's profit being shifted out of the Philippines? and (3) Are not the Dolefil workers receiving a less-than-fair share of the fruits of their labor because of this "legal but unfair" profit transfer out of the country?

Dolefil's presence in the area is alleged to discourage local entrepreneurs, particularly those trying to penetrate the pineapple market. In the export market, local entrepreneurs face the problem of dealing with foreign buyers, particularly when their volume is small. Dolefil sells no fresh pineapple locally; nevertheless, in the local market, the local farmers allegedly face extreme competition both from Dole and from Del Monte. They are alleged to have stated that Dole was "dumping" its product. "So they taught us how to plant pineapples—they call that transfer of technology. What good is it if we can't sell them?"

As for future availability of economic opportunities, Polomolok has often been viewed as an area where a person not only can sustain himself, but can also get ahead by taking advantage of the opportunities present. First of all, there is employment directly with Dolefil. Second, the company contracts out work to various local businessmen (see table 3). For example, machine shops do repair work, and the company leases a large number of vehicles from private owners. In the case of trucks to transport workers and fruit, the owners also furnish the drivers. Third, there is the area of providing food, clothing, hardware, transportation, and recreational and professional services to the residents of Polomolok. Many residents see Polomolok as an area possessing many more opportunities to be taken advantage of than almost anywhere else in their experience.

Whether this attitude will continue for very much longer remains to be seen. Dolefil representatives say their expansion has stopped and that they can meet their personnel needs from the population already present. Nevertheless, Polomolok's reputation is still attracting immigrants. Further, approximately 50 percent of the current population is under fifteen years of age, and not yet in the work force. Many of these persons, who may not be absorbed into the local work force, will have to seek employment or their opportunities elsewhere. Little thought seems to have been given to where that "elsewhere" might be, except perhaps Manila. This attraction of "primate cities" throughout the countries of South and Southeast Asia has been recognized for years, and it is viewed as causing development problems in these countries.

For years the Philippine government has been attempting to discourage further immigration to Manila. In July 1980 newspaper headlines announced that the government was, in fact, forbidding further immigration to that city. As it is, the news stories recounted, 10,000 new jobs a year are already needed to support the current Manila population. Regardless of whether such a ban can be enforced, its issuance indicates the seriousness of this pattern of attraction to Manila.

Dolefil, as an agricultural operation supporting an urban-like concentration of population, is a rural alternative to concentrating further industrial and commercial developments in urban areas, even outside Manila. Polomolok faces the prospect in the future of having to send its currently young residents outside its boundaries to make their fortunes.

In this connection, then, what are Dolefil's responsibilities to the community as it faces the future? Can Dolefil be expected to expand its employment opportunities within the Polomolok municipality? Can and should Dolefil attempt to attract other employers to the municipality? Is Dolefil responsible for educational programs to prepare the children of the area to discover new opportunities in the future?

Conclusions

We think that our exploratory case study could provide valuable information and assistance to groups trying to develop some kind of constructive dialogue. We are aware of the many ambiguities and the complexities of the issues surrounding the multinational corporate impact on Third World peoples in the years approaching 2000. Some of the history and specific facts surrounding the issues in this case study can provide possible directions for the development of creative dialogue on multinational corporate responsibility in the Third World. Nevertheless, some basic questions persist.

We have been challenged by our discovery of the sincerity of the people on both sides of this debate. Given such sincere belief in their positions and interpretation of evidence, we are compelled to wonder if it is possible to have a dialogue between the multinational corporate managers and social critics representing the interest of the Third World poor, when public statements from the company and church groups take on the flavor of those in Exhibits B and C. How can the parties avoid, or break, the impasse caused by such rigid and polarized positions?

In the study, we have raised a variety of questions about basic issues, as well as about issues specific to the Dolefil case. There are many more issues, to be sure. More importantly, in the specific context of this study, have we identified *all of the truly central issues* which would encourage a meaningful exchange of viewpoints about different interpretations of evidence?

Finally, we must clearly delineate the world views of the parties to the debate. Only when each party becomes aware of the philosophical stances of the other parties involved, can a truly constructive discussion take place. Effective ways must be found to discern "where everyone is coming from."

This case study itself might help shed light on these basic questions.

Statement of Principles
CASTLE & COOKE, INC.

CASTLE & COOKE, INC. SUPPORTS THE FOLLOWING PRINCIPLES:

(1) Respect for the basic civil, social and economic human rights of every individual and protection of these rights for the Company's employees.

(2) Harmonious relationships between employer and employees based on good will and mutually agreed contracts strictly observed.

(3) Recognition of the need to maintain levels of wages, benefits and general working conditions that provide a decent standard of living in terms of the area involved and are competitive in the industry and area involved.

(4) Freedom of the individual worker to join the union of his or her choice (or to refrain from such membership) and for employees lawfully to bargain collectively through representatives of their own choosing.

(5) Condemnation of all use of intimidation or violence in labor-management relations.

(6) Cooperation with governments, civic groups, and employee associations, in the development of employment and general economic opportunities.

(7) Recognition of the important role of stockholders in the corporate enterprise system, and the positive role of good labor relations in ensuring a fair return on their capital and the long-term growth of their company.

(8) Any and all payments made to government officials will be legal and proper in the country where made; will comply with the terms of the Foreign Corrupt Practices Act; will be made pursuant to close financial controls requiring prior approval of appropriate

senior executives of the company, including the president, and will be clearly and accurately accounted for on the books of the corporation. In addition, compliance with this policy will be audited by the Company's internal auditors and reviewed by its independent public accountants and will be reported to the Finance and Audit Committee of the Board of Directors of the Company.

EXHIBIT B
Anti-Business Radicals in Clerical Garb
D. J. KIRCHHOFF

Castle & Cooke has been in business since 1851. We are perhaps better known by our brand names than by our corporate name. We produce and market Dole bananas, pineapple, and mushrooms, Bumble Bee seafoods, and Bud of California vegetables. They account for about 85 percent of our $1.3 billion in revenues. We operate worldwide.

We have 31,000 stockholders, 42 percent are women. Our shares are typically held by small investors. Half of our stockholders own fewer than 200 shares each. Only 10 percent own 1,000 shares or more each.

Some among our stockholders, who own relatively small holdings, say they represent certain church groups and purport to reflect in their resolutions and other actions the attitudes of churches throughout the world. For over three years we have been the target of slander and unwarranted attacks from representatives of some of these church groups and from nonchurch institutions who obviously shroud their anticorporate operations under, or with the assistance of, the clerical garb.

I also want to say that we are encouraged by the responsible and concerned attitude shown by other church leaders, particularly some among the Passionists, the United Christian Missionary Society, and the United Church Board for World Ministries, who do not agree with the radical political posture of some of their peers. We have initiated a constructive and positive dialogue with them, which, hopefully, will lead to a better understanding of the role of the corporation in the

Reprinted by permission from *Business and Society Review,* Winter 1979–80, Copyright 1980, Warren, Gorham and Lamont Inc., 210 South Street, Boston, Mass. D. J. Kirchhoff is president and chief executive officer of Castle & Cooke.

Third World and to the identification of areas of our mutual interest where church and corporation could improve their respective community work.

Yet the attacks continue. Profits, we are told, are immoral; business is ripping off the people; and we are told this also by some of our elected officials and appointed regulators. The successful entrepreneur, yesterday's hero, is today's villain. How did this come about? Is it an awakened public? A better-educated citizenry? Or is there a dedicated, motivated movement attempting to get that message across? I have come to the latter conclusion.

WHERE IS THE MAJORITY?

I am convinced that the majority of church members neither supports nor agrees with the political excesses of some in the clergy, and I am happy to say that we have initiated a good dialogue with responsible leaders in the same church groups who sponsored [the above] resolutions against our management. During our 1979 stockholders' meeting we reiterated a statement of principles, spelling out our corporate beliefs and the ethics that have guided us in the past. The statement satisfied the concerns of those responsible church leaders with whom we are in contact, and we hope that their criteria and better judgment will prevail.

I am still concerned, however, with the persistency and activity of a highly vocal and political minority within those groups. With the support of various pro-Marxists, this activist minority has created tax-exempt institutions to develop strategy, to select target companies, and to coordinate the overall effort of church radicals. One of these institutions, the Interfaith Center for Corporate Responsibility (ICCR), a project of the National Council of Churches, is based in New York City. It is well-financed and staffed, and it counts on extensive research support from the North American Congress on Latin America (NACLA) as well as other organizations in the new left camp, such as the Institute for Policy Studies. That organization has been prominent on the Op-Ed page of the *New York Times* in recent months, defending Vietnam and Afghanistan while attacking U.S. motives in the world.

The World Council of Churches is another source of support for the anti-business movement. Its increased interest in the Third World has been marked by a radical theology and has led to its involvement in direct support of the South African Marxist guerrillas with funds and other resources obtained from various religious congregations. The World Council of Churches has repeatedly protested violations of human rights and directed protests against western democracies and allies for violations of human rights, but it has ignored grievous infractions in Marxist states, such as North Vietnam's treatment of the boat people.

No Gunboats

The age of gunboat diplomacy is over—and a good thing, too. Concerned shareholders and citizens have a right to ask MNCs to be moral in their dealings with employees, customers, and communities in every host nation, according to the needs and priorities established by the government and people of that nation. But shareholders should not in fairness ask businessmen to spearhead political action in foreign countries. They do not have the right to ask an MNC to be an instrument of their personal foreign policy.

Those Marxists who frankly want to end political and economic freedom, and to impose their own values on society, are engaged in a constant search for divisive and abrasive issues that will destabilize free societies. And they are using corporate annual meetings as a primary battleground. The anti-corporate movement blames capitalism for the evils in contemporary society—greed; materialism; fraud; for a growingly inhospitable environment; for the gap between the haves and the have-nots; for society's frustrations and despair. Since capitalism is such an easily identifiable target as the possible cause of humanity's malaise, the solution in the eyes of the critics of our system is an easy one: the replacement of capitalism with a "justice and peace" egalitarian economic system, which can be easily recognized as a centrally controlled economy. I ask those who advocate such a change to show where it has worked for a free people. I have yet to hear an answer from them.

There is mounting opposition in the church's hierarchy

and membership to political church activists who are trying to preach a "contemporary faith" by embarking on social and political causes. Because of this opposition, responsible church leadership will have to cope with the rebellion within its own ranks led by those who, although belonging to a political minority, have announced plans for a continuation of their anti-corporate activity.

Is it not time we ask these church activists to state their vision of society—and what it takes to arrive there? They are always on the attack, but will never indicate their ultimate objective. They love publicity when attacking, but they avoid it like the plague when asked about their real motivation, their objectives, and their ultimate solutions to the problems they are bringing to everyone's attention.

Earlier I alluded to the disenchantment of businessmen with the anti-business feeling of the general public. But could the public feel any differently when avowed enemies of the free enterprise system can impose a tyranny of ideas and push their positions and attitudes into the halls of Congress, the newspapers and broadcast media of America, and the pulpits of our churches?

EXHIBIT C
Multinationals Are Liabilities to the Republic of the Philippines on a Long-Term Basis

Along the highway from Tupi to the wharf in General Santos City, trucks and trailers traverse back and forth. They may be carrying workers to the farms, delivering containers to be loaded on ships, or transporting pineapples straight from harvest.

At the wharf, week after week, boats load the pineapples to overseas export destinations.

In the cannery, as in the surrounding areas, thousands of laborers work, orchestrated so efficiently that today DOLEFIL is reputed, the "IBM" of plantations.

On the surface these are the faces of progress. Employment, taxes, and exports deceive the ordinary Filipino that DOLE is an economic miracle, not only for South Cotabato but for the Republic of the Philippines [R.P.] as well.

There is a growing number of people who refuse to be deceived. We readily concede that DOLEFIL and its sister corporation STANFILCO have provided employment and its benefit to thousands of workers. That it pays taxes and earns badly needed dollars for our government is beyond dispute. That it has done a lot to many people around will be admitted even by the company's harshest critics.

Against the seeming immediate benefit and advantages derived from DOLEFIL and STANFILCO operations, must be weighed the long-term interest of the country's coming generations.

At the heart of the historic continuing dispute in the Philippines are the problems of land holdings and the equitable distribution of the fruits of production.

President Ferdinand E. Marcos staked his martial law and

Translated from *Concern-Marbel Prelature Newspaper* (Marbel, So. Cotabato, Philippines), 2–8 June, 1980, p. 3.

New Society on Presidential Decree No. 27 which is land reform. This is what he calls progress—the emancipation of tenants and distribution of land to the poor. In this light, the operation by DOLE and STANFILCO of thousands of hectares for a highly profitable pineapple and banana export are in the long-run counterprogressive and inimical to national interest. The threat of revolution will hang over the country so long as multinationals operate plantations while many Filipinos remain poor, hungry, and landless.

By its manipulative pricing transfer mechanism plus liberal incentives from the government, DOLEFIL and STANFILCO remit big profits abroad to the mother company, Castle & Cooke in the U.S.A. In effect the DOLE and its mother corporation prosper while poverty remains in the Philippines. The remittances of such profits contribute to social unrest. Again we say that in the long run DOLEFIL and STANFILCO will be a national liability.

A host of other evils attends DOLE's operations which makes this multinational a true enemy of R.P.'s national interest on a long-term basis.

First, it creates ecological damage. The great floods that DOLE has caused in Tupi, Polomolok, and General Santos City are now well-known facts. Erosion has been increasing and right now there are two cases against DOLE in the court of First Instance. The case arose when rampaging torrents of water from the plantation virtually wiped out big portions of productive farms of farmers. To keep production at its peak, even from sandy and non-fertile fields, the company uses highly toxic chemicals which eventually are carried to creeks and waterways which in turn have decimated marine life.

Second, through its pricing transfer the company in effect manipulates our government, and this with impunity.

Third, DOLE, despite its huge profits, has repeatedly violated R.P. labor laws. In 1978 the Ministry of Labor ordered DOLE to reinstate workers it fired in 1966 and told the company to pay millions of back wages and other benefits it unjustly withheld from thousands of laborers.

Fourth, in view of the law of diminishing returns, DOLE and STANFILCO through intensive cultivation exhaust the soil nutrients. Authoritative sources note the increasing use of inputs. If ever the company will pull out, the soil shall have been exhausted. This is dangerous for future generations.

WE PRESENT NO ALTERNATIVES

It is beyond our competence as Christian social workers to present viable economic alternatives. However, we draw from the wealth of both our Christian and cultural heritage certain criteria which should influence more competent bodies in determining viable alternatives. Such alternatives should have the following criteria:

(1) The big plantations must be broken up into small compact farms to be given to Filipino families.

(2) The plan must uphold human dignity, personhood, autonomy, and self-reliance—age-old cultural values. This is in contrast to the regimentation and automation and depersonalization that DOLE's agri-business has made of thousands of workers. Note that R.P. has a 10 percent unemployment problem.

(3) The plan must demechanize work. Energy conservation is a priority national policy.

(4) The alternative plan must place less emphasis on imported farm inputs than the ecological disorder that they cause. Indigenous and organic inputs must be emphasized.

(5) To offset the so-called dollar losses that DOLE eviction might trigger, export crop production should be emphasized. Note well that R.P. now is a rice-exporting country. Rice produced by small farmers is centrally collected, distributed, and marketed by the National Grain Authority. It should be clear once and for all that small farmers can earn dollars for the country, too.

(6) The alternative plan must see to it that cereals and protein in big quantities wouldn't leave our shores to feed overfed first world countries.

I submit that the question of multinational corporations is hard to resolve. The government is in a squeeze. On one hand, the government upholds nationalism, dignity, and rights of the Filipino workers and must protect ecology and the national patrimony. On the other hand, the country immediately needs precious dollars and a disruption of operation of these multinationals will cause massive unemployment and social unrest.

It will take a lot of wisdom for the people and the government to make up their minds on what to do with multinationals operating in our country. A tremendous national will and sacrifice is needed to resolve the issues.

Physical Quality of Life Index (PQLI)
(Selected Countries)

Countries (by income)	Population Mid-Year: 1976 (millions)	Per Capita GNP: 1974 (dollars)	PQLI	Per Capita GPN Growth 1965–1974 (percent)	Birth Rate Per 1000
HIGH (37)[1]	1057.0	4361	95	4.0	17
United States	215.3	6670	96	2.4	15
Netherlands	13.8	5250	99	4.1	14
USSR	257.0	2600	94	3.4	18
UPPER MIDDLE (35)[1]	470.6	1091	67	4.7	36
Brazil	110.2	920	68	6.3	37
Taiwan (ROC)	16.3	810	88	6.9	23
Algeria	17.3	710	42	3.5	49
LOWER MIDDLE (39)[1]	1145.4	338	59	4.4	30
Cuba	9.4	640	86	.3	25
Philippines	44.0	330	73	2.7	41
Low (49)[1]	1341.3	152	39	1.7	40
India	620.7	140	41	1.3	35
Sri Lanka	14.0	130	83	2.0	28
Mali	5.8	80	15	.4	50

EXHIBIT D

Physical Quality of Life Index (PQLI)
(Selected Countries)
(Continued)

Countries (by income)	Death Rate Per 1000	Life Expectancy at Birth (Years)	Infant Mortality Per 1000 Live Births	Literacy (percent)	Per Capita Public Education Expenditure: 1973 (dollars)
HIGH (37)[1]	9	71	21	97	217
United States	9	71	17	99	348
Netherlands	8	74	11	98	331
USSR	9	70	28	100	172
UPPER MIDDLE (35)[1]	10	61	82	65	28
Brazil	9	61	82	66	20
Taiwan (ROC)	5	69	26	85	9
Algeria	15	53	126	26	43
LOWER MIDDLE (39)[1]	11	61	70	34	10
Cuba	6	70	29	78	31
Philippines	11	58	74	83	7
LOW (49)[1]	17	48	134	33	3
India	15	50	139	34	2
Sri Lanka	8	68	45	81	7
Mali	26	38	188	5	2

Source: Compiled from Overseas Development Council, *The United States and World Development: Agenda 1977.*

1. Total number of countries in income bracket.

13. The Impact of the Dolefil Presence: Three Presentations

JOHN B. CARON, WILLIAM P. GLADE, AND

REV. PETER J. HENRIOT, S.J.

I: JOHN B. CARON

WHEN THE SEMINAR WAS initiated Father Hesburgh asked, "Can multinational companies help solve the problem of world poverty?" There was a positive response on the part of many of us in attendance. We shared a feeling that multinationals do have the resources and talent to have some positive impact.

In the attempt to separate rhetoric from the facts, this group inaugurated the Dolefil Study with excellent cooperation from Castle & Cooke. Dolefil was not singled out as being typical of all multinationals but because there has been criticism of Castle & Cooke, both in this country and in the Philippines, so it seemed to be a good case to study.

The results indicate that Dolefil has had a very positive effect on the area of the Philippines in which it is operating and that its workers have acted as good citizens. Land was not taken away from small landowners nor was it diverted from local food production. Jobs were created at wage rates higher than previously available. Education, health services, and recreation were all improved. The puzzling thing is, then, why the condemnation? We could dismiss it as being irrational and uninformed, but I would feel uneasy leaving it at this.

"Multinational" is a dirty word today in many circles. The recent visit of Pope John Paul II to Brazil received extensive press coverage in this country. There was an article in a September 1980 issue of *Forbes* magazine entitled "When

232

Capitalism and Christianity Clash" in which Paulo Evaristo
Cardinal Arns, O.F.M., Archbishop of Sao Paulo, referred to
"savage capitalism." In the interview Cardinal Arns said: "The
church criticizes the consequences of economic systems when
they damage large segments of society. The church also has
criticized hyperconsumption many times as a consequence of
capitalism, especially the multinationals." He said, moreover,
that problems such as inflation and unemployment are "consequences of the installation of the multinational corporations
and of savage capitalism that can produce these ills in order to
reap greater profits later." This is strong condemnation.

The Philippine newspaper *Concern*, published by the
Prelature Social Action Center in Marbel, South Cotabato, acknowledged that Dolefil had done many good things, but it
concluded that multinationals such as Dolefil are bad for their
country even though *Concern* was not able to present an alternative. (Exhibit C)

There seems to be a feeling that development is a zero
sum game, i.e. if somebody is going to profit, another person
is going to lose. Hopefully, everyone can profit—both the
multinational and the people in the country in which the multinational operates. But, first, the facts must be known. Is it
true that development involving multinationals is *not* a zero
sum game? If so, the strident rhetoric of exploitation and de-
humanization must be confronted.

On a global level, the United Nations is calling for the
equivalent of "affirmative action" in the economic policy of
developed countries relative to the Third World. The U.N.
believes that such a plan is called for to compensate for the
years of exploiting cheap raw materials in the Third World
and then selling them back as manufactured products at high
prices—a process that supports the standard of living of the
Western world at the expense of the less-developed countries.
This affirmative action would include higher prices for raw
materials, preferential access to markets for Third World
manufactured products and transfer of technology at little or
no cost.

Multinationals have a stake in these debates. They need to
seriously consider the charges.

The research report itself raises a number of questions
that must be addressed. I would like to add two more basic
issues of my own.

What are the criteria for determining whether a multina-

tional benefits or hinders a country? Usually the effect on balance of payments and standard of living, statistically measured, are the criteria used. More recently, merely operating
in a country that has an oppressive political regime is considered support of that regime. We need to develop better
criteria so that the effect of a multinational company can be
judged.

Another key question refers to profit. A frequent comment made is that the workers are not getting their fair share
of the profits. We need to ask an even more basic question.
What is a fair profit? To answer this we must include the elements of risk/reward, inflation, need for reinvestment,
priorities of workers and stockholders, etc.

The effect on relationships between countries, due to the
presence of American multinationals, should be considered.
The multinationals often have a negative effect because of the
"ugly American" problem, but I suspect our presence can have
a more positive effect.

A few years ago I was a member of a group that evaluated
the Peace Corps. In the original legislation, Congress provided
that the Peace Corps was to be periodically evaluated to see if
it is still fulfilling its original purpose or whether the original
purposes should be changed. One of the most positive aspects
of the Peace Corps is the effectiveness of the American presence in the developing countries. Some U.S. ambassadors to
developing countries were appalled when the suggestion was
made that perhaps the United States should pull out of a
number of these countries, especially those that were making
economic progress on their own and where the standards of
living had increased. The ambassadors pointed out that the
Peace Corps is the most effective U.S. presence in those countries, and that it would be a tragic mistake from a perspective
of relationships between countries if the Peace Corps were
withdrawn.

I do not mean to imply that a multinational company
could have the same effect as the Peace Corps. I do suspect
that more people getting to know each other better will
enhance the prospects for peace. Having American multinational companies operating throughout the world might be
having some positive effects in this matter.

The evidence is that a country is better off with a multinational than without it; but we must be careful here not to

arrive too quickly at conclusions that elsewhere might be considered a whitewash. We need to better understand why there are such strong anti-multinational feelings.

II: WILLIAM P. GLADE

OVER THE MIDDLE DECADES of the twentieth century, three types of foreign investment have proved to be especially vulnerable to political risks in less-developed countries: utility companies, extractive enterprises, and plantations.

Utility enterprises, caught between regulated rates and endemic inflation, saw net earnings dwindle; and when, predictably, service did not expand to keep pace with a rapidly growing demand, nationalization was often the result. Industry-specific factors have played a role as well. In the case of railway lines, problems associated with defects in initial systemic design and construction, exacerbated by low maintenance outlays and geographical shifts in traffic patterns, have forced line after line into bankruptcy and public ownership. In the case of electric power companies, a development-inspired desire to subsidize certain energy users has compounded the difficulties of regulation-*cum*-inflation and led governments to transfer the industry from private to public hands.

The two other investment fields which have been demonstrably open to expropriation, or subjected to a variety of discriminatory policies short of outright take-over, are both classic cases of the enclave phenomenon. In these instances, location is determined by where minerals are to be found or inexpensive usable land is to be had. Such locations are often, though not always, in relatively remote and less-developed areas in which the disparity between intra-mural and extra-mural economic and social organization is intensified. This highlighted disparity is, indeed, one of the perils of paternalism for it serves to raise the awareness by those outside the enclave of their unfortunate circumstances.

One such enclave is the large, export-oriented minerals operation in which, to judge from the record, extraction of a non-renewable resource can evidently be made to appear very much like the unrequited draining away of a valuable national patrimony. That such enterprises may confer some benefits on certain, usually small, groups in the host society does not prevent their being depicted, for political purposes, as Jacobs who are given to tricking Esau of his birthright. Victimization, it would appear, is an inexhaustible flow resource for the political leaders of troubled lands.[1]

The other classic enclave case that has served so often as a lightning rod for political discontent is the large agricultural operation geared to the export trade. While here a renewable resource is involved rather than a fund resource which evokes images of asset loss, there are nevertheless problems, many of which have, seemingly, a sort of historical inevitability about them. For one thing, such enterprises necessarily make extensive use of the prime asset of any pre-industrial society: land, an asset over which there is customarily an almost continuous stream of disputes even in the absence of foreign capital. For another, such operations have almost invariably been labor intensive, so that all the problems associated with dealing with large numbers of people alien to the culture and social situation of the managers are involved. Convincing research in the field of industrial relations has shown that the propensity to strike or to engage in other forms of industrial conflict tends to be highest among isolated masses of workers, even in societies where employers and employees share a more-or-less common culture.

It is essential to view the Dolefil operations in the context of this historical experience. No matter what the company may do, there is a high probability that it will be the focus of a certain amount of social antagonism and criticism — whether from the Passionist fathers or those imbued with other passions. Such problems, so to speak, come with the turf, and they delineate a set of inter-institutional frictions that are, essentially, structured into the social setting of the world economy as it has been organized for well over a century. This being so, problems of this sort, being more or less unavoidable, are more or less irrelevant to the examination of an individual company's policies.

If this were not enough, export-oriented plantation operations have often, in the absence of effective local government and given the weakness of the domestic private sector, had to supply their resident labor force with a whole variety of social and economic overhead services: housing, medical care, education, public utilities, and even, in many instances, retail outlets for consumption goods. Understandable though this blanket involvement of the company in the life of its workers has been, it is charged with enormous risk. Simply put, all the grievances that people may have with their employer, with their landlord, with the physician, with the school principal, with town hall, with the shopkeeper, and so forth, come home to roost on one doorstep, that of the omnipresent company. Small wonder, then, that plantation enterprises have so often been places to raise Cain as well as to raise cane.

While there are specific labor and other grievances the company could probably deal with, as by improving the quality of the truck transportation used to take workers to and from the fields or by indexing land lease payments to reflect changes in the general price level, it seems safe to predict that various elements of Dolefil's community program will, as have paternalistic policies everywhere no matter how well-intentioned, eventually backfire and saddle Dolefil managers with a new set of accusations and denunciations. Doubtless the company would face swelling community indignation if it did not provide water, some housing assistance, schooling, medical aid, and so on; but each of these good works is, for the reasons noted, virtually certain to become, sooner or later, an additional occasion for reproach. One is reminded of the truth of the old Eastern European adage that no good deed goes unpunished.

By the same token, an historical approach places what we might call a generic interpretation on certain other problem areas revealed in the field study. The gross inadequacy of the region's public services and infrastructure, the shortcomings of provincial government, the inability or disinclination of neighboring farmers to install advanced systems of erosion control like those used by Dolefil, routine inter-union conflicts between competing labor organizations, neither of which may stand as a paragon of leadership integrity and both of which take frequent potshots at the company—all these are pretty much standard features of the operating environment of Third World plantation undertakings, not a function of Dolefil policies as such. These difficulties, too, may therefore be set aside as having to do with the nature of the case.

Further, a number of the criticisms of Dolefil operations tell us more about what the critics think of the global regime of capitalism than they do about particulars of the Dolefil enterprise; i.e., about anything that is subject to control by Dolefil policymakers. Such, for example, is the objection that wage levels in the Philippines are substantially below those of equivalent jobs in Hawaii, and that the Filipino workers are still low-income workers, if not "poor," in spite of the progress of the enterprise. Such also is the complaint that a highly capitalized foreign enterprise has been able to make more effective use of the land than did the earlier cultivators thereof. All these features of the situation are the normal results of market forces.

For present purposes, such criticisms may be disregarded, since we are presumably talking about what multinational managers can or cannot do to improve matters in the Third World, not about the injustices, real or imagined, of the overarching institutional order of which multinational corporations are but a part. The data provided in this, as in any case study, are more relevant to assessing micro-economic level issues than they are for settling the issue of systemic efficacy and legitimacy. This is not to deny an interest in, or even the desirability of, confronting the more cosmic or systemic question on some other occasion. But it is to point out that the quite excellent set of observations contained in the Dolefil study simply does not and cannot provide an evidentiary base for arguing either one way or the other the social usefulness of capitalism.

Let me suggest that one further aspect be dropped from consideration; namely, what impact, if any, a multinational operation like Dolefil has on human rights and freedom. Granted that there are historical instances in which business enterprises have been vested with certain trappings of sovereignty, as in the case of the East India Company during part of its operations; in those instances such a consideration might be germane. The facts as presented, however, suggest that underdeveloped though the Philippines may be, there is nevertheless sufficient institutional differentiation that one can distinguish between social organizations that pertain to the exercise of sovereignty (i.e., the customary realm of issues of human rights and freedom) and those that have to do with the production of goods and services. There is no evidence that Dolefil operates directly in such a way as either to reduce human rights and freedoms or to enhance them. Whatever may be the *indirect* repercussions of its operations, these would be systemic in character and hence beyond the scope of any discussion built on a case study for the reasons mentioned previously. For what it is worth, however, it does seem relevant to observe that, within the context of the prevailing institutional system, Dolefil appears to have increased local employment and earnings as well as the array of local investment options so that, relative to the previous era, there has at least been some expansion of the material basis of choice and freedom—the aspect of human rights on which Marxian social analysts have often dwelt.

In the context of a world economy organized primarily on a market basis, this achievement in itself may be worth some reflection by those who argue for the existence of moral obligations to alleviate world poverty. Let me explain. Despite the remarkable growth of technology, it is still true that the numbers of the poor still vastly exceed the presently available means of eradicating their poverty, as the world economy is ordered today. Moreover, even if one accepts the existence of a moral obligation to relieve poverty, there is no specific obligation to prefer one set of the poor over another, to prefer poor Filipinos, say, to poor Bolivians. Under the circumstances, there may be some validity in asking which poor can be helped by the available instruments of relief and which are, at least for the time being, situated beyond the reach of those instruments. In other words, it seems reasonable to ask among which populations of the poor conditions are most favorable for the application of business enterprise, the principal resource-organizing and poverty-alleviating mechanism of a market system.

From this standpoint, an interesting moral counterpoint stands revealed. Whether Dolefil operates in South Cotabato or in Nigeria, the direct effect of its choice in either event would seem to be more or less equally poverty-relieving and freedom-amplifying (in the aforementioned sense of expanding the material basis of choice). Not so, however, the moral choices confronting the writers in *Concern*. So long as these critics are unable to substitute another more humane economic system for the present one or to move credibly in that direction, they would appear to have only two alternatives. They can either work to attract and build upon the poverty-relieving ministrations of multinational managers or else they can drive them away. The cost of the latter course of action is the continuing poverty of their local working class, to the impoverishment of which they would then have contributed.[2]

The basic question finally comes into focus. Is everything

so historically and circumstantially determined that little or no discretionary latitude remains for devising policies that contribute significantly to social and economic amelioration, over and beyond what Dolefil already does in the routine course of its business operations and its sundry good works? Conceding, as David Vogel has recently put it, that "profitability can be regarded as a necessary condition of responsible social performance" by corporations,[3] one can still query whether, constrained as they are by profitability considerations, corporations can make any real difference beyond handing out, as a charity transfer, a few schools, water systems, and baseball diamonds. The question is especially pertinent for enclave operations which, virtually by definition, have not usually served as platforms for broader development in their vicinity, where lasting spill-over effects have been limited, and where the surrounding institutional milieu has not ordinarily received much nurture from their operations.

Curiously, certain policy elements that quite conceivably have long-term survival value for the firm (a performance criterion which is self-validating) may not be altogether unrelated to behavioral standards held up for emulation in the traditional moral economy based on a sharing of talents—to resort to biblical language. There is not space to explore the notion fully in this paper, but a few suggestions may be in order to indicate the connection which subsequent discussion might develop in more detail.

As remarked previously, overseas operations like that of Dolefil are fraught with considerable risk on account of their enclave nature, in which the alignment of the foreign institutional complex with its "host" society produces almost continuous friction at a number of points. A reduction in the alien character of the enclave is no guarantee of long-term staying power, particularly if the general environment has deteriorated so far that a comprehensive social-political upheaval results. But under modern political conditions those decisions which maintain a distinct separation between the foreign enterprise and adjacent social organizations are virtually certain to produce increasing difficulty (and higher costs) in preserving the operation as a going concern.

What, we must ask, lies at the heart of the enclave's distinctiveness?[4] Wherein lies its comparative advantage, its particular talent, as it were? We have been habituated by the way we conceptualize the factors of production to seeing the distinctiveness of the enclave operation in terms of its contribution to savings and capital formation or in terms of the complexity of its technology. Yet it is clear that in economies characterized by highly unequal income distribution there exists a potential to save much more than they commonly do, while access to off-the-shelf technology is no longer always predicated on the admission of direct private foreign investment. For that matter, a given transfer of material capital cannot be the basis of a foreign firm's most significant contribution as nowadays the injection of a given technology confers at best a fading advantage. What is more important is the linkage the foreign firm supplies with a flow of technical advances, a more dynamic and processual advantage deriving from the organizational/informational capabilities of the firm.

If we conceptualize "organization" as a distinctive factor of production (even though it be less amenable to measurement than labor, capital, and land), and if we take more seriously what various social observers have pointed out for years (that information has become the critical resource in the modern economic system), then the defining characteristic of an enclave enterprise becomes much clearer.[5] As the Dolefil case study makes abundantly plain, the organizational efficacy of Dolefil as an information gathering and information processing system is almost light years ahead of the other social organizations that populate the Mindanao region in which Dolefil conducts its business. And enjoying such a superiority in its capacity to process information, Dolefil enjoys, as a derivative advantage, a considerable superiority in organizing the co-operant resources of land, labor, and capital as well. The disparity between Dolefil and its environment in this respect is well illustrated throughout the study. Among other things, this disparity constricts the transfer of labor skills from enclave to non-enclave operations, hampers the shift of land from pineapple production to alternative uses that would be at least equally remunerative, throttles down the diffusion of innovation (such as erosion-control techniques), and reduces the ability of local entrepreneurs to respond to the new investment opportunities created as spin-offs of Dolefil activities.[6] In short, organizational capacity would appear to be of pivotal importance in determining whether an industry functions as a growth pole contributing to local development or as an enclave contributing to local resentment.[7]

Given the limited absorptive capacity of Dolefil's environment for productive transfers of capital, labor, and land resources, it should be of interest to explore the possibilities for designing and costing-out an alternative program centered on local organizational development, to build up the information processing capacity of the host economic region. To be sure, other organizations—for example, the National Development Corporation, trade union programs similar to the American Institute for Free Labor Development, and business development ventures such as the Latin American Agribusiness Development Corporation (with which there is, apparently, already some corporate linkage)—might usefully be enlisted in the effort. But it is precisely the ability to monitor the horizon for relevant expertise and to establish and capitalize on such inter-organizational linkages that differentiates a modern economic system so markedly from its antecedents—as, indeed, this seminar itself so well illustrates.

More often than not, multinational enterprises have built their local good works programs around gifts of products and money, with only limited impact on the poverty of the societies in which they operate. Were they, so to speak, to give more of themselves, i.e., their "talent" for organizational design and management, they might well reduce the institutional disparity that renders them so conspicuous and vulnerable while more surely supplying the critical factors needed to launch Third World economies into a growth trajectory characterized increasingly by organization-intensive and information-intensive methods of production.

An appropriate agenda for research (and, possibly, action), then, might well focus on the uses of multinational corporations as organizational catalysts: e.g., the degree to which they serve as a springboard to enhance the local production of technology (not just how they function as vehicles of technology transfer); the ways in which they might integrate, or at least interlink, their company information systems with those of national development authorities (as, for instance, through co-participation in joint ventures); the means through which multinational corporations, as a beachhead of advanced organizational capability in less-developed countries, may be serving to upgrade the management information systems of national firms in the vicinity; and so on.

Notes

1. The formidable size of such operations also makes them suspect, a point which is surely not incomprehensible in a country which has known anti-chain store regulations in the not-too-distant past and which still has restrictions on branch banking.

2. Lest all this be construed as an apologia for a world regime dominated by multinational enterprises and rich nations, it should be said again that the systemic level of judgment, like the systemic level of analysis, simply cannot be accommodated by the methodology of a case-study approach.

3. See "Foreword" in Thornton Bradshaw and David Vogel, eds., *Corporations and Their Critics* (New York: McGraw-Hill, 1980).

4. A first clue as to the source of an enclave's distinctiveness can be gained from a pair of simple observations: not all export industries even in the Philippines have an enclave character, and not all Dole Pineapple operations (such as those in Hawaii) would appropriately be described as having such a character.

5. While Leibenstein's notion of X-efficiency and the secular growth studies of Dennison and others have acknowledged the importance of organization and information, international trade theory has not as yet fully incorporated these insights into its framework. To be sure, the place of service sector exports is recognized in the balance of payments, the role of entrepôts is a standard element in economic history, and empirical studies have revealed that some firms have been able to capitalize to advantage a dominant position in the international marketing process (rather than direct control of production processes) so that they, like financial intermediaries, have organization as their principal asset. Still, most international economic analysis is built mainly on a two- (labor, capital) or three-factor (labor, capital, land) conceptual basis.

6. These new local business opportunities, which could become the basis of a more generalized economic expansion, are, for example, reflected in reported complaints about the rising cost of housing and food—a sign that demand has outstripped supply.

7. Foreign ownership is not, it should be remarked, an invariable concomitant of enclave operations. Recent studies of the development of the Las Truchas iron-and-steel complex on the Pacific coast of Mexico, a project launched under auspices of the Mexican government, indicate that it has also developed more as an enclave than in the growth-pole role originally envisioned for it.

III: REV. PETER J. HENRIOT, S.J.

On May 22, 1980 Father Loreto G. Viloria, a Filipino priest who is director of the Social Action Center of the Prelature of Marbel, wrote to a gathering of Passionist priests in New Jersey (which included many who had worked in the Philippines, among them Bishop Reginald Arliss of the Prelature) the following critique of Castle & Cooke's operation in his area: "Dolefil is in the long run a national liability. Therefore the people and the country should evict the company from the country." This and similar critiques of Dolefil have been reiterated by many church and social groups in recent years. To understand and evaluate the critiques has been one of the aims of the Notre Dame seminar's case study on the Dolefil operations in the Philippine Islands.

The purpose of these reflections is to react to the paper prepared by Yusaku Furuhashi, Father Don McNeill, and John Thorp. Having studied the paper, as well as additional material received from church and social groups, I want (1) to point to three needs which I feel are not adequately discussed in the paper, and (2) to raise a few questions for additional focus in discussions of the paper.

The paper is well-researched and persuasively argued. The comments I make here come from my consultation of secondary sources and my own particular views on development. Though lacking in first-hand experience of the South Cotabato situation, I believe that my comments nevertheless raise serious issues.

International

The discussion needs to be placed in the context of the international debate. It is not possible to get an accurate picture of the benefits or nonbenefits of Dolefil's operations without situating it within the larger context of the North/South debate. Either in the short term or in the long term, Dolefil does not carry on its economic efforts in a vacuum. Hence I believe that the basic New International Economic Order (NIEO) issues raised in my seminar paper "Restructuring the International Economic Order" still stand.[1] We must ask ourselves whether Dolefil's operations contribute to forward progress of true interdependence and a self-reliance which promotes the best welfare of the Philippines. The call for restructuring North/South relationships presents a perspective within which to view the activity of Dolefil, since such a large and influential multinational as Castle & Cooke is a key factor in any NIEO discussions.

I find this perspective absent in the paper. It attempts to do a micro-economic analysis without adverting to the macro-economic issues. Thus it cannot adequately come to grips with the question of the impact of Dolefil on a development process which meets the challenge of poverty.

Of particular import for us, for example, is an awareness of the current breakdown in North/South negotiations as a result of the failure of the recent United Nations General Assembly Special Session on Economic Issues (UNGASS). This forum closed without reaching agreement on laying strategies for the Third Development Decade or procedures for a round of global negotiations on economic issues (including energy).[2] The United States stood almost alone in withholding consensus on a final document, objecting particularly to points affecting decision-making power in international institutions. All multinational corporations, including Castle & Cooke, must be alert to the implications of continued stalemate in the international development debate if they seek to evaluate their activities in terms of addressing global poverty issues.

Political

The presentation needs to take more serious account of the political context in the Philippines. While the paper addresses the "socio-cultural" context of Dolefil, it does so in a disturbingly *a-political* analysis. Certainly no discussion of significant economic activity in the Philippines today can be carried on without serious consideration given to the present effects of martial law and the future prospects of the overthrow of the dictatorship of President Marcos. A front-page article in the September 10, 1980, *Wall Street Journal,* entitled "Bedeviled Dictatorship," cites U.S. business projections (by Frost & Sullivan, a research firm) that estimate only five years, at the most, before the Marcos regime is toppled. The Roman Catholic hierarchy has recently called for an immediate end to the repressive martial law in order to avert violent revolution. Comparisons are readily made between U.S. government and business support of President Marcos and the support given to the Shah of Iran. The Island of Mindanao, where Dolefil is located, is particularly unstable.

What is Dolefil's relationship to the Marcos regime? Any stability martial law does impose (e.g., strikes banned) may be a short-term advantage. But is it an advantage Dolefil can take uncritically in the light of repeated analysis of a bad human rights situation in the Philippines (e.g., that done by Amnesty International)? Dole has several connections with high Philippine government officials. For example: in 1978 Defense Minister Juan Ponce Enrile had done the corporation's legal work; the government's energy expert, Geronimo Velasco, was a former president of the board of Dolefil; and the Minister of Finance had been part of Dole's auditing firm. Mention of this is not to offer a "conspiracy" thesis or to overemphasize a "power elite" argument. Rather it is simply to point out that Dole can be and is perceived by many as one more U.S.–based corporation whose presence in the Philippines is supportive of the Marcos regime.

Because the paper adverts to none of this political context, it tends to give the impression that it could have been written about operations in some other country where the political situation was not so volatile.

ECONOMIC

The discussion needs some fundamental critique of the economic development model being pursued. The great contribution of the paper is to focus the discussion of the pros and cons of MNC operations in less-developed countries—specifically, Dolefil's presence in the Philippines—in the light of more detailed ethnographic information about the concrete situation. But in order to address the issues of corporate responsibility and social justice that have been the major concerns of this seminar, some basic questions have to be asked about the consequences of the development model being pursued by the present activity of Dolefil. A socio-cultural context cannot abstract from the economic context since the latter has an impact on every aspect of the former.

For the sake of our discussion, let me illustrate this point with four issues.

Castle & Cooke Throughout the Philippines

Dolefil is a subsidiary of Castle & Cooke, which is a major presence in the Philippines. In recent years it has ranked around 75th in total sales among the top 1000 corporations in the Philippines. Besides pineapple operations, Castle & Cooke's business in the Philippines includes bananas (Stanfilco), cattle raising, sugar (shares in Hawaiian-Philippines Sugar Co.), investment banking (joint venture with House of Investments), glass manufacturing (Republic Glass Corp.), and land development (holdings in Manila Memorial Park and Holy Cross Memorial Park). The Philippine publication *Business Day* of 9 June 1980 reported that Stanfilco had dissolved its corporate existence (effective 17 May 1980) and would be merged with Dolefil in an effort by Castle & Cooke to cut costs since Stanfilco had been incurring substantial losses in the past few years. Additionally, Dole has begun expanding its tuna fishing and canning operations in the South Cotabato Province.

This brief description is mentioned here simply to remind us that in terms of economic development in the Philippines, Castle & Cooke is a major factor. Its impact on South Cotabato's development has to be seen as part of a piece of its overall impact on Philippine development.

Economic Development Versus Return to Shareholders

Dolefil is present in South Cotabato because of "comparative advantages" arising from the availability of cheap land and cheap labor. The obvious needs restating simply to remind us of an important economic fact. Dolefil's primary reason for being in the Philippines is not economic development of the country but a return on investment for stockholders. This is the proper role of foreign multinationals. But we should therefore remember that an upward adjustment of land prices or an improvement in wages is not to the direct advantage of the company even if they would improve the condition of workers and local residents.

Exports as an Engine of Development

Export-oriented development, particularly of luxury commodities, is increasingly being critically examined as an engine of development which benefits all the people of a poor country. Agricultural land in the South Cotabato Province is devoted to pineapple production rather than to basic food production for locals (many of whom suffer serious malnutrition in their poverty state). Unequal distribution of wealth and income in Mindanao—heightened by economic structures reinforced by MNC presence—affects the entire population, with the deprivation of the great majority of people being a stark reality and social unrest an ominous potential. Dependency relationships on foreign capital and on Western technology and managerial expertise, mean a national economic formation which is heavily influenced by foreign interests.

The central question for evaluating any development approach is: What is happening to people? The thrust of the recent development debate has been toward an examination of the social consequences (e.g., income distribution) of certain policies as well as of the economic consequences (e.g., increases in gross national product). (See my paper "Restructuring the International Economic Order," chapter 3.) "Development as if people mattered" is the only socially just approach. In that light, export-oriented development, such as is promoted by Dolefil's operations, must be seriously evaluated. As a major study produced in July 1980 by the Afrim Resource Center, Davao City (*Mindanao Report: A Preliminary Study on the Economic Origins of Social Unrest*) explains:

> Ultimately, the question concerns not whether or not the Philippines should produce for export, but rather what are the types of export products, who benefits from export earnings, and are the domestic resources being allocated properly so that the needs of the local population, especially the poor, are being sufficiently met. (p. 11)

Possibility of Departure

A closely related economic issue which has immediate consequences for the socio-cultural context of development is the potentiality/possibility/probability of an eventual pull-out by Dolefil from South Cotabato. Aside from the volatile political situation mentioned earlier, two other key questions raise this question of pull-out: How long will the soil, already heavily fertilized, remain usable? and, What is the potential for a declining market in the face of increasing competition (already a fact with Stanfilco's banana operations)? A development model skewed toward export of luxury agricultural commodities and generating large-scale dependency relationships may in the short-term bring some economic advantages to the region but in the long-term it is at least highly questionable.

Additional Comments on Direct Consequences

Since I am not able here to go into greater detail, let me simply indicate two additional issues which I feel the paper raised but did not treat in an altogether satisfactory fashion.

First, I would like to hear more about the issue of ecological damage resulting from Dolefil's operations. From other sources I have been informed that the flooding and erosion problem is really quite serious and that Dolefil's responsibility is widely recognized in the area. Similarly, in order to keep production at peak in sandy and nonfertile land, Dolefil uses highly toxic chemical fertilizers which are washed into the low lands and down into Sarangani Bay, eventually affecting the fishing there.

Second, I was less than comfortable with the paper's discussion of the cultural concept of poverty. At least it could give rise to the impression that local attitudes mean that destitute conditions such as exist in "Little Tondo" (near the Cannery Site) are really not so bad because of the "opportunity" offered for inhabitants to work for Dolefil. Although I have not personally visited the area spoken of in the paper, I have lived for some time in extremely impoverished situations in Latin America and know of the deeper consequences of such inhuman conditions. Friends of mine who have visited the Dolefil area have reported to me an impression different from that conveyed in the paper about the consequences of the poverty conditions there. Therefore I believe that a discussion of the policy implications of the cultural concept of poverty needs more attention from this seminar.

Conclusion

In these remarks I have deliberately tried to be provocative. The paper on the socio-cultural context of Dolefil raises extremely important questions for our general discussion of the multinational corporations and Third World poverty. But I feel that certain additional questions need to be raised for a more complete discussion.

We need to recall the purpose of this seminar: to address very directly the relationship between the multinationals and the problems of poverty in the less-developed countries. In examining the case study, then, we have to take a look at the larger picture. In summary, I would suggest three questions for our discussion. Obviously, they are questions which can be asked of almost any multinational corporation's operations in almost any Third World country:

(1) What is the relationship of Dolefil's operations in the Philippines to the NIEO issues of structural changes in North/South relationships?
(2) Can Dolefil be politically neutral in the present situation of the Philippines, or is its presence actually supportive of the current regime?
(3) What model of economic development does Dolefil promote and who benefits from the model?

Notes

1. See chapter 3.
2. The Center of Concern has available several analyses of UNGASS.

PART IV:
Summary Observations

14.   The Nature of the Debate

REV. DONALD McNEILL, C.S.C.,
AND LEE A. TAVIS

WHY IS THERE SUCH antagonism in the discussions about the role of multinational corporations in the Third World? Through the discussion of the material presented in this volume the seminar participants grew in their appreciation of the difficulties in addressing this question.

This concern, of course, was one of the precepts upon which the seminar was formed. The participants came from different backgrounds with vastly different views of the world. For most of us the experience has been truly unique in terms both of the topic coverage and of the nature of the discussion. Our attempts to understand one another formed a microcosm of the broader debate around us. As individual participants committed themselves to the understanding of contrary views, and as the group grew to be more trusting and cohesive, a structure for understanding evolved.

LEVELS OF ANALYSIS

The three levels of analysis introduced by Glade in the panel on "A Role of Multinationals" provide a structure for analyzing the reasons for this general lack of communication.

(1) The micro-economic or atomistic level: An examination of the individual enterprise as in the Dolefil case.
(2) The categorical level: Analysis of multinationals as a group, as in the case of the Francis-Manrique study.
(3) The systemic level: Evaluation of the impact of the

multinational at the global market level as in the
Henriot paper "Restructuring the International Economic Order."

As one proceeds from the first to the second level, the
focus shifts from the smallest element (a single subsidiary) and
an indepth analysis of how that element of the system inter-
faces with its environment, to the systemic level where the emphasis is more on how the total system interacts with all of its
environments. A person's observations about the proper role
of multinationals may well differ depending upon the level of
analysis that one chooses. As Glade predicted, we found increasing difficulty in our comprehension and degrees of controversy as we moved from the micro to the systemic level.

Atomistic

At the case level there was little disagreement over the
fact that the presence of Dolefil was contributing significantly
to meeting the basic human needs of people in the surrounding area, and that people in those barrios perceived the Dolefil
presence to be a "good thing." Surprisingly little of the seminar discussion was directed to the specifics of the Dolefil actions, such as the adequacy of their community service or the
problem of erosion. The panel evaluating the Dolefil impact
asked why the level of criticism was intense. Caron makes the
point well when he states:

> The results seem to me to indicate that Dolefil has had a very
> positive effect on the area of the Philippines in which it is
> operating and its workers have acted as good citizens. . . . The
> puzzling thing then is, why the condemnation? We could dis-
> miss it as being irrational and uninformed but I would feel un-
> easy leaving it at this.

Two answers are suggested: one addressing the concerns
of religious communities, and the other dealing with the nature of the Dolefil investment. One reason for differences has
to do with the forms of "pastoral" involvement of the religious
working in the Third World. When missionaries deal with the
poor in those countries, they generally deal with them closely
as individuals. The missionary hurts when his or her people
hurt and will struggle to alleviate that hurt, whatever the di-

rect cause. This pastoral response often tends to be sympathet-
ic, immediate, and to focus on the direct cause. Missionaries
try to work in "solidarity with the poor." Therefore, their confrontation with the multinational corporation often stems
from a desire to help the poor participate in decisions concerning the basic human needs which affect them and their
future.

The second reason for conflict in the case of Dolefil can
be attributed to the "enclave" nature of this investment. Glade
points out in his response to the Dolefil evidence that large
agricultural operations geared to export serve as lightning
rods for political discontent. Their extensive use of labor, their
isolation, their investment in social infrastructure, all lead to
antagonism. Glade maintains that in these cases "no good deed
goes unpunished."

There seemed to be a clear understanding of the various
views relative to the Dolefil influence on its immediately surrounding area. Moreover, we sensed a convergence of opinion
as to the proper role for a multinational in this interaction.
Thus, we would conclude that the rancor of the debate lies at
a different level.

Categorical

The Francis-Manrique study crisply sets forth the debate
at the categorical level. The paper identifies areas of disagreement and agreement as well as those areas where the debate was simply not enjoined. For areas of disagreement, the
belief systems studied provide a solid structure for empirical
verification and an opportunity to move the debate to an objective level. For other topics where the debate is one-sided,
there is little hope of moving beyond the accuser phase until
the "other" side is taken up.

Francis and Manrique helped the seminar to understand
better our own debate. The connection between the nature of
goods produced by multinationals and the rigidity of class
structures in the Third World is an example. An analyst concerned with class structure views the kinds of goods produced
and the manner in which they are advertised as reinforcing
the local class structure. Others, not versed in, nor directly
concerned with, class structure find it difficult to see the connection or the importance.

A second dimension of the conflict at the categorical level has to do with the interface between the multinational corporation and the nation-state. Through direct investment multinationals tie nation-states into the international economic system, often in ways that the nation's government officials resist and resent. While the national sovereignty of a government is bounded by geographical limits, the economic span of a single multinational embraces a number of countries. Throughout history, overlapping systems of this nature have created conflict when the goals of the two systems diverge. As the multinational attempts to manage its system to satisfy economic goals, survival, and long-term returns on capital employed, and as the national government attempts to serve a range of economic social and political objectives, conflict is inevitable.

Conflicts resulting from overlapping systems with divergent goals tend to be resolved as a function of the balance of power between the participants. This balance is gradually shifting in favor of Third World countries as more multinationals from more countries gain strength in the international markets. Powers noted that this shift in the balance is one point of agreement among both the detractors and supporters of the multinationals' presence in the Third World. In their study Doubet and Tavis found that in all the cases studied, the nation-states held the balance of power, at least for entry conditions. In his presentation for the panel "A Role for Multinationals," however, Glade argued that for many developing countries (i.e., those with less economic presence than say, Brazil, Mexico, or Venezuela) four factors will tend to keep the balance on the side of the multinationals: their relative size, stability, mobility, and accessibility to resources of money, organization, and information.

Throughout the seminar, our discussions at the categorical level converged in terms of understanding the various views of the issues, although not necessarily agreeing upon the most desired solutions.

Systemic

The systemic level is where the strongest conflict was generated, and where the seminar participants seemed to have the greatest difficulty communicating with one another. As indicated, the multinational corporation is an integral component of the global system. Thus, one's view of the corporation is closely tied to one's view of the global social-political-economic system, and a preference as to the desired balances within the system becomes a criterion for judging the existing or potential impact of the multinational presence. Three balances were of importance to the seminar participants: (1) competing goals of the economic system; (2) the proper role of the marketplace and national regulation in guiding the allocation of resources; and (3) participation of the poor in corporate or government planning.

There are two overarching goals for economic systems at both the international and national levels: economic growth, and meeting the basic human needs of the people. These goals are not mutually exclusive. Economic growth increases the resources available for distribution to the poor, while a focus on consumption at the lowest economic levels may well slow the rate of growth. Thus, in spite of their congruence, these goals are competitors at the margin for economic resources.

At the heart of the seminar concern over these two goals was the "trickle-down" theory. One set of participants stressed economic growth as the critical requirement, claiming that the benefits of this growth would trickle down to help those at the lower end of the economic spectrum. Another group of participants challenged this scenario on the basis that the benefits of economic growth in the Third World have gone more to the upper classes and have contributed little or nothing to alleviating conditions for the destitute. Moreover, even if the benefits were to trickle down, they argue, this would not take place in an acceptable time frame.

There was a surprising level of agreement that multinational corporations did, indeed, contribute importantly to economic growth in the Third World areas where they operate. There was less agreement as to whether economic growth would naturally contribute to an equitable distribution of resources, or as to how multinationals could or should contribute in a direct way to meeting the basic human needs for the poor in the Third World.

The second systemic balance considered was the role of economic markets and governmental regulations as a structure within which the dual economic goals should be pursued. Attitudes toward the proper role of governmental bodies in allocating resources to meet basic human needs were mixed.

Few participants saw national governments as serving them well. In general, supporters of the trickle-down theory would argue that regulation should be minimized, while critics of that theory would stress the importance of efficient national and local regulation. Most participants supported the need for some form of government involvement to ensure minimum standards of survival.

The third type of balance in the system that influences one's view of the multinational corporate role is the amount of participation to be allowed in the decision process by those who will be affected by the decisions. In our case the issue is how much control the poor should have over corporate and governmental planners that are deciding on their future. This concern has to do with the characteristics of the planning process both in the private and public sector.

Corporate decision models tend to follow a sequence of five steps: (1) formalizing objectives, (2) anticipating uncontrolled constraints on action alternatives, (3) deciding on an action plan, (4) implementing that plan, (5) evaluating the results. Although good planning loops back through this process a number of times between the initial goal setting and the final implementation, the general sequence is usually in evidence. In these procedures, the decision-maker decides on the trade-offs among the constituencies within the constraints imposed by their relative strength. That is, the decision-maker sets his objectives and pushes for their accomplishment. The constituencies are not consulted beyond their ability to enforce the demands in and on the corporations.

The process does not allow for the idea that those who will be affected by a decision should participate in setting the objectives in the decision process. Powers stated this need in terms of "freedom of choice" for those whom an action affects as a fundamental requirement in his principle for moral action. This participatory process is at odds with most corporate decision procedures.

Governmental planners tend to follow the same general decision-making sequence. They may measure characteristics or attitudes of the affected parties, but they seldom include them in their deliberations. This basic distinction, particularly as it is worked out in the structure of the existing economic-political systems, repeatedly led to fundamental and hard-to-define disagreements among the participants.

Thus the experience of this seminar group, as reflected in

the materials published in this volume, support Glade's observation that the level at which the debate takes place—micro, categorical, or systemic—is a major determinant of the problems encountered in attempts to discuss the role of multinational corporations and their impact on the Third World. The ability to understand and to communicate the various views of the multinational firms becomes more difficult and more value-laden as the discussion moves from the micro level to a systemic view.

Choosing the Appropriate Level

The level at which multinational corporate activities in the Third World could be meaningfully evaluated was a major point of contention among the participants. One group believed that an appropriate focus for evaluation was the individual subsidiary, whereas another was convinced that any realistic evaluation must put its major emphasis on the global economic-political system of which the individual multinational is a part.

The micro (atomistic) group would concentrate on the firm's constituencies and on the broader society only as it is directly influenced by these constituencies. For example, they would focus on the workers and their communities, and on the national or international system only as seen through the perspective of the workers. Their concern would be with the working and living conditions of the firm's employees, its suppliers, and the surrounding community.

The systemic-oriented group would begin their evaluation with, or at least, carry the evaluation of the firm through, a series of linkages to the global system. Either way, the economic and social results of the global system would be an integral part of the group's analysis.

Those in the micro group were more likely to see the firm as having some flexibility within the existing economic-political system to implement a program of developmental responsibility. And they see managers as having an opportunity to influence the actions of their firms. Systemically oriented evaluators would be more concerned with constraining the actions of the firm through national governments or the United Nations.

The level at which we as analysts or decision-makers in

our own fields choose to exert our efforts is perhaps the most basic personal issue we must address. As we move to translate our better understanding of the potential role for multinationals into our own action plans, or into the activities toward which we would direct the institutions or groups of which we are members, we will always face this choice.

As an example, consider the case of a missionary working in an area surrounding a large agribusiness plantation. Suppose that, in the performance of his pastoral concerns, this missionary identifies a worker or a group of workers that he believes is receiving unjust treatment from the foreign investor. This injustice could be perceived as caused by the lack of morality or judgment on the part of the corporation's local management, or as the result of an unjust system. Depending upon one's own viewpoint, actions could be quite different. For a local redress, the missionary would attempt to work with local management. Whereas, for systemic relief, the emphasis would be on broader structural change in the form of union legislation or other national laws, or on pursuit through other avenues, such as shareholder resolutions in the parent country or in the United Nations.

For the manager of a multinational corporation, the same choice exists. To improve performance at the micro level, the manager would attempt to incorporate a broad range of developmental concerns into the firm's decision processes. Micro focused managers would monitor the full impact of the firm at its local operating sites and ensure that a concern for the overall social as well as economic impact is included in decisions. If the issues are viewed in a systemic light, the manager would probably work more with national laws and regulatory structures, required codes of conduct, disclosure rules, or participate in United Nations' activities as in the case of the United Nations Conference on Science and Technology for Development. Emphasis would be on systemic changes that affect all multinationals, thus modifying the whole system and not placing any one firm at a competitive disadvantage.

CONCLUDING OBSERVATIONS

We trust that this shared seminar experience will contribute to understanding the knotty issues surrounding multinational corporation presence in the poorer countries of our world. Virtually all global, economic, political, and social issues are, in some way, tied to this presence.

Our focal point has been on the poor within the less-developed world, a group of desperate human beings surely deserving of our best effort. The volume began with a capsule view of their poverty, considered the factors that mold the local and international environment within which the multinational firm interacts directly or indirectly with them, and presented a number of views on multinational capability and responsibility to respond positively to their needs. The conceptual discussion has been complemented by a case study of a multinational operation in the Southern Philippines.

In this final part of the volume, we have attempted to share our sense of why the debate over multinational presence in the Third World has not contributed more in a positive way to the plight of the poor. We suggested that a first step is to clearly identify the level of analysis, ranging from a response at the local operating site to the global economic system. The nature of the debate is different at each level, as are the opportunities and approaches for responding to the needs of the poor. Those who view multinational managers and their corporations as bounded by the dictates of the national or international system, would concentrate on changing that system. Others who perceive flexibility for action, seek opportunities for local response.

Against this background, the seminar is now focusing on the implementation of the developmental responsibility outlined in this volume. Activities are under way in two areas: modification of the corporate decision processes to enhance the firm's ability to respond to local development needs, and seeking means through which multinational corporations can interact meaningfully with local institutions.

Too often, outside observers view the multinational corporation simplistically as a monolithic whole—as a unified system. They forget that a multinational firm, like any other organization, has no life of its own but reflects the interaction of a great many people joined together in some organizational structure. Any action on the part of the institution must be agreed upon and managed by a group of individuals working together. If the institution moves in the intended direction, it is only because it is well-managed. For the multinational, the uniqueness of its various operating locations dictates that an appropriate response at one location may not fit the needs of another. Combined with the responsibility for development this environmental uniqueness poses a massive challenge to the management of a multinational firm.

Multinational activities in the Third World must be worked out in conjunction with local constituents and institutions such as governments, labor, and religious groups. The more sophisticated these institutions, and the more they are effectively targeted toward local development, the easier it is for the multinational to meet its developmental responsibility. Indeed, the key to meeting a firm's developmental responsibility may well lie in working to enhance the effectiveness of these local groups.

We plan to report the results of these seminar efforts to improve internal decision processes and to find pathways to work with local institutions in later volumes.

Appendix

Individuals who have participated in all or some part of the seminar are listed below. Although many have moved on to new responsibilities over the course of the seminar, their titles reflect their involvement in the Third World. The contribution by these people has, indeed, been great. Theirs is the credit for the insight shared in this book.

We hope that the seminar proceedings reported here will encourage dialogue and will help to avoid the prolonged discussions with the repetition of biased and unfounded claims from both sides. No one person or firm should be held accountable for the final product. Given the intensity of the interaction, that would be impossible.

J. Joseph Anderson	Executive Vice President Multinational Banking Continental Bank
Jean-Marc Bara	Vice President International Banking Chase Manhattan Bank
Simon Bourgin	Senior Adviser to U. S. Coordinator of Preparation for United Nations Conference on Science and Technology for Development
James L. Burtle	Vice President Economic Group W. R. Grace & Company

John B. Caron

President
Caron International

A. J. Costello

Vice President-Agricultural,
Americas
Far Eastern Division
American Cyanamid Company

Joseph P. Cummings

Deputy Senior Partner and Partner
in Charge of International
Relations, Peat, Marwick, Mitchell
and Company; Retired

Shaun E. Donnelly

Financial Economist
Office of Development Finance
U. S. Department of State

Earl W. Doubet

President
Caterpillar Americas
Caterpillar Tractor Company

Wolfgang
Fenkart-Froschl

Vice President
International Banking
Chase Manhattan Bank

Michael J. Francis

Chairman
Department of Government
and International Studies
University of Notre Dame

A. Blake Friscia

Vice President
Economic Group
Chase Manhattan Bank

D. W. Furbee

Vice President
Castle & Cooke, Inc.

Yusaku Furuhashi

Associate Dean
College of Business Administration
University of Notre Dame

Animesh Ghoshal	Assistant Professor of Finance and Business Economics University of Notre Dame
William P. Glade	Director Institute of Latin American Studies The University of Texas
J. Peter Grace, III	Executive Vice President Restaurant W. R. Grace & Company
Frank Grimsley	Vice President Caterpillar Tractor Company
Samuel L. Hayden	Director of Washington Programs Council of the Americas
Rev. Peter J. Henriot, S.J.	Director Center of Concern
Rev. Theodore M. Hesburgh, C.S.C.	President University of Notre Dame
Andrew Hodge	Senior Economist W. R. Grace & Company
Kenneth P. Jameson	Associate Professor of Economics University of Notre Dame
Gerard M. Keeley	Senior Vice President Commercial Banking Continental Bank
Roger T. Kelley	Vice President Caterpillar Tractor Company
Kenneth A. Lawder	Top Management Corporate Consultant W. R. Grace & Company

David C. Leege   Director
                              Center for the Study of Man in
                              Contemporary Society
                              University of Notre Dame

Cecilia G. Manrique   Doctoral Candidate
                              Department of Government and
                              International Studies
                              University of Notre Dame

Leonard T. Marks,   Executive Vice President
Jr.   Castle & Cooke, Inc.

Rev. Arthur   Population and Development Office
McCormack, M.H.M.   Rome, Italy

Rev. Donald McNeill,   Director
C.S.C.   Center for Experiential Learning
                              University of Notre Dame

John R. Mullen   Vice President of Corporate
                              Relations
                              Johnson & Johnson

Sylvain Plasschaert   Professor of Economic Science
                              University of Antwerp

Charles W. Powers   Executive Director of Corporate
                              Action
                              Cummins Engine Company

Rev. John J. Ridyard,   Coordinator
M.M.   Corporate Social Responsibility
                              Maryknoll Fathers

Norlin G. Rueschhoff   Chairman
                              Department of Accountancy
                              University of Notre Dame

J. H. Schriever   President
                              Americas Far Eastern Division
                              American Cyanamid Company

Harold R. Sims	Sims International Ltd.
Vernon L. E. Stisser	Vice President and Managing Director Asia-Pacific Division and Canadian Division Ralston Purina International
Lee A. Tavis	C. R. Smith Professor of Business Administration University of Notre Dame
John P. Thorp	Assistant Professor of Anthropology St. Mary's College
Csanad Toth	Special Assistant and Director for Policy Planning Bureau for International Organizations U.S. Department of State
Louis A. Van Houten	Vice President and Managing Director South & Central American Division Ralston Purina International
John A. Weber	Associate Professor of International Business University of Notre Dame
Charles K. Wilber	Chairman Department of Economics University of Notre Dame
Jean Wilkowski	Ambassador United Nations Conference on Science and Technology for Development
Rolando M. Zosa	Manager East Asia Division International Finance Corporation